Sacred Debts

The North's Civil War Series
Paul A. Cimbala, series editor

SACRED DEBTS

State Civil War Claims
and American Federalism,
1861–1880

KYLE S. SINISI

Fordham University Press
New York
2003

The North's Civil War series, No. 23
ISSN 1089-8719

Library of Congress Cataloging-in-Publication Data

Sinisi, Kyle S.
    Sacred debts : state Civil War claims and American federalism,
1861–1880 / Kyle S. Sinisi.—1st ed.
      p.   cm. — (The North's Civil War series ; no. 23)
    ISBN 0-8232-2259-4 (hard cover : alk. paper)
      1. United States—History—Civil War, 1861–1865—Claims.   2.
United
States—Politics and government—1861–1865.   3. United
States—Politics
and government—1865–1900.   4. Federal government—United
States—History—19th century.   I. Title.   II. North's Civil War;
no. 23.
E480.S56   2003
973.7′1—dc21   2003008816

Printed in the United States of America
07   06   05   04   03   5   4   3   2   1
First Edition

Dedicated to
Rocco J. Sinisi
and
Judith J. Sinisi

CONTENTS

ACKNOWLEDGMENTS

As ALWAYS, there are acknowledgments that should be made in a project of this length. While numerous archivists and librarians have provided help, I want to recognize the efforts of several in particular. They include Cindy Stewart of the Western Historical Manuscripts Collection, Marie Concannon and Mark Thomas of the State Historical Society of Missouri, Martha Clevenger of the Missouri Historical Society, Ron Bryant of the Kentucky Historical Society, Claire McCann of the University of Kentucky, Rod Rust of the National Archives, and John Caldwell of the Carl Albert Center for Congressional Research and Studies. I accomplished much of the actual research for this book without having to wander too far afield from my various places of study and employment. In this, no one has been of as much help as Debbe Causey and Electa Hoyle of the Inter-library Loan Department at The Citadel's Daniel Library. They have, with good cheer and wit, always gone an extra step to acquire all that I needed.

An important part of this study has been Donald Mrozek. His incisive commentary on the manuscript and the time he devoted to just talking about history and what it means to be a historian went well beyond what I could have expected of a graduate advisor. He exemplifies professionalism, and I can think of no higher praise. Others who have commented on, and molded, this book include Aruna Michie, Marion Gray, and Robin Higham, all of Kansas State University. Rod Andrew, Robert Steed, Peter Knupfer, William R. Roberts, Louis Gerteis, Thomas Mackey, and Jamie Woods have helped by either commenting on various conference presentations or reading the manuscript. Special thanks should also be given Edgar Raines of the U.S. Army Center for Military History. Dr. Raines took interest in this research in an early period of its development, and many of his comments sparked a major revision of what became chapter 4. No less important in shaping the final version of this manuscript has been Paul Cimbala and his reader for Fordham University Press.

Paul, especially, deserves credit for the good-natured encouragement that led me to finish the work.

Personal support came from all the expected places. My colleagues at The Citadel, but especially Keith Knapp and Kathy Grenier, have offered, through the years, encouragement and friendship that cannot be matched. They and my cadets have made The Citadel the best place to be. Final thanks, of course, go to family: my wife for her love and sacrifice, and my mother and father for the example of their lives.

INTRODUCTION

WHEN THE CIVIL WAR ended, a long line of creditors and claimants piled up at the door of the United States Treasury. Contractors, banks, bond holders, and aggrieved citizens all wanted their share of the Union government's money. Also in line, but certainly not new to it, were the states themselves. Since the very beginning of the war, the states had been the primary vehicles through which the United States had recruited and organized its armies. This cost the states money, and a lot of it. By one congressional estimate, the states could claim over $468 million. But that was hardly the beginning of what they might demand. Several states had become active war zones, leading not only the call for state-sponsored local defense forces, but also the invariable destruction of private and public property. Add in the accumulating monetary interest on these costs, and more than one lawmaker thought there might be no limit to what the states could claim. For a treasury that had already spent in excess of $3 billion on the war by June 1865, even the low estimate of $468 million was an amount that could not be repaid quickly. In fact, it was a figure that would never be repaid.[1]

This book tells the story of state attempts to recoup the costs of fighting the Civil War. It is an examination of the little-known financial contributions of the states to the Union war effort. More importantly, the book provides a window into the even lesser-known administrative operations of U.S. federalism from 1861 to 1880. Despite a recent explosion of scholarly interest in the government of this period, there has been little attendant research into, or acknowledgment of, federalism. To be sure, authors have written about the federated states and their constitutional relationship with the national government.[2] However, this is not the same as treating federal-

---

[1] U.S. Congress, House Report, 39th Cong., 1st sess., 1866, H. Doc. 16, serial 1272; *The Statistical History of the United States from the Colonial Times to the Present* (Stamford, Conn.: Fairfield Publishers, 1965), 718.

[2] Works that touch upon state government collectively include Ballard Campbell,

ism as a working system of intergovernmental operations.[3] Simply stated, scholars have shed little light on an administrative system involving both state and national governments.[4] An exploration of state war claims provides that opportunity because the claims represented the most sustained and expensive intergovernmental contact of the three decades following the war.[5]

My initial research into the claims was framed by the basic question of discovering how the claims system worked. It was followed quickly by the more substantive question of what determined success in a process that clearly had winners and losers among the states. This, in turn, led to the idea that the court system and political parties would be central to an issue that appeared to involve the United States' historical litigiousness and its distributive party politics. It was also a framework for analysis at the core of the most recent works on

---

Representative Democracy: Public Policy and Midwestern Legislatures in the Late Nineteenth Century (Cambridge, Mass.: Harvard University Press, 1980); William R. Brock, *Investigation and Responsibility: Public Responsibility in the United States, 1865–1900* (Cambridge: Cambridge University Press, 1984); and John Duffy, *The Sanitarians: A History of American Public Health* (Urbana: University of Illinois Press, 1990). Ballard Campbell discusses some of the ideological ramifications of federalism in *The Growth of American Government: Governance from the Cleveland Era to the Present* (Bloomington: Indiana University Press, 1995). Richard Hamm has dealt extensively with the constitutional aspects of federalism in the period after that under discussion in this book. See his *Shaping the Eighteenth Amendment: Temperance Reform, Legal Culture, and the Polity, 1880–1930* (Chapel Hill: University of North Carolina Press, 1995).

[3] The term *intergovernmental operations* describes the administrative interaction of the national government and states. It should not be confused with the terminology of some scholars, who have used "intergovernmental relations" to describe the existence of a postfederal system. For an overview of this approach, consult Deil S. Wright, "A Century of the Intergovernmental Administrative State: Wilson's Federalism, New Deal Intergovernmental Relations, and Contemporary Intergovernmental Management," in *A Centennial History of the American Administrative State*, ed. Ralph C. Chandler (New York: The Free Press, 1989), 219–21.

[4] One of the few works to examine the administrative interaction between the states and the national government in the nineteenth century is Daniel Elazar, *The American Partnership: Intergovernmental Co-operation in the Nineteenth Century United States* (Chicago: University of Chicago Press, 1962).

[5] There is some debate about the birth of modern cooperative federalism and the attendant flow of federal dollars to the states. Works that represent varying opinions on this include Harry Scheiber, "Federalism and the American Economic Order, 1789–1910," *Law and Society Review* 10 (1975): 108, and his *The Condition of American Federalism: An Historian's View* (Washington: Government Printing Office, 1966); James Q. Wilson, "The Rise of the Bureaucratic State," *The Public Interest* 41 (1975): 91; Daniel Elazar, *The American Partnership*.

government in the Gilded Age. More particularly, in 1984 Stephen Skowronek helped usher in a new age of research in political development with his statement that "courts and parties" controlled nineteenth-century U.S. government.[6] Using a thoroughly modern definition of the function of political parties, Skowronek found that parties in the nineteenth century brought "cohesion to national politics," while "facilitating working relationships within and among the branches and levels of the constitutional structure." Although the modern United States has sprouted numerous other linkage structures to order governance, Skowronek found only one other institution that mediated public life in the nineteenth century: the courts. According to Skowronek, the courts were really the "surrogate for a more fully developed administrative apparatus."[7] Richard L. McCormick did not come from the same "new institutionalist" background as Skowronek, but he did reach a similar conclusion about the importance of parties in his equally influential article on the "party period." To McCormick, parties were not only electoral machines, they were also the vehicles that organized governments and distributed its largess to the electorate.[8]

The United States' experience with the claims, and hence its administration of the federal system, shows that such an emphasis upon courts and parties needs to be modified. Although the claims appear to model McCormick's description of a distributive state, it was nonetheless a state that relied little on courts and parties to distribute wealth. These institutions do appear within the claims narrative, yet they are of secondary importance within the actual process. Corrupt officials, for example, were tried in the courts, and Democrat-con-

---

[6] The literature on this historiographical revolution is large. A good place to start is David B. Robertson, "The Return to History and the New Institutionalism in American Political Science," *Social Science History* 17 (1993): 1–36.

[7] Stephen Skowronek, *Building a New American State: The Expansion of Central State Authority, 1877–1920* (Cambridge: Cambridge University Press, 1982), 25. A discussion of parties as a modern linkage structure can be found in Samuel J. Eldersveld and Hanes Walton Jr., *Political Parties in American Society*, 2nd ed. (Boston: Bedford/St. Martin's, 2000), 1–3.

[8] Richard L. McCormick, *The Party Period and Public Policy: American Politics from the Age of Jackson to the Progressive Era* (New York: Oxford University Press, 1986), 209. The influence and complementary nature of McCormick's and Skowronek's scholarship is best exemplified in Theda Skocpol's influential *Protecting Soldiers and Mothers: The Political Origins of Social Policy in the United States* (Cambridge, Mass.: Belknap Press of Harvard University Press, 1992), 68–71.

trolled states sometimes complained of mistreatment at the hands of Republicans in Washington. But beyond this, there was nothing. Neither courts nor parties were terribly important in the handling of a potential transfer of $468 million from Washington to the states.[9]

Absent a governing system defined by courts and parties, what then is the conceptual framework to understand the claims? The answer to this question lies in the contradictory popular demands of the post–Civil War United States. On the one hand, the end of the war found the national government with a greatly expanded role and set of responsibilities. Washington began to operate, if imperfectly, in a wide variety of areas, including banking, land grants, the enforcement of civil liberties, and the regulation of interstate commerce. Naturally, public expectations of what the national government could then do rose concurrently. The frontiersman's demand for land, the veteran's demand for pensions, the railroad's demand for cash or land subsidy, and the loyal state's urgent demand for war reimbursement all neatly represented society's newly expressed, if not discovered, sense of what Washington could provide.

On the other hand, the new expectations were more than balanced by older impulses in U.S. political culture.[10] First, for every demand on the government there was an equal demand for what many Americans called retrenchment. After the great spending spree that was the Civil War, it did not take the citizenry long to call for frugality and a return to an ideal of limited government that echoed the nation's republican heritage. The claims experience demonstrated what would happen when these contradictory demands met in one issue.

---

[9] Not all recent scholarship supports the monolithic concept of courts and parties. At the municipal level, see Stanley K. Schultz, *Constructing Urban Culture: American Cities and City Planning, 1800–1920* (Philadelphia: Temple University Press, 1989) and Jon C. Teaford, *The Unheralded Triumph: City Government in America, 1870–1900* (Baltimore: Johns Hopkins University Press, 1984). For the national government, consult Daniel P. Carpenter, *The Forging of Bureaucratic Autonomy: Reputations, Networks, and Policy Innovation in Executive Agencies, 1862–1928* (Princeton, N.J.: Princeton University Press, 2001), 64. I agree with much of Carpenter's discussion of the role of bureaucracy within the period. However, later in this book I will dissent from his assessment of that bureaucracy's capabilities.

[10] Morton Keller has examined this tension in *Affairs of State: Public Life in Late Nineteenth-Century America* (Cambridge, Mass.: Harvard University Press, 1977). However, Keller argues that America oscillated from a period of progressive state expansion to one of retrenchment between 1865 and 1880. The example of the claims shows no such oscillation. See also McCormick, *The Party Period*, 216.

At the state level there would be a continual drumbeat for reimbursement, but the public cry for retrenchment produced an indemnification effort that depended upon the limited administrative structures of the past. The desire to retain the basis of the older system did not, however, prevent the states from experimenting. In a manner reminiscent of what Stephen Skowronek has described as "patching" various agencies of the post-1877 national bureaucracy, the states chose often to hire outside professional agents to manage the claims. This privatization of government function aimed to cut costs and gain efficiency while not further encrusting a state's existing bureaucracy. Nevertheless, the electorate never warmed to such an innovation. Notions of retrenchment caused many to look upon agents as a corrupt extravagance. The price of corruption was therefore not worth the promise of reimbursement.[11]

A second long-standing impulse that complicated the process and effectiveness of any state's push for reimbursement was the presence of a host of local concerns, including, among many others, Indian raids, fears of debt repudiation, overburdened officials, and a simple distrust of the national government. Not surprisingly, the end result was a distracted bureaucratic and political effort. State activity directed toward Washington thus became an ad hoc affair, with state leaders creating temporary administrative structures with each new cycle of claims that needed prosecution. Fearing permanent governmental innovations, state leadership repeatedly seemed to assume or hope that each attempt at indemnification, and its attendant contact with the federal government, would be its last.

In Washington, the demand for retrenchment proved a powerful brake on all attempts to access public money. Always concerned with a depleted treasury, Congress and the executive departments resisted the states' disjointed efforts to modify administrative structures, procedures, and precedents in their attempts to facilitate reimbursement. Any money returned to the states would have to be

---

[11] Skowronek, *Building a New American State*, 37–162. The efforts to privatize claims administration was a part of a nascent privatization movement in subnational governments in the years following the Civil War. For other examples, see Timothy J. Gilfoyle, *City of Eros: New York City, Prostitution, and the Commercialization of Sex, 1790–1920* (New York: Norton, 1992) and Anne-Marie Szymanski, "Dry Compulsions: Prohibition and the Creation of State-Level Enforcement Agencies," *Journal of Policy History* 11 (1999): 115–46.

pried from the hands of an army of clerks, patronage appointees, and even elected officials, all anxious to defend the treasury.

The administration of the claims system can be illustrated by looking at any number or combination of states. For this study I have chosen Kansas, Missouri, and Kentucky. Although they were border states, these states are broadly representative of all Union states in their efforts to gain reimbursement. First, Kansas, Missouri, and Kentucky relied upon commonly used officials and methods to prosecute the claims. Second, they filed collectively for every type of claim seen in the postwar era. Third, these states had contrasting financial conditions involving debt and taxation that could determine just how vigorously any given state would have to pursue its claims. Finally, and relevant to determining the role of political parties in the claims process, these states represent most of the different permutations of partisan political competition and domination seen between 1865 and 1880.

Against this background, the states pursued indemnification. It was an activity that certainly reveals much about the nature of relations between Washington and the states. But the pursuit of indemnification also provides insight to a series of broader questions involving the study of government in the late nineteenth century. How well, for example, would the states work together on an issue of mutual concern? How did the states lobby their interests in an era notorious for its corporate business lobbying? Just how efficient was a clerk-dominated bureaucratic system when faced with an unprecedented volume of work?[12] Did it grind to a halt? Was it riddled with corruption? The answers to these questions are complex and sometimes contradictory, but that is at least fitting for an era whose electorate wanted many things from its government but was also uncomfortable with any concurrent growth in that government. It was, in other words, a familiar situation in U.S. history and one that would be seen again. This book chronicles just how the states and Washington operated in a system defined by conflicting public demands over the size and function of government.

---

[12] Daniel Carpenter has coined the term "clerical state" to describe the governmental bureaucracy of the nineteenth century. See his *The Forging of Bureaucratic Autonomy*, 37–64.

1

Origins of the Civil War Claims System

ON APRIL 13, 1861, war fever gripped the United States. One day after the Confederate attack upon Fort Sumter, popular sentiment in the North erupted in a show of support for the idea of Union. As men rushed by the tens of thousands to hastily set up recruiting offices, the governors of the states agitated and rode this tidal wave of excitement. Caught in the euphoria of the moment and believing, as most people did, that the rebellion would be short lived, the governors gave little thought to the long-term financing of the war. Oliver P. Morton of Indiana, for example, declared that his state was willing to spend its "best blood and treasure without limit." Alexander Randall of Wisconsin spoke for many when he cried out: "What is money? What is life—in the presence of such a crisis?"[1]

Early fiscal abandon knew few bounds. Where money was short, some governors, such as William A. Buckingham of Connecticut and Erastus Fairbanks of Vermont, bought the necessary supplies with their own personal cash and credit. Other state officials concluded that Washington's financial assistance was unnecessary. Writing in May 1861, Col. Ambrose Burnside of Rhode Island refused a War Department offer to requisition supplies for his regiment. An indignant Burnside spurned the offer, noting that Rhode Island's troops "need nothing . . . from the government; Rhode Island and her governor will attend to their wants." A similar situation occurred in the

---

[1] Two states, New Jersey and New York, did have early reservations about state spending. See War Department, United States, *War of the Rebellion: The Official Records of the Union and Confederate Armies*, 3 series, 70 vols. (Washington: Government Printing Office, 1880–1901), 3:1:73, 83. Hereafter cited as *OR*. The enthusiasm of other governors is covered in William B. Weeden, *War Government, Federal and State, in Massachusetts, New York, Pennsylvania, and Indiana, 1861–1865* (Boston: Houghton, Mifflin and Company, 1906), 163–64. Morton quoted in *OR*, 3:1:126. Randall quoted in Walter S. Glazer, "Wisconsin Goes to War: April 1861," *Wisconsin Magazine of History* 50 (1967): 152.

Midwest. Mixing personal disdain for Abraham Lincoln with his belief that Illinois alone could crush the Confederacy, Republican governor Richard Yates attempted to raise a private army of 100,000 men without financial assistance from Washington. In yet another twist in federal relations, John Andrew of Massachusetts bombarded President Lincoln with not only military advice but offers of unconditional grants of money. To Andrew, the war was from the first day a holy crusade for abolition that should not be impeded by worries over the availability of revenue. A state's troops should go forward, he proclaimed, and "the question of who shall pay for them afterwards, is of secondary importance. . . ."[2]

Eventually, this impetuousness waned. A number of states continued to suffer from the effects of the nationwide economic panic that had begun in 1857. The Old Northwest, especially, entered the war in a cash-starved condition. Shaky antebellum credit and traditionally unstable currencies joined together with the lingering effects of the panic to push several states to their financial limits. As early as July 17, 1861, Ohio let it be known that the state needed help to pay its war-related bills.[3] In Wisconsin, Governor Randall's early war enthusiasm, which had led him to ask "What was money?" faded by summer when he realized that his state had literally no money. Other states, ranging from Iowa to Maine, soon found themselves in a similar plight. Confederate victory at Manassas on July 21 sealed the financial fates of the states as they then understood that this war would be neither short nor cheap. Their governors then turned to Washington for help.[4]

---

[2] Burnside quoted in William B. Hesseltine, *Lincoln and the War Governors* (New York: Alfred A. Knopf, 1948; reprint, Gloucester, Mass.: Peter Smith, 1972), 170. Jack Northrup, "Governor Richard Yates and President Lincoln," *Lincoln Herald* 70 (1968), 196. Andrew quoted in William Schouler, *A History of Massachusetts in the Civil War*, 2 vols. (Boston: E. P. Dutton, 1868–1871), 1:123. See also Edith Ware, "Political Opinion in Massachusetts During the Civil War and Reconstruction" (Ph.D. diss., Columbia University, 1916), 67.

[3] The financial conditions among midwesten states are examined in William G. Shade, *Banks or No Banks: The Money Issue in Midwestern Politics, 1832–1865* (Detroit: Wayne State University Press, 1982), 221–22. For the condition of Ohio, see William Dennison to John Sherman and C. S. Wolcott to John Sherman, July 17, 1861, John Sherman Collection, Library of Congress (LC), Washington, D.C.

[4] Randall's fiscal frustrations are covered also in Richard N. Current, *The Civil War Era, 1848–1873* (Madison: State Historical Society of Wisconsin, 1976), 302–5; Frank L. Klement, *Wisconsin and the Civil War* (Madison: State Historical Society of Wisconsin, 1963), 24–27. The financial distress of other states can be glimpsed in

As Congress and the treasury crafted their responses to states now desperate for money, they had a long trail of experience to fall back upon. Throughout the nineteenth century, the U.S. government relied upon the states to advance their own money to pay the costs of all military conflicts. Whether in Indian uprisings or formally declared wars, the states expended millions of dollars for self-defense with little or no complaint. That the states did not complain indicated that the national government eventually reimbursed the cost. Moreover, the American experience with reimbursement predated the Revolution. In many cases, the English Parliament saw fit to reimburse the colonies for war-related expenses during the many Indian and French conflicts of the eighteenth century. In the French and Indian War alone, Parliament reimbursed over one-half of all colonial expenses. The American experience of paying for the cost of the Revolution did not deviate from this tradition. As early as 1783, James Madison proposed that the Continental Congress assume all state debts caused by the war. This proposal then formed the basis of the better-known plan of debt assumption that Alexander Hamilton put forward in 1789. Hamilton's plan, when ultimately approved in January 1790, reimbursed over $20 million to the states. Vital to the establishment of a national credit for the fledgling nation, the reimbursement obviated the need for any increases in state taxation until well after the War of 1812. Just as significantly, it also helped pave the way for future congressional acts of indemnification that would make up the majority of the roughly $17 million in cash grants provided to the states before the Civil War.[5]

Hubert H. Wubben, *Civil War Iowa and the Copperhead Movement* (Ames: Iowa State University Press, 1980), 34; Dan Elbert Clark, *Samuel Jordan Kirkwood* (Iowa City: State Historical Society of Iowa, 1917), 173–219; Michael W. Whalon, "Israel Washburn and the War Department," *Social Science* 46 (1971): 81.

[5] Evidence of colonial reimbursement can be found in E. James Ferguson, *The Power of the Purse: A History of American Public Finance, 1776–1790* (Chapel Hill: University of North Carolina Press, 1961), 19–20; Benjamin U. Ratchford, *American State Debts*, 6, 10–11; Charles J. Bullock, *Historical Sketch of the Finances and Financial Policy of Massachusetts from 1780–1905*, Publications of the American Economic Association, series 3, vol. 8, no. 2 (New York: MacMillan Co., 1907): 4; E. P. Tanner, "Colonial Agencies in England," *Pacific Studies Quarterly* 16 (1901): 33. Information on the Revolutionary War debt can be found in Kenneth R. Bowling, *Politics in the First Congress, 1789–1791* (New York: Garland Publishing, 1990), 202; William C. Anderson, *The Price of Liberty: The Public Debt of the American Revolution* (Charlottesville: University of Virginia Press, 1983); U.S. Congress, *Resolutions, Laws, Ordinances Relating to . . . Funding the Revolutionary Debt* (Washington:

Initially, such acts of indemnification covered the military expenses of the states that had furnished militias to engage hostile Indians. The types of expenses included most things required to mobilize, equip, transport, and employ a fighting force. These costs could add up quickly. For example, in 1797 Congress issued over $70,000 to Georgia for the services of its militia along the state border. In another, and much later, example, Congress disbursed almost $1 million to California in August 1854 for the purpose of paying that state's expenses in quelling all Indian disturbances prior to January 1, 1854. Both of these cases, though separated by fifty-seven years, illustrate the periodic costliness of indemnification for the treasury. Georgia's reimbursement in 1797 accounted for almost 7 percent of that fiscal year's War Department budget, while California's reimbursement totaled 8 percent of the budget in 1854. Georgia and California were not the only states to receive reimbursement from the general government. By the end of 1860, Congress had passed more than thirty separate appropriations totaling more than $3 million for state war claims related to Indian uprisings. Although other military expenses during this period dwarfed the size of these claims, the government also had to pay the states for other military costs.[6]

Indeed, although Indian troubles produced claims from the largest number of states, America's formally declared wars accounted for the most expensive claims. Pennsylvania, for example, received $743,000 to defray the costs of calling out its militia during the War of 1812. By 1817 alone, Congress had reimbursed other states in excess of $3.5 million for fighting that war. Congress continued the indemnification practice with most state militia expenses incurred during the Mexican War. Because of the advent—and widespread usage—of state volunteer units that were organized by the state and then mus-

---

Thomas Allen, 1838; reprint, New York: Research Reprints, 1970), 26–59. Evidence of the influence of indemnification upon state taxation can be found in Elazar, *The American Partnership*, 88. Calculations of the national government's outlays to states do not include President Andrew Jackson's distributions from the defunct Bank of the United States in 1837. See Scheiber, "American Federalism and the Distribution of Power," 70 n.

[6] A compendium of legislation relating to state claims for suppressing Indian invasions can be found in J. B. Holloway, ed., *Laws of the United States and Decisions of the Courts Relating to War Claims* (Washington: Government Printing Office, 1908), 139–49. Percentages of the War Department's budget were calculated from statistics in *The Statistical History of the United States from the Colonial Times to the Present* (Stamford, Conn.: Fairfield Publishers, 1965), 718–19.

tered into national service, Congress expanded its indemnification coverage beyond state militias originally designed strictly for local defense. By the end of the Mexican War, Congress had assumed most state expenses accumulated in the recruiting, equipping, and transportation of volunteer units prior to their incorporation into national service.[7]

Though a viable arrangement, indemnification also revealed some of the strains in the newly created American federal system. Most antebellum claims problems developed out of political conflict and constitutional interpretation. Not surprisingly, the first incidence of difficulty arose when Alexander Hamilton proposed indemnification of the states for their Revolutionary War debt. Hamilton's initiative generated heated opposition, much of which was tangential to any dispute over the concept of indemnification. Some resistance came from a number of southern states that saw any national assumption of the debt as a backdoor method of subsidizing northern commercial interests that had speculated in the debt. More resistance came from Virginia, North Carolina, and Georgia, which had paid off most of their debts by 1790 and thus did not see it as their responsibility to pay those of other states. Still more opposition came from scattered Anti-Federalists who saw the act as an unconstitutional consolidation of power in the federal government. Sentiment against assumption of state debts ran high enough to defeat Hamilton's first attempt to force legislation through the House of Representatives.[8]

The eventual passage of the assumption act in 1790 represented a triumph of practical politics. States dominated by the Anti-Federalists, such as Massachusetts and South Carolina, were also those states more than likely to have great debts. In the end, the need for money outweighed most fears of governmental consolidation. Similarly, proponents of assumption gained most of the necessary southern support

---

[7] Examples of the federal assumption of state expenses can be found in *United States Statutes at Large* 5 (1817): 251–52, 378; 10 (1846): 111, 115. For the War of 1812, see also the communication of James Madison to Senate, January 27, 1817, in Benjamin F. Cooling, ed., *The New American State Papers: Military Affairs*, 19 vols. (Wilmington, Del.: Scholarly Resources, 1979), 5:72.

[8] Noble E. Cunningham Jr., *The Jeffersonian Republicans: The Formation of Party Organization, 1789–1801* (Chapel Hill: University of North Carolina Press, 1957), 3–8; Bowling, *Politics in the First Congress, 1789–1791*, 200–211; Whitney K. Bates, "Northern Speculators and Southern State Debts, 1790," *William and Mary Quarterly*, 3rd series, 19 (1962): 30–48.

with two practical compromises. One saw the government reimburse
the southern states for any war-related debts that they had already
paid off. The other compromise delivered the future federal capital
to the shores of the Potomac River.[9]

Lost in the debate over the Revolutionary War debt were the ramifications for future acts of indemnification. When justifying indemnification, few supporters varied from Hamilton's recitation of the
necessity of the establishment of a national credit. It was only after
this debate that interested parties attempted to justify the concept of
indemnification in terms other than Hamilton's. Though the states
would in future instances refer to the precedent of the Revolutionary
War claims, they usually placed more emphasis upon indemnification
simply being a matter of equity and justice. Moreover, advocates of
indemnification turned readily to the Constitution and its "guarantee
clause" of Article 4. That clause guaranteed each state a republican
form of government. States seeking indemnification interpreted this
as meaning the federal government would provide the money necessary to protect republicanism when threatened by armed invasion.
Such an interpretation stood as the principal application of the "guarantee clause" until the 1830s, when abolitionists used the clause to
rationalize the destruction of slavery in the name of defending republicanism.[10]

Once indemnification had been justified by precedent, equity, and
the Constitution, problems shifted from conflicts between groups of
states to conflicts between the national government and the states.
Friction between the two levels of government was most obvious
during and after the War of 1812 in the case of Massachusetts. In
this example, the claims dispute merged administrative, political, and
constitutional questions as Massachusetts sought indemnification for
militia that did not serve the federal government and, in fact, was
mustered in direct defiance of that government. At the outset of the
War of 1812, Massachusetts stood at the center of Federalist resis-

---

[9] Charles A. Beard and Mary R. Beard, *The Rise of American Civilization*,
1:342–47; Noble E. Cunningham Jr., *The Jeffersonian Republicans*, 3–8; Bowling,
Politics in the First Congress, 1789–1791, 200–211; Whitney K. Bates, "Northern
Speculators and Southern State Debts, 1790," 30–48.

[10] For the use of the guarantee clause in antislavery constitutionalism, see William
M. Wiecek, *The Guarantee Clause of the U.S. Constitution* (Ithaca, N.Y.: Cornell
University Press, 1972).

tance to the war policy of President James Madison. This resistance included a denial that an emergency actually existed in 1812 warranting President Madison's calling of the state militia. Massachusetts ultimately rejected the constitutional authority of the president to call out the militia and have regular officers placed in command.[11]

Massachusetts and Madison did not solve the dispute during the war. Between 1812 and 1815 the Massachusetts militia served in a variety of situations, but only rarely under the command of regular United States officers. Militiamen spent most of their time guarding the Canadian border and the Atlantic seacoast under the direct command and authority of the Federalist governor Caleb Strong. In the years following the war, Massachusetts' resistance to national authority on this issue thawed considerably, especially when Republicans gained power in the state in 1823. Led then by James Madison's onetime secretary of war, William Eustis, Massachusetts disavowed the right of the governor to interpose his military authority over that of the president. To some extent, this decision stood as an obvious repudiation of the Federalists, who had also just been defeated at the polls.

More importantly, the decision recognized the constitutional and administrative realities of the postwar world. Constitutionally, Eustis's repudiation of Strong's policy confirmed an 1820 United States Supreme Court opinion, which also invalidated state military interposition. Administratively, the move was a necessary precondition for Massachusetts to be indemnified for its war expenses. In an action that provoked much contemporary astonishment, Massachusetts, beginning in 1814, sought reimbursement of its militia expenses from the same government it chose to disobey during the war. A running political and administrative feud ensued for the next ten years as Massachusetts tried repeatedly, and unsuccessfully, to persuade the federal government of its ultimate responsibility to reimburse any state that had mustered troops in a declared war. During that time, United States Treasury officials and the president affirmed a salient point regarding indemnification; that is, reimbursement would go

---

[11] The following discussion of Massachusetts' claims difficulties is based primarily upon Leonard White, *The Jeffersonians: A Study in Administrative History, 1801–1829* (New York: The Free Press, 1951), 539–45. See also W. Edwin Hemphill, et. al., eds., *The Papers of John C. Calhoun*, 16 vols. (Columbia: University of South Carolina Press, 1975–), 8:xxxv–xxxvii.

only to those states that mustered troops under the president's call. States such as Massachusetts, and Connecticut to a lesser extent, that called forth troops only to deny the president their use forfeited Washington's financial support.[12]

With the principle thus firmly established, Congress could grant exceptions through special legislation. In the case of Massachusetts, the government delayed any serious consideration of the claims until the Bay State repudiated Governor Strong's wartime actions. When that happened in 1823, President James Monroe, soon to retire, prodded a reluctant Congress to authorize indemnification for the purpose of equity and political peace. Monroe ultimately saw Massachusetts no differently than most states. Massachusetts had been harmed by the financial cost of the war, and the time had arrived to soothe partisan feelings. Although permeated with the broader constitutional overtones that often dominated federal relations in the new republic, Massachusetts' claims illustrated a key point about future claims settlements. The settlement of claims was predicated upon either the actual national service of state militia or the president's specific authorization that the militia take the field in the absence of federalized troops. Without these preconditions, states such as Massachusetts had to pursue their claims interests in the political forum of Congress.[13]

For the remainder of the antebellum period, this system of indemnification functioned with few noticeable problems. For the most part, this resulted from fewer conflicts that necessitated reimbursement from the United States government. Regular troops handled Indian uprisings with greater frequency, and the states played a short-lived, and restricted, role in troop mobilization during the Mexican-American War. Regular Army commanders Zachary Taylor and Edmund P. Gaines mounted early recruiting drives that allowed many state units to muster almost directly into national service. Consequently, after Congress authorized the reimbursement of states be-

---

[12] *Houston v. Moore,* 5 Wheaton 1 (1820). Congress controlled the specific appropriation of national dollars for the war. See for example, *Statutes at Large* 5 (1816): 252–53; 5 (1817): 378.

[13] *Statutes at Large* 5 (1817): 378. One future example of the necessity of national authorization can be found in Florida's claims from the Seminole Wars. See U.S. Congress, House Report, 28th Cong., 2nd sess., 1845, H. Doc. 108.

ginning July 1846, the treasury received only a limited number of claims. The volume remained small for the next fourteen years. By 1860, the government had processed and approved only $152,108 in claims with no state expressing any great dissatisfaction.[14]

Thus, at the outbreak of the Civil War, there were few apparent problems within the claims system. Numerous wars and one constitutional test had established a series of precedents and procedures that seemed to operate with little controversy. However, the reality of the Civil War's early months revealed a claims system that not only had yet to be tested, but one that was largely foreign to most state executive officials and legislatures. One reason helps explain the situation. Despite the constant—albeit diminished—flow of claims to Washington during the late antebellum period, most northern states that would be in position to file claims had very little actual experience with the system. America's military conflicts in the nineteenth century involving state troops, especially in the years following the War of 1812, had been fought almost exclusively by southern and border states. Whether in the Seminole or Black Hawk Wars, the mobilization of state troops occurred primarily in the South. In the Mexican War, this was even more evident. Only six of the twenty-two states that would remain loyal to the Union in the Civil War had filed claims of any kind. Of those that had filed, only Ohio pressed a claim of any significance ($14,000).[15]

Although lacking any real experience working within a claims system, the states were anxious for that chance following the Union debacle at Manassas on July 21, 1861. Six days later on July 27, Congress responded with an act to indemnify the states. As with the thirty-four other pieces of war legislation enacted during the crisis that followed Manassas, this indemnification act passed without the normal legislative scrutiny of the antebellum period. Congressional committees examined and reported the bill within twenty-four hours, and neither House nor Senate debated it. The level of legislative scrutiny for this bill was, however, greater than that given to other bills passed in July 1861. During those fitful days, the House of Rep-

---

[14] *Statutes at Large* 10 (1846): 111; U.S. Congress, Senate Report, 50th Cong., 1st sess., 1888, S. Doc. 1286.

[15] U.S. Congress, Senate Report, 50th Cong., 1st sess., 1888, S. Doc. 1286.

resentatives generally suspended its rules, bypassed the committees, and introduced the emergency legislation directly into the Committee of the Whole.[16]

Befitting much congressional legislation, the indemnification bill was vague and offered a large amount of hope to the states that Washington would reimburse a broad array of military expenses. The bill authorized treasury officials to reimburse costs associated with "enrolling, subsisting, clothing, supplying, arming, equipping, paying and transporting" state troops "employed in aiding to suppress the present rebellion. . . ." Confusion immediately arose among the states and the executive departments as to the effective date of these claims, but Congress moved quickly to pass an amendatory act. The new bill allowed the states to press such claims covered in the original legislation retroactive to President Lincoln's April 1861 call for volunteers.[17]

The passage of the first Civil War reimbursement act seemed to minimize the potential for controversy. The wording of the act was broad, and most states applied quickly for reimbursement under its terms. Indeed, the indemnification bill touched off an early rush by the states on the treasury. Less than one year after the passage of the act, fifteen states had petitioned the treasury with claims totaling $23.9 million. But the highest expectations of the states were not to be realized. Congress had disposed of the bill quickly and left no record of its intentions as to how exactly it should be interpreted. With no committee reports or floor debates, the limits of the legislation then depended exclusively upon the treasury's interpretation of the bill. Secretary of the Treasury Salmon P. Chase quickly filled the interpretive void when he published a list of rules for the settlement of state claims. Chase's rules satisfied few states, and they became the basis of most claims disputes between the states and the United States government for the remainder of the century.[18]

Though the rules generated almost immediate friction, their strict

---

[16] *United States Statutes at Large* 12 (1861): 276; Congressional Globe, 37th Cong., 1st sess., 253, 276, 362. For an examination of these events and their place within the administrative history of Congress, see Thoman F. Broden, "Congressional Committee Reports: Their Role and History," *Notre Dame Lawyer* 33 (1958):209–38.

[17] Ibid.

[18] Treasury Department, *Report of the Secretary of the Treasury, 1862*, 82. Chase's ryles in "Report of the State Agent," January 1, 1868,. Doc. #18, vol. 2, *Kentucky Documents, 1867*, 16–18.

nature might have been predicted. Secretary Chase assumed control of the treasury at a time when it seemed that the entire country demanded money from the government's coffers. Upon Lincoln's inauguration, the treasury was spending almost $172,000 a day. Just three months later when Congress passed its claims legislation, the treasury was then spending over $1 million a day. During the early days of the war, the government did not have enough money in the treasury to pay congressional salaries, let alone the claims of anxious states. For a government that was now hemorrhaging money, Salmon Chase was the right man to stanch the flow. Ill-tempered and humorless, Chase craved power but not popularity. Even a personal admirer termed him "cold-hearted, obstinate, and enormously self-conceited." He was, in other words, the perfect bureaucratic chief.[19]

Chase's natural unwillingness to spend scarce public dollars was magnified by his belief that Congress had erred in its July 27 legislation authorizing reimbursement. Although Congress had filled the July 27 bill with far greater detail than the indemnification authorizations for the War of 1812 and the Mexican conflict, Chase believed the legislation still too broad. He concluded that fraud and extravagance would result without strong interpretive rules. Consequently, his rules carefully detailed an administrative process grounded in antebellum precedents. Chase required, for example, that the states present original vouchers, or receipts, for every transaction, and that the states then classify and abstract all claims into separate categories of pay, subsistence, clothing, transportation, and equipment. The vouchers themselves had to specify the particular troops, by regiment or corps, on whose behalf the state spent money. Claims for pay also had to be accompanied by payrolls similar to those used by the regular United States Army.[20]

As other paragraphs established reasonable rates for transportation and the accepted costs allowable for a soldier's daily subsistence, the net effect of the rules was to restrict severely the amount of a state's reimbursable expenses. It was a situation made evident by the frantic nature of the war's mobilization and the haphazard method by which

---

[19] An admirer quoted in P. J. Staudenraus, *Mr. Lincoln's Washington: Selections from the Writings of Noah Brooks, Civil War Correspondent* (South Brunswick, N.J.: Thomas Yoseloff, 1967), 340.

[20] "Report of the State Agent," January 1, 1868, Doc. #18, vol. 2, *Kentucky Documents, 1867,* 16–18.

the states gathered their troops and provided for their expenses. Popular enthusiasm early in the war generated numbers of troops and logistical difficulties that the states could scarcely handle. They adapted well, but the rush to absorb units into state service also led to a rush to accept costs. In many cases, documentation of state expenses did not exist. In other cases, when the documentation did exist, it was not in the form specified by Chase.

Burdened now by a level of proof that often could not be met, the states realized that the procedures established by Chase created an administrative tangle that would take years to straighten. To some degree, the problem stemmed from a lack of cash. By the fall of 1861 the states needed money badly. Chase offered small percentage rebates on the direct tax levied upon individual states if those states met their troop quotas on time. Chase offered additional cash advances to the states based upon estimations of how much the states spent and would, therefore, be eventually reimbursed. By the end of June 1862 alone, the treasury had advanced over $4.5 million to thirteen states. But these measures were not enough. With $23 million in claims pending, Chase's rules did not offer the hope of a speedy reimbursement. In fact, they necessitated clerical work that some within the Congress thought would take twenty-five years to process.[21]

Here then was the first major claims controversy, as many states mounted a concerted campaign to have Chase's rules either overturned or relaxed. Congressmen and state officials lobbied the treasury directly, but, more importantly, beginning in January 1862 they concentrated their efforts in Congress. Chase's voucher requirement concerned them most. Republican representative William Kellogg of Illinois led the charge against Chase by introducing legislation that allowed governors to certify claims as just and proper without any recourse to specific vouchers. Debated at length, Kellogg's legislation revealed immediately that Congress still contained a vocal opposition. Although Kellogg argued for reform in the name of administrative efficiency, a coalition of Democrats and Union Whigs joined to denounce legislation that, they thought, subsidized fraud and poor

---

[21] Treasury advances to the states are covered in *Report of the Secretary of the Treasury, 1861*, 144–45. Regarding the time necessary to settle claims, see the comments of William Kellogg and William Dunn in *Congressional Globe*, 37th Cong., 2nd sess., 567.

accounting in Republican-dominated midwestern state governments. Representative Charles A. Wickliffe of Kentucky charged Indiana with fraudulent war expenditures. William S. Holman of Indiana, a man referred to by his friends as "the watch-dog of the Treasury" and by his enemies as "The Great Objector," claimed that Kellogg's home state of Illinois paid over $130,000 in inflated costs for military supplies. Democrat William A. Richardson of Illinois embellished this accusation when he charged that the Republican administration in his state had rung up over $2.5 million in unauthorized expenses. According to Richardson, an "entire tribe of State officers . . . [had] engaged in plundering the public Treasury."[22]

Kellogg tried in dramatic fashion to rebut the charges. After regaining the floor, he proclaimed the opposition's accusations "all saturated with slander, green, slimy, and reeking with falsehood and abuse. . . ." But such protests were futile. Though outnumbered heavily in the 37th Congress, Democrats and Union Whigs succeeded in casting doubt upon the propriety of the reform. The House tabled the bill, and it never surfaced again. It was also the last time that any effort to change Chase's rules made it to the floor of Congress. The controversy swirling over Illinois and its state military contracts no doubt played a significant role in undermining the assault on Secretary Chase's rules. Of equal importance was Congress's own institutional culture and adherence to a traditional Republican ideology that, despite the pulls of pork-barrel legislation, emphasized frugality and accountability. Here, in the debate over Kellogg's bill, there was a sense that the original legislation of July 27, 1861, had been overly generous and that Chase's regulations were a necessary check. Speaking again for the opposition to Kellogg's bill, Congressman Richardson criticized the original legislation, declaring "God knows that it is broad enough—that it covers ground enough. We have opened the doors to all the thieves on the earth to plunder this Government."[23]

---

[22] Report of the Secretary of the Treasury, 1861, 144–45; Richardson quoted in Congressional Globe, 37th Cong., 2nd sess., 568. It can be noted that Richardson competed with others for the title of "watch-dog of the Treasury," including Senator Elihu Washburne. See George W. Julian, *Political Recollections, 1840 to 1872* (Chicago: Jansen, McClurg, and Co., 1884), 367. For the negative assessment of Holman, consult P. J. Staudenraus, *Mr. Lincoln's Washington*, 305–6.

[23] Kellogg quoted in Congressional Globe, 37th Cong., 2nd sess., 565. Richardson quoted in ibid. Allan Bogue discusses the activities of the various congressional

Ultimately, this opening battle over Chase's rules revealed a Congress that not only conformed to traditional attitudes about public spending, but one that also rejected its customary inclination to intervene in executive administration. The hesitancy, however, was by no means universal. Throughout the war, Congress spasmodically resisted the increasing power of the executive branch. The meddlesome activities of the Joint Committee on the Conduct of the War serve as but the most prominent example. The creation of numerous House and Senate special committees designed to investigate alleged misconduct in some executive offices serve as other examples. Nevertheless, congressional deference on the claims issue fit a more prevalent wartime role that emphasized a loosening of congressional scrutiny of executive spending and resulted in a general rubber-stamping of the administration's military actions and requests. Frequently, Congress had little choice but to approve the decisions of the Lincoln administration. This was especially true of the entire list of extraconstitutional measures that Lincoln used at the beginning of the war when Congress was not in session. To have opposed the president after this would have been to deny that by July 1861 Congress no longer shaped events. To some extent, however, congressional deference in the arena of war claims demonstrated its acceptance of the executive branch's power to interpret legislation and attach rules. At no point during the debates over Chase's rules did the opposition dispute the secretary's administrative authority to mold the law as he saw fit. But perhaps most important, congressional deference revealed a basic political realization that certain war-related business had best be left to the executive. As stated by Representative William Dunn in the debate over Kellogg's claims bill, "One man [Chase], with a good head, is better to manage this matter than all of us together."[24]

---

committees in *The Congressman's Civil War* (Cambridge: Cambridge University Press, 1989), 60–109. For a general discussion of congressional control of executive spending, see Lucius Wilmerding, *The Spending Power: A History of the Efforts of Congress to Control Expenditures* (New Haven, Conn.: Yale University Press, 1943). The continued resonance of republican ideology during the Civil War and Gilded Age can be glimpsed in Campbell, *The Growth of American Government*, 17.

[24] For a discussion of congressional intervention in nineteenth-century executive operations, see Leonard D. White, *The Republican Era: A Study in Administrative History, 1869–1901* (New York: The Free Press, 1958), passim, but most especially 54–57, and Bruce Tap, *Over Lincoln's Shoulder: The Committee on the Conduct of*

Congressional willingness to accept the claims system as interpreted by Chase solidified throughout the remainder of 1862 regardless of party. At one point the Senate buried an attempt by Kentucky's delegation to bypass both Congress and Chase in the claims process when it suggested a presidential commission to audit all state claims. But more importantly, during July of that year Congress passed new legislation that essentially confirmed the most important feature of Chase's rules concerning the original claims bill of July 27, 1861. Chase, in paragraph two of his rules, interpreted the original general authorization of claims for state troops "employed in aiding to suppress the present rebellion. . . ." To Chase, this was a far too liberal allowance. It appeared to authorize the states to file for an unprecedented variety of expenses for troops called out by state and local authorities to perform tasks that were only tenuously related to the war. Chase believed, instead, that only the expenses of organizing two types of troops had to be reimbursed. In the first case, the treasury secretary stated that indemnification should apply to the expenses of those troops actually mustered into national service. State troops that merely cooperated with the army without being physically mustered into the service of the United States were thus disqualified. In the second case, and providing for the sole exception to the first rule, Chase authorized reimbursement for unmustered state militia called out only at the request of either the president or the secretary of war.[25]

Difficulties with the interpretation arose quickly. At the outset of the war, chaos in several areas, particularly the border states, led to situations where state governments provided for a great many troops that never actually mustered into service. Some state troops died in skirmishes with the enemy prior to their mustering. Others simply died before mustering as a result of the various diseases that swept the camps. Some states had paid the expenses of people who had unsuccessfully attempted to raise units. Though such circumstances

---

the War (Lawrence: University Press of Kansas, 1998). Morton Keller argues, however, that Congress was reinvigorated by war, especially on the tariff. See his *Affairs of State*, 22–25. Dunn quoted in *Congressional Globe*, 37th Cong., 2nd sess., 1862, 567.

[25] The proposal of a presidential commission is described in the *Congressional Globe*, 37th Cong., 3rd sess., 155. Chase's rules in "Report of the State Agent," January 1, 1868, Doc. #18, vol. 2, *Kentucky Documents, 1867*, 16–18

meant that the states would lose a considerable amount of money under Chase's rules, a greater difficulty pertained to the service of nonfederalized militia that had not been called out at the specific request of either the president or secretary of war. Throughout the border area, governors and provisional legislatures had responded to frequent military emergencies that lasted but a short period of time. The emergencies were nevertheless usually accompanied by the appeals of local army commanders for state troops to act in concert with federal troops. Never mustered into United States service and not called out by the proper authority in Washington, these troops—and the states they served—were two-time losers under Chase's rules.[26]

Chase's restrictive rules did not, however, spell the end of a state's chances to be reimbursed. Indeed, a whole new avenue for indemnification opened for the states when in July 1862 Missouri successfully petitioned Congress for reimbursement of certain militia expenses disallowed by Chase because some of the state troops called out did not meet the tests of rule two. Though this bill established a precedent that allowed the states to bypass the treasury, it also established a precedent that forced the states to seek their redress through Congress on a state-by-state basis. Furthermore, Chase's rules had not been overturned. The rules had, in actuality, been given congressional approval in a move that only restored a traditional feature of the antebellum reimbursement process where more and more claims money came to depend upon the judgment of Congress rather than the executive bureaucracy. That Congress now assumed a larger role in the claims process helps to explain further the willingness of Congress to let Chase interpret its legislation without any substantive congressional challenge. An institution ever watchful of its prerogatives, Congress, by virtue of Chase's rules, gained back part of what it had forfeited through the vague claims legislation of July 27, 1861.[27]

Still, very little had changed in terms of actual reimbursement. Quite simply, Congress made few settlements. At least two situations explain such a lack of action. First, many in Congress shared Secretary Chase's fears of whether a depleted wartime treasury could meet the demands of states bent upon the reimbursement of a host of ex-

---

[26] For an example of an unsuccessful attempt to raise troops, see the case of Massachusetts in Schouler, *A History of Massachusetts in the Civil War*, 1:433–35.

[27] *Congressional Globe*, 37th Cong., 2nd sess., 3039, 3272, 3379.

penses. More specifically, the granting of one state's exceptions to Chase's rules meant that other states could quickly seize upon that dispensation as precedent for their own particular situations. Speaking shortly after the war, Representative Roswell Hart of New York noted that Congress "was very much against the allowance of war claims of any kind, owing to the fact that they were so enormous in magnitude that to open the door for the payment of one claim would be to involve the country in national bankruptcy. . . ."[28]

A second reason to explain the small number of settlements stemmed from congressional methods of conducting business. Despite increases in the amounts of legislation passed during each of the war years, Congress did not substantively alter its patterns of operation, especially with the claims. There had been some movement within Congress during the antebellum period to reform a process that even in peacetime was overly cumbersome, as all claims against the government—private and state—had to be decided and disposed by Congress. But these reform efforts did not alter the system significantly. Although Congress created the United States Court of Claims in 1855, the court possessed no actual judicial standing. Anxious to preserve its own authority and the separation of powers, Congress had empowered the court only to investigate the private claims of individuals and then recommend actions to Congress. Unfortunately for both the power of the court of claims and the workload of many congressmen, the House and Senate usually ignored the recommendations and conducted new investigations anyway. Though interested in lightening its administrative burdens, Congress never intended to surrender its power to award money to a judicial body appointed by the executive.[29]

Thus, all claims traveled to Congress for investigation and disposition. The House and Senate normally referred each claim—whether private or state—to either one of two standing committees: claims or military affairs. The process did not lend itself to speedy resolution. Private citizens fully exercised their First Amendment right to "peti-

---

[28] Hart quoted in *Missouri House Journal*, 1871, 517.

[29] For a discussion of the court of claims, see Stanton J. Peele, "History and Jurisdiction of the United States Court of Claims," *Records of the Columbia Historical Society* 9 (1915): 2–21; Edward I. Renick, "Assignment of Government Claims," *American Law Review* 24 (1890): 442–56; William M. Wiecek, "The Origin of the United States Court of Claims," *The Administrative Law Review* 20 (1968): 387–406.

tion the government," deluging Congress with hundreds of claims each session for items ranging from the costs associated with the destruction of an individual's private property to the granting of a widow's pension. Antebellum state military claims mingled with private claims in the committees, with the private claims often receiving more attention due to the pressures of an individual congressman's constituent service.

The Civil War magnified the burdens of such a system, as claims flooded into Congress only to be submerged in the committees, with most never being reported out. Work patterns within the committees guaranteed this. For example, the nine-member House Committee on Claims, like most committees, convened two times per week. It then met for one hour, during which time it distributed new claims for examination to individual members, heard reports on old claims, and, on rare occasions, listened to claims-related testimony. This crowded schedule allowed little time for deliberation, which meant that judgment on a particular claim resided with the member who received it for initial investigation. No documentation exists to show that an individual's conclusions were questioned within the formal meeting of the committee. Facilitating the control of individual members over individual claims was the standard committee practice of not requiring a formal disposition of the case, let alone a disposition accompanied by a written report.[30]

The power of the standing committees was such that few members of Congress ever challenged their decisions on the floor of either the Senate or the House. But that power generally did not mean that all legislation reported favorably by a committee would then pass into law. Here the parliamentary procedure of the period led to bitter battles between chairmen for a limited number of slots on the legislative calendar. Assuming, however, that a bill for state indemnification had indeed run the legislative gauntlet and reached the floors of Congress, it usually met one of two possible fates. Either the bill was debated to death, like most financial legislation, or it was killed by

---

[30] U.S. Congress, House, Minutes, Committee on Claims, 39th Cong., 2nd sess., through 42nd Cong., 3rd sess., RG 233, NA. There were exceptions to the work schedule mapped out above. The House Committee on Military Affairs met three times weekly, two hours per session. See U.S. Congress, House, Minutes, Committee on Military Affairs, 39th Cong., RG 233, National Archives (NA), Washington, D.C.

some members—such as Senator Benjamin F. Wade of Ohio—as a matter of mere local or "pecuniary interest."[31]

The lack of any broad congressional remedy during the Civil War forced the states to focus their efforts within the parameters of the July 27, 1861, legislation as interpreted by Secretary Chase. For states presenting their claims, the paper trail started in the treasury's Office of the Third Auditor. After accounting clerks officially logged the claims, the paperwork passed to the War Department to determine the general validity of the claim. For claims pertaining to state volunteer units, examiners searched for evidence of each unit's actual time of muster. For claims pertaining to militia, the examination searched for evidence that the governor had the proper authorization from Washington to call out the militia. When the clerks and assigned special duty army officers in the War Department completed this screening, the claims traveled back to the Treasury Department and the third auditor's office.[32]

Assuming that the War Department certified the validity of a state's claims, the most difficult and time-consuming part of the process had now begun. Clerks examined every expenditure contained within a state's claim. The level of scrutiny was painstaking because the states had to provide—among other things—physical proof of each expenditure, as well as its necessity. Accordingly, the clerks examined everything that a military unit in the nineteenth century needed to become organized and then operational, including ice, lightning rods, recruiting posters, candlesticks, coffins, tobacco, food, and musicians. It was a time-honored, yet mind-numbing, process. Nonetheless, the clerks persevered and sorted each expense into the categories of approved, disallowed, and suspended claims. Subse-

---

[31] George Galloway recounts the strength of the standing committees in his *History of the House of Representatives* (New York: Crowell, 1961), 89. Lee Robinson has described a considerably weaker committee system in the Senate. See his "The Development of the Senate Committee System" (Ph.D. diss., New York University, 1954), chapter 3. See also Walter Kravitz, "Evolution of the Senate's Committee System," *The Annals of the American Academy of Political and Social Science* 411 (1974): 27–38. The difficulty in gaining space on the legislative calendar is recounted in Margaret S. Thompson, *The "Spider's Web": Congress and Lobbying in the Age of Grant* (Ithaca, N.Y.: Cornell University Press, 1985), 110. Wade quoted in *Congressional Globe*, 38th Cong., 2nd sess., 513.

[32] For an example of the confusion in the offices of the auditors, see R. J. Atkinson to second comptroller, February 15, 1862, Letters Received, vol. 1., E. 604, RG 217, NA.

quently, the third auditor allowed the states to investigate further each of the disallowed or suspended claims in order to provide evidence that would answer the objections of the accounting clerks. The auditor then forwarded to the office of the second comptroller all of those claims that had been approved. In this office another set of clerks descended upon the claims, checking the work of the previous office. For those claims that survived this process of attrition, the comptroller forwarded them to the secretary of the treasury for final approval.[33]

Such a system, used with some degree of efficiency during the antebellum period, struggled now to perform its assigned tasks. By the end of 1862 the treasury had processed and settled only one-quarter of all claims filed. Two years later over $18 million in claims remained unsettled. The problem was most acute in the third auditor's office because it supervised a variety of accounts not related to state claims. Numbered among them were quartermaster, commissary, pension, and engineer accounts, as well as Mexican War claims, all of which totaled nearly one-half of all governmental expenditures. Repeated complaints by the third auditor about the workload throughout the Civil War resulted in congressional authorization for incremental increases in the number of clerks. In April 1861, for example, the budget authorized sixty-one clerks. By 1863 the number had almost doubled to 121. But these increases did not solve the burden of clerical duties. At no time during the war did the office ever reach an authorized level of manpower, which increasingly spent much of its time answering executive, congressional, and state queries as to the status of claims, large and small. Even the treasury's controversial decision in 1861 to hire female clerks failed to alleviate the personnel shortage. These new clerks remained far away from the third auditor's office, trimming and clipping treasury notes. Culminating the list of its difficulties, the third auditor's office—as did the rest of the treasury—had to cope with a change of buildings in the middle of the war, which, the auditor noted, "retarded" operations significantly.[34]

---

[33] For examples of items generally claimed by the states, see the abstracts and vouchers contained in Records of the Accounting Officers of the Department the Treasury, State Claims, 1861–1890, Kentucky, E. 759, Boxes 30–41, E. 759, RG 217, NA.

[34] *Report of the Secretary of the Treasury, 1862*, 82; *Report of the Secretary of the*

Difficulties persisted throughout the war and into the Gilded Age. During the war there were other attempts by the various third auditors to deal with the workload. Most efforts addressed the division of labor within the office and the actual methods of auditing the claims. But others dealt with what one auditor thought to be the root cause of much of the office's trouble—Chase's rules. In December 1864, John Wilson requested that Chase's successor as secretary of treasury, William P. Fessenden, modify the rules to create a more flexible method of presenting evidence. Fessenden refused, becoming the first of many future secretaries of the treasury who did not want to overturn Chase's rules. A record of why Fessenden refused does not exist, but his rationale could not have deviated too much from the two reasons normally cited by subsequent secretaries. First, there invariably appeared the matter of opening the treasury to an increasing number of claims, which ultimately might have bankrupted the government. Second, with the rapid turnover in civil servants resulting from the patronage practices of the nineteenth century, executive branch officials—both inside and outside the treasury—relied upon administrative precedent as the glue that kept their departments together. Though enthusiastic for the changes that brought them into office, winners of executive appointments generally avoided operational changes that might disrupt the tried, or codified, practices of previous officials. Against such resistance, and although some secretaries of the treasury allowed changes in the auditing procedures following the war, Chase's rules remained substantially unchanged for as long as states continued to file their claims.[35]

However, in 1865 the reliance upon administrative precedent did not overly impress Auditor Wilson. Still deluged with claims, and displaying considerable sympathy toward the states, Wilson for-

---

Treasury, 1863, 98; *Report of the Secretary of the Treasury, 1864,* 102. Female clerks covered in Cindy S. Aron, *Ladies and Gentlemen of the Civil Service: Middle-Class Workers in Victorian America* (New York: Oxford University Press, 1987), 6, 69.

[35] John Wilson's attempt to modify the auditor's procedures can be found in John Wilson to William P. Fessenden, December 29, 1864, Letter Book, Third Auditor, vol. 2, 224–25, E. 617, RG 217, NA. The primary change in Chase's rules occurred on March 21, 1868, when the treasury allowed the use of certified copies of vouchers. For a compilation of changes to the accounting procedures, see "Regulations of the Second Comptroller," 1–24, E. 758, RG 217, NA. For the issue of precedence outside the treasury, see the example of the post office in Carpenter, *The Forging of Bureaucratic Autonomy,* 91.

warded an annual report, through Fessenden, to Congress that contained seventeen surprising proposals. Among the more important were requests that Congress pass specific legislation allowing the states reimbursement for a variety of expenses prohibited by Chase. Besides guaranteeing money for troops not actually mustered into service, the proposals promised money for property damage and interest payments on state bond issues, two areas that were only beginning to attract the serious attention of the states. Wilson concluded the report with his boldest suggestion, recommending that state claims be removed from the treasury's jurisdiction entirely. In its place, he proposed that the government establish a separate bureau of claims, where adverse decisions involving over $200 could be appealed to the United States Court of Claims.[36]

Congress never seriously considered Wilson's proposals. Not only did the proposals lack the support of the secretary of the treasury, they also asked Congress to do two things it had always been loath to do: open the treasury to the states and surrender congressional disbursing powers to a judicial body appointed by the president. Like the states that sought wholesale changes in the claims system, the third auditor had no chance. However, and if Wilson were so inclined, he could look around the government and find comfort in numbers. He was not the only mid-level bureaucrat of the period to fail at policy innovation. From the General Land Office to the Pension Bureau, mid-level officials such as third auditor proposed administrative reforms that languished and died in Congress. It was, according to the political scientist Daniel P. Carpenter, the principal failure of a bureaucracy that lacked the autonomy to shape its own programs. In the conceptual framework of Carpenter, a bureau or department chief such as Auditor Wilson was little more than glorified clerk, and "clerks did not innovate; they took orders."[37]

With reform unlikely from within the executive branch, Congress would try its own hand at innovation. In 1866, some members of Congress made a serious attempt to alter the process of claims administration. At that time, the states had begun to make a full accounting of their wartime expenses. Powerful House Republican James G. Blaine of Maine then assumed control of efforts to total the

---

[36] *Report of the Treasurer, 1865*, 133–35.
[37] Carpenter, *The Forging of Bureaucratic Autonomy*, 60.

war cost and offer a way of resolving state claims quickly. The result was the formation of the Select Committee on the War Debts of the Loyal States. Created in 1865, the committee submitted its report in February 1866. The report was both ominous and innovative. Blaine's numbers revealed the extent of state expenditures and the concurrent national liability. According to Blaine, the states had spent at least $468 million. The number was comprehensive and included many expenditures that had not previously been considered reimbursable expenses. The states had spent large amounts on enlistment inducements, or bounties, and dependent compensation. Blaine believed it only just and equitable that the Union as a whole absorb some of this cost. He also deemed funding of the war debt vital to the financial health of the United States.[38]

Blaine then proposed what would be the most innovative method of dealing with the debt. Realizing that the full cost was beyond the capability of the government in the foreseeable future, he moved that the government establish a simple formula based on a state's total contribution of troops. He then calculated that each state spent, on average, $220 per soldier furnished to the federal government. From this figure Blaine calculated that a flat 25 percent, or $55, was an equitable portion for the United States to reimburse. Despite Blaine's attempt to create a formula for what he called an "impartial reimbursement," there were many people left dissatisfied. The calculation considered neither regional differences in costs nor the types of expenditures made by the individual states. Blaine had simply divided the total number of troops that had served in the Union army by the reported accumulated war expenditures of the states. Blaine further compromised the plan by deferring true payment to the states. The government would issue bonds to the states that could be redeemed in twenty years while paying 5 percent interest available semiannually.[39]

Problems were threefold. Not only was payment in a circulating currency delayed for twenty years, the states could not resell the bonds until the treasury actually redeemed them. Aiming to stifle speculation, Blaine unintentionally killed state interest. For many op-

---

[38] U.S. Congress, House Report, 39th Cong., 1st sess., 1866, H. Doc. 16, serial 1272; *Congressional Globe*, 39th Cong., 1st sess., 2201, 2902, 3440, 3902.
[39] Ibid.

erating within the nineteenth century's financial markets, the most attractive feature of a bond was its speculative value. Lacking an allowance for investment or usage, the proposal inspired little excitement among the states or their representatives. A second reason for the failure of the bill was that not all states were terribly interested in maximizing their monetary return. Here, the demands of fiscal restraint and retrenchment influenced the idea that the federal government was not responsible for all the debts covered by Blaine's legislation. In particular, some states, such as Ohio, rebelled against any indemnification for state and local bounties for voluntary enlistments. The final difficulty concerned basic politics and simple constituent service. In the House, one of the chief opponents of the bill was Columbus Delano of Ohio. Delano believed—erroneously—that claims for the seizure of private property would total far more than those of the states for financing the war, which led him to protest any attempt to adjust state claims ahead of those for private property. As a result of these types of considerations, various House and Senate committees then bounced the bill around Congress until it finally disappeared, dying from what its sponsor blandly called "an indisposition to consider and press it at this time."[40]

Lacking a collective solution to the problems of expediting the claims, the individual states turned once again to Congress for reimbursement. However, the end of the war had not eased the process. In fact, new problems surfaced to distract legislators from the business of the state claims. American government had grown significantly during the war. Whether owing to the magnitude of the war effort or its attendant nationalizing momentum, Congress, in particular, found itself with a variety of responsibilities that were either new or expanded in scope since the beginning of the war. Its list of obligations was imposing: civil rights agency, employment office, constituent ombudsman, watchdog of the executive, and preserver of public morality. Congress demonstrated that it recognized the new realm of

---

[40] U.S. Congress, House Report, 39th Cong., 1st sess., 1866, H. Doc. 16, serial 1272; *Congressional Globe*, 39th Cong., 1st sess., 2201, 2902, 3440. Ohio's resolution opposing the bill found in U.S. Congress, House Miscellaneous Document, 39th Cong., 1st sess., 1866, H. Doc. 43, serial 1270. Delano covered in Albert S. Bolles, *The Financial History of the United States from 1861–1885* (New York: D. Appleton and Co., 1886), 246–48. Blaine quoted in *Congressional Globe*, 39th Cong., 1st sess., 3902.

its powers when it established, between 1863 and 1871, a set of bureaus or commissions dealing with education, statistics, fish, immigration, science, and the newly freed slaves.[41]

Congress would have difficulty functioning effectively. This situation was most evident in the matter of claims. In 1865, Americans had awakened to a seemingly infinite variety of things that they could claim from their governments. Even though, as noted earlier, claims against the different levels of government had existed since the Revolution, the sheer number and variety of claims in the postwar era was startling. Social and economic conditions in the postwar era were conducive to these new expectations of what government could provide. The historian Daniel Boorstin once described the period as possessing a "Go-Getter" spirit in which thousands of Americans sought and exploited the bounty that awaited them in new western lands and resources. So it is not surprising that an equally large number of Americans found opportunity in a wide variety of claims against their state and national governments. There appeared to be a class of claims for every American, all of which were described carefully in a 477-page handbook entitled *The War Claimant's Guide*, published in 1866. There were homestead claims, bounty claims, subsistence claims, pension claims, dependent widows' claims, property compensation claims, horse claims, contractor claims, claims for loyal southerners, and a multitude of others. Claims opportunities were particularly ripe at the state level. According to one contemporary observer, "legislatures have ceased to create or concentrate pubic sentiment; they have become clearing houses for the adjustment of claims." Well beyond the boundaries of any given state, America's wars and foreign policy could even be understood in terms of claims. There were still outstanding Revolutionary War, French Spoliation, and Mexican War claims. There were also the *Alabama* Claims, which developed out of Britain's role in the construction of Confederate naval commerce raiders. Ultimately, claims defined the function of government for many Americans. Some observers thought such a culture of claims unique only to their state or territory. For example, Sol Miller, editor of a small frontier newspaper in Kansas, thought it the exclusive practice of Kansans when faced "with losses

---

[41] The expanded federal bureaucracy is described in Keller, *Affairs of State*, 101.

of any kind to at once petition the Legislature or Congress to reimburse them." He could not have been more wrong.[42]

Claims of all varieties preoccupied most representatives and senators. The average congressman, according to one estimate, received at least fifty letters a week from constituents. Some requested patronage or letters of recommendation for patronage. But most sought special, or private, legislation dealing with war-related compensation such as that for veterans, businesses, churches, schools, and homesteads. Congressmen rarely took the requests lightly. Private legislation thus clogged the legislative calendar of both houses of Congress. For example, between 1873 and 1875, Congress passed a total of 833 bills. Private war-claims legislation accounted for over 53 percent of this number. Ten years later, the numbers had not been reduced. In fact, private claims legislation had increased. In the first session of the 49th Congress alone, 66 percent of the 7,885 bills introduced into the proceedings were private claims. This morass was enough to lead Senator William Warner of Missouri in 1886 to note that "an ordinary lifetime is far too short to get a claim through Congress."[43]

Notwithstanding Senator Warner's pessimism, some scholars have placed the origins of the modern state in the years immediately following the Civil War. To the extent that the Civil War destroyed a federal system dominated by peripheral states and created a new world of finance capitalism, the idea of modernization stands on solid historical ground. However, the modernization thesis is subject to qualification. Although America may have been on the verge of modernizing its constitutional and economic structure, the administrative structure of Congress changed little during the nineteenth century. The Speaker of the House and the party caucus still determined the all-important committee chairmanships. High electoral turnover fre-

---

[42] "Go-Getter" spirit covered in Daniel J. Boorstin, *The Americans: The Democratic Experience* (New York: Random House, 1973), 3–88. George W. Raff, *The War Claimant's Guide: A Manual of Laws, Regulations, Instructions, Forms and Official Decisions . . . Growing Out of the War of 1861–1865* (Cincinnati: Robert Clarke and Co., 1866). "Observer" quoted in Alan Trachtenberg, *The Incorporation of America: Culture and Society in the Gilded Age* (New York: Hill and Wang, 1982), 165. Contemporary front-page reporting of the *Alabama* Claims can be found in the *Times and Conservative* (Leavenworth, Kans.), December 23, 1869. Sol Miller quoted in the *Kansas Chief* (White Cloud), February 23, 1871.

[43] Thompson, *The "Spider's Web,"* 42–43, 50, 106. Information on the 49th Congress found in *Congressional Record,* 49th Cong., 1st sess., 1886, 2497. Warner quoted in same.

quently resulted in sparse knowledge of parliamentary procedure and a lack of substantive expertise on many issues. There were no staffs to either bridge the gaps in knowledge or alleviate the workload. It was only the rare representative or senator who employed a private secretary. For those people interested in the passage of private legislation in the House, these problems were particularly acute. The committees most responsible for private bills, especially those bills pertaining to claims, were also the least desirable in the eyes of individual members. The work was excessive and the secretarial help no different from that of other committees. Only freshmen and those men who had fallen out of party favor filled the ranks of the committees working on claims.[44]

The ability of Congress to function effectively was severely taxed in the postwar era, but the institution did not grind to a halt. In an ironic fashion, the same forces that helped to strain the engine of government also managed to grease the wheels of its operations. As the demands upon government exploded following the war, so too did the number of lobbyists who sought to represent those demands. By the hundreds, agents flocked to Washington on behalf of individuals and business with interests in veterans' pensions, land grants, railroad subsidies, and mail contracts. While government thus ran the well-documented risk of being sunk by a tidal wave of special-interest representatives, all governing institutions managed to stay afloat because the lobbyists provided at least one unexpected benefit. Whether in the executive departments or the Congress, most officials came to rely upon the lobbyist as both a means of information and a bridge to constituents.[45]

The states were situated no differently from individual citizens and

---

[44] For works emphasizing modernization, consult Richard Bensel, *Yankee Leviathan*, passim, but especially ix–x, 2–17; Samuel P. Huntington, *Political Order in Changing Societies* (New Haven, Conn.: Yale University Press, 1968), 46; and Raimondo Luraghi, "The Civil War and the Modernization of American Society: Social Structure and Industrial Revolution in the Old South Before and During the War," *Civil War History* 18 (1968): 230–50. Margaret S. Thompson presents the best description of congressional administrative structure in her *The "Spider's Web,"* 105.

[45] Thompson, *The "Spider's Web,"* passim, but more particularly, 54, 164, 256; David J. Rothman, *Politics and Power: The United States Senate, 1869–1901* (Cambridge, Mass.: Harvard University Press, 1966), 192; Summers, *The Era of Good Stealings* (New York: Oxford University Press, 1993), 107–21. See also Harry James Brown's "Garfield's Congress," *Hayes Historical Journal* 3 (1981): 66 for a description of the available clerical help in Congress.

businesses. In some sense, though, the states were in a more difficult position. Although congressmen represented the particular needs of specific areas within states, and senators theoretically represented the states as a whole, the immediate and persistent pressures of individual constituent service—usually presented by an agent or lobbyist—pulled congressmen away from state-related duties. In but one example, while the minutes of the House Committee on Claims are replete with representatives and senators testifying on behalf of constituents with claims, there is no evidence that they did so on behalf of their states. Therefore, in a chorus of voices all demanding something from the government in Washington, states would suffer without special representation. This was never more true than with the issue of reimbursement. Its complexity required expertise, and its subject, the appropriation of money, required access to congressmen and executive branch bureaucrats.[46]

To some degree, the governors came to understand this during the war. Encouraged by the complete early wartime reliance of the federal government upon the states, and then facilitated by newly available railroad connections, most governors had made numerous trips to the nation's capital. In some cases, they sought the president directly to offer advice and, whether subtly or explicitly, remind him of the power of the governors. In most cases, the governors entered the president's office and one administrative office after another in search of weapons and funding, often finding exactly what they wanted. John Andrew of Massachusetts, Thomas Carney of Kansas, James Nye of Nevada, and Alexander Randall of Wisconsin all spent substantial, and successful, time in the capital searching for military and financial assistance.[47]

The immediate close of hostilities did not lessen the pull of Wash-

---

[46] The pressures of constituent service and the response of congressmen during the Gilded Age can be glimpsed in U.S. Congress, House, Minutes, Committee on Claims, 39th Cong., 2nd sess., through 42nd Cong., 3rd sess., and the correspondence of Senator John White Stevenson of Kentucky. See his correspondence of 1873 and 1874, but particularly Quartermaster General Montgomery Meigs to Stevenson, March 12, 1873, and J. D. Bingham to Stevenson, December 11, 1873, Stevenson Collection, vol. 30, LC.

[47] Kyle S. Sinisi, "The Political Career of Thomas Carney, Civil War Governor of Kansas" (master's thesis, Kansas State University, 1990), 40–44, 52–55; Current, *The Civil War Era*, 305; Jud Samon, "Sagebrush Falstaff: A Biographical Sketch of James Warren Nye" (Ph.D. diss., University of Maryland, 1979), 288.

ington upon the governors. Throughout 1865, for example, Henry Crapo of Michigan made a number of trips to the capital to press his state's case for reimbursement. Rumors that Governor Andrew had paid a personal visit to Washington originally spurred Crapo's frenetic mission. Upon hearing that Andrew had successfully pressured the government into assuming its war debts, Crapo rushed to Washington to get the same deal. After all, Crapo declared, "I shall not quietly submit to remain passive and wait the slow tedious process of the Government . . . when it permits itself to be bullied into the payments of the claims of Massachusetts. . . ." During his many visits, he received reassurances of eventual payment, but no money. Crapo ultimately concluded that the secretary of the treasury paid Andrew the money simply "to get rid of him."[48]

As the activities of Andrew and Crapo illustrate, the personal touch, and pressure, applied by governors could have mixed results. Though the results varied—and they did so for a variety of reasons, including a state's relative importance and the persuasiveness of the particular governor—state executives did not forget the value of personal contact. The lesson of an incident such as that involving Crapo and Andrew was that unremitting pressure needed to be applied upon administrators to get the required result, or, in this case, reimbursement. The problem for the governors was beyond their relative individual stature and ability to bring pressure. It was also a simple matter of expertise and time. Although state governors in the Gilded Age slipped into virtual policy-making irrelevance when compared with their legislatures, clerical minutiae and patronage disbursement alone constrained their time. The time restriction was especially great on a subject that required extended visits to the nation's capital. The governors would have to find some other way to apply pressure and represent their respective state's needs.

For some states, this meant hiring lobbyists, or agents. It was not a new practice. During the seventeenth century, the colonies used agents to represent their grievances, present evidence in intercolony disputes, and generally lobby the English government. For most of that century the colonies made only scattered use of the agents. But in the eighteenth century, the tightening bonds of empire, and the

---

[48] Crapo quoted in Lewis D. Martin, *Lumberman from Flint: The Michigan Career of Henry D. Crapo 1855–1869* (Detroit: Wayne State University Press, 1958), 167.

attendant controversies, forced the colonies to increase their dependence upon the agents. This was especially true in royal and proprietary colonies where the assemblies appointed the agent and saw him as a check upon the power of the royal governor or proprietor in London. However, and regardless of the shape of a colonial charter, by the time of the Revolution, most colonies maintained agents in London. Edmund Burke and Benjamin Franklin were but the two most prominent examples.[49]

The creation of a separate American government did not spell the end of agents. The Constitution of 1787 only loosely defined the governing operations of the federal republic. When necessary, the states would only logically seek extraconstitutional methods to represent their interests before the general government. During the early republic there was little necessity for an agent, but there were circumstances that warranted it. A state with war claims against the government often found it wise to appoint special commissioners, or agents, to prod Washington. After the War of 1812, Virginia, especially, found great success with its agents. A succession of state agents worked diligently on a difficult claim, piecing together documentation that had been either destroyed or lost during the war. These agents also successfully lobbied executive agencies and the presidency.[50]

Despite such visible activity, the states never relied greatly upon the agents during the antebellum period. This want of administrative importance descended from a simple lack of claims to prosecute. Under these circumstances, the business of representing the states on complicated administrative matters fell into the hands of Washington-based lawyers who worked only part-time on behalf of their states. The system worked well during the antebellum period, but a decreasing volume of state claims against the government failed to tax either the stamina or the ingenuity of the agents. Employed sporadically, the agent became a shadowy figure in the operation of the

---

[49] Beverly Bond, "The Colonial Agent as a Popular Representative," *Political Science Quarterly* 35 (1920): 372–92; E. P. Tanner, "Colonial Agencies in England," *Pacific Studies Quarterly* 16 (1901): 24–49; Michael G. Kammen, *A Rope of Sand: The Colonial Agents, British Politics, and the American Revolution* (Ithaca, N.Y.: Cornell University Press, 1968), passim.

[50] Information on Massachusetts agents can be found in Hemphill, *The Papers of John C. Calhoun*, 3:xxxv–xxxvii. Daniel Elazar describes Virginia's agents in his *American Partnership*, 103–9.

antebellum federal system. Georgia perhaps best illustrated the states' antebellum experience. Having incurred expenses in a number of Indian conflicts during the 1830s, the state legislature authorized the appointment of an agent in 1834. By 1842, the legislature and the governor had completely lost track of the agent and any of the work he had accomplished; nor could they even determine his name. The governor eventually handled most business related to the prosecution of the claim.[51]

The Civil War altered this type of loose relationship between agents and their states. Faced with a mass of expenses and the limited ability of governors to deal personally with the claims, the states could no longer depend upon lawyers in Washington who represented the state only part-time. As state claims piled up, so too did the demand for full-time agents. In response to the demand, a whole profession of claims agents sprouted. Unlike their antebellum predecessors, this class of agents generally had no experience in the law. Many were former soldiers. Some of the more successful agents were former clerks in the executive offices of the state and national governments. Claimants were eager to use agents with this type of experience and the connections it theoretically brought. Agents with clerical experience in the government never hesitated to advertise that fact prominently.[52]

When states did turn toward full-time agents, they bestowed vary-

---

[51] Hemphill, *The Papers of John C. Calhoun*, 3:xxxv–xxxvii; Elazar, *American Partnership*, 103–9; *Acts of the General Assembly of the State of Georgia, 1842*, 198; Secretary of War Spencer to the Speaker of the House, April 20, 1842, and Spencer to Speaker, January 31, 1843, in Cooling, *The New American State Papers: Military Affairs*, 9:356–58, 365–67; U.S. Congress, Senate Committee Report, 32nd Cong., 1st sess., 1852, S. Doc. 329.

[52] But one example of soldiers turned agents can be found in the circular from the "Office of Weston Flint, Late Colonel and State Military Claims Agent for Ohio, Michigan, and New York," Lewis V. Bogy Papers, 1866, Missouri Historical Society (MHS), St. Louis, Mo. Another soldier turned agent, who would also turn adjutant general of the state of Kansas, was Thomas L. Moonlight. He advertised his business in the *Leavenworth Times*, February 9, 1866. Clerks turned agents can be found in J. M. Trimble to Charles Hardin, January 6, 1876, Governor Hardin's Correspondence, R. 152, F. 15278, Western Historical Manuscripts Collection (WHMC), Columbia, Mo.; *Leavenworth Times*, February 8, 1866, contains a frequently run add for T. M. O'Brien, "Formerly Clerk in the Pension Office"; Adjutant of Indiana to "to whom it may concern," June 17, 1868, Letters Received, vol. 1, E. 604, RG 217, NA; Theodore S. Davis to J. S. Williams, September 26, 1885, and T. W. Palmer to J. S. Williams, May 13, 1886, Letters Received, vol. 5, E. 604, RG 217, NA.

ing degrees of responsibility upon them. Some assumed total control, from the collection of individual vouchers to the actual lobbying of Congress and the executive. Others concentrated more exclusively on their lobbying function, leaving collection and sorting to state adjutants, quartermasters, and auditors.

Nonetheless, despite the increasing importance of the agents, the states did not use them exclusively. In fact, a number of states tended to depend upon their own militia officers for both the collection of information and its presentation through lobbying in Washington. This choice was logical. State adjutants and quartermasters occupied the first line of state military spending. Theoretically, these officials knew the numbers of troops mustered and the amount of money paid to mobilize them.

There were other reasons as well. With neither Confederates nor Indians to fight, there was some political sense in the East and Midwest that state militias were no longer needed. One manifestation of this sentiment was a movement to eliminate the militia outright. Another, and ultimately more popular manifestation, was that state military officials could best spend their time fighting the claims battle against the government. Once occupied in the crusade to gain reimbursement, the militia officers relieved the legislatures of the responsibility of paying agents their commissions. In a political culture that emphasized the importance of fiscal and bureaucratic retrenchment, this use of militiamen satisfied a chief popular concern: they served cheaply. Although some state adjutants complained bitterly that their offices had been turned into claims factories, the complex and time-consuming process of claims indemnification proved ultimately beneficial. It contributed to the institutional survival of the militia hierarchy until the labor agitation of the late 1870s demonstrated yet another function for a military force tottering on the edge of extinction.[53]

Whether or not the states relied upon agents or military officials,

---

[53] For brief descriptions of the decline of the militia in the immediate postwar period, see William H. Riker, *Soldiers of the State* (Washington: Public Affairs Press, 1958; reprint, New York: Arno Press, 1979), 41–45; John K. Mahon, *History of the Militia and the National Guard* (New York: Macmillan Publishing Company, 1983), 108–24; Richard G. Stone, *A Brittle Sword: The Kentucky Militia, 1776–1912* (Lexington: University Press of Kentucky, 1977), 74; M. D. Morgan to George C. Bingham, March 19, 1875, Missouri Adjutant General's Office, Box 210, RG 133, Missouri State Archives (MSA), Jefferson City.

successful reimbursement depended most upon the organization and persistence of the individual state. Ironically, as the individual states thus labored against an uncooperative national government, they also cooperated little among themselves. Too many claims competed with too few appropriated dollars in a federal system where interstate cooperation was often confined to the exchange of Thanksgiving proclamations, compendiums of statutes, and gubernatorial addresses. Minus a history of interstate cooperation, the states pursued their claims in a political and governing vacuum. Legislative logrolling and the formation of state coalitions remained conspicuously absent as the separate states first ignored each other and then battled Washington on issues of mutual interest. In this context, while the framework of claims adjustment was national, the execution was driven by a number of local issues, including partisan politics, fiscal pressures, and the press of other administrative business not related to the claims. Missouri would be but the first example of this.[54]

---

[54] The level of administrative contact, or coordination, between the states early in the Gilded Age is suggested, in part, by the correspondence files of most governors. See, for example, a variety of courtesy letters in Governor's Correspondence, Thomas Bramlette, Box 1, F. 3, 6, 7, 8, 9, and 10, Kentucky State Archives (KSA), Frankfort, and the "out-of-state" file in Governor's Papers, Thomas C. Fletcher, F. 14620, CFD-159, MSA.

2

Missouri's Precedents
and Lobbyists

IN THE BATTLE for claims indemnification, Missouri was a victim of
its own success. Much of the state had endured war firsthand through
either pitched battles or bloody guerrilla conflict. The cost of the war
to the state government was inordinately high, and Missouri would
eventually possess the largest claims of any state. To its credit, Missouri wasted no time or effort in working for its reimbursement. By
the end of 1862, Missouri achieved victories in Congress and the
treasury that also set precedents for other states to follow. Better yet,
in 1867 alone the United States Treasury reimbursed Missouri over
$6 million. It was an amount that made other states jealous and Mis-
souri anxious for more. Though Missouri continued to generate
claims following the war, the Show Me State would never again see
such a dollar figure. Just as bureaucratic tendencies in Washington
would influence how much money a state could get, so too would a
number of state and local issues. In Missouri's case, nothing would
shape the claims more than the clamor for retrenchment, intragovernmental squabbles, interest-group politics, and political scandal.

The demand for retrenchment was very acute in Missouri. The war
had drained the state of its financial resources. Stricken by numerous
Confederate invasions and possessing a substantial number of pro-
Confederate citizens, Missouri had to fund a wide variety of militia
for home defense. Frequent diversions of Union troops to other the-
aters of the war increased the state's reliance upon its citizen soldiers.
In fact, by the end of 1865 the Missouri government had gone bankrupt supporting 52,000 militiamen. Few other states had called up
that large a militia, and even fewer were in such dire financial
trouble.[1]

---

[1] It is difficult to compare the numbers of militia mobilized because the states
tended to categorize their troops differently. Perhaps the only state that exceeded

By itself, Missouri's wartime expenditures were not that unusual. The midwestern states in particular spent far beyond what they possessed to help prosecute the war. However, unlike the other midwestern states, Missouri started the war in a bankrupt condition. At the end of December 1861 Governor Hamilton Gamble was pained to note that Missouri carried a debt of $24.7 million. Of this debt, only $700,000 was for costs associated with the war. The remainder represented state bond issues floated to finance antebellum railroads. At different times Missouri had provided these bonds to various railroad companies with the understanding that the railroads would assume both the principal and interest on the bonds when they came due. Unfortunately for Missouri, most of the railroads went bankrupt, leaving the state liable. Aside from the principal, this left Missouri in the unenviable position of having to pay over $5 million per year in interest.[2]

The outbreak of the war created an even greater burden upon the state's economy. Both the general economy and the public treasury suffered. Agriculture witnessed the loss of men to the army and slaves to emancipation. Bushwhackers disrupted all forms of business and commerce outside of the major population centers, and as early as November 1860 all of the state's banks suspended specie payments. Missouri had quickly become a cash-starved state that soon saw postage stamps substituted for coins, and banks flooding the streets with bank notes and fractional paper currency.[3]

Missourians readily sensed the government's dire financial position. This was especially true of young loyal men. Many stayed away from the militia because of the state's inability to pay for their services. All too frequently, young men anxious to serve enlisted in volunteer and regular regiments only after being told by federalized officers and recruiters that the state of Missouri would not pay its militia. Against such a background, and given the state's already di-

---

Missouri's numbers was Ohio, which mobilized 50,000 men in 1863 to fend off John H. Morgan's raid. See Robert S. Chamberlain, "The Northern State Militia," *Civil War History* 4 (1958): 108–10.

[2] Ibid.; Grace Avery and Floyd Shoemaker, eds., *The Messages and Proclamations of the Governors of the State of Missouri*, vols. 3, 4, 5 (Columbia: State Historical Society of Missouri, 1922–1924), 3:438–39; 4:23–24.

[3] William E. Parrish, *A History of Missouri, Volume 3, 1860–1875* (Columbia: University of Missouri Press, 1973), 55, 80.

vided loyalties, Governor Hamilton Gamble's August 24, 1861, call for 42,000 militia netted only 6,000 men.[4]

Badly in need of cash, the state took several steps to right its sinking finances. Initially, Governor Gamble approached the federal government in August 1861 for loans. A personal visit to Washington provided some success, as Gamble met with President Abraham Lincoln and members of his administration. By the end of the governor's visit he had obtained promises for a loan of $200,0000. However, upon Gamble's return to Missouri, it quickly became evident both to the governor and the ruling state convention that more money would be needed. Union general Nathaniel Lyon's rash campaign to purge the state of Confederate sympathizers had backfired. His crushing defeat at Wilson's Creek signaled a need for more troops and the money to support them. Lincoln's promise of $200,000 would simply not be enough. Meeting in October 1861, the ruling Unionist state convention, or provisional government, experimented with a number of measures to bring in the necessary revenue. It looked first to fiscal retrenchment and abolished a number of administrative bureaucracies and positions, including the Board of Public Works, the superintendent of common schools, and the state geologist. Furthermore, the convention reduced the salaries of all state employees by 20 percent. The convention looked also to increased taxation. It levied a general state tax, increased the state property tax, and added fees for certain state-authorized licenses. But all of these measures still left the state unable to fund its debt. Relatively small though the taxes might have been, they proved notoriously difficult to collect throughout the war. In many cases, if the unsettled nature of the countryside did not prevent collection, the ever-present cash shortage would. The difficulty of collecting revenue was, in the end, best illustrated by the state accepting as tax payment its own paper scrip, or IOUs.[5]

As did many other loyal states, Missouri chose finally to fund the war through massive bond issues. Beginning in October 1861 the state offered its first issue of Union Defense Bonds. Redeemable in ten years at 7 percent interest payable semiannually, the bonds filled the immediate hole in the state treasury. This action, coupled with

[4] William E. Parrish, *Turbulent Partnership: Missouri and the Union, 1861–1865* (Columbia: University of Missouri Press, 1963), 54–55; Marguerite Potter, "Hamilton R. Gamble, Missouri's War Governor," *Missouri Historical Review* 35 (1940): 39.

[5] Parrish, *Turbulent Partnership*, 55, 78, 79, 199.

future issues that offered redeemability in one year, allowed the government to function and essential military activities to continue. But problems persisted. Although the willingness to use bonds in lieu of taxation reflected the conventional wisdom of the period, it brought added difficulties for Missouri. Because of the state's assumption of the railroad debt at the outset of the war and its attendant inability to pay that debt, Missouri's credit rating in the financial markets plummeted. Wall Street's bearish attitude frequently forced the state to discount its bonds well below the face value. Sales of between 75 and 85 percent of par were not uncommon as Missouri struggled to sell its issues. Problems with the bonds were not confined to their reception within the nation's financial markets. The state legislature lessened the attractiveness of the 1861 bond issue by barring its redemption in paying the state's general tax. Under such circumstances, by November 1865 Missouri had accumulated a combined war debt of $7 million sustained with annual interest payments in excess of $390,000.[6]

The burgeoning state debt did not go unnoticed. As the war ended, many within Missouri realized that the debt would have a significant role in the state's postwar economic development. To a succession of governors and state legislatures, the debt threatened to ruin any future prosperity. Concern over the impact of the debt also united both the moderate and radical wings of the ruling Republican Party. In January 1865, radical governor Thomas C. Fletcher decried the debt, stating that it was "one of the great calamities of the war." Speaking two years later, Fletcher thought the loss of public credit "the greatest loss entailed on us by the civil war." The nature of this calamity was twofold. On the one hand, the debt was a purely economic burden. Massive debt in an era of deflationary money meant that the cost of paying that debt was going to increase dramatically in real dollars. Furthermore, future private investment in Missouri seemed to depend upon funding the debt. Postwar interstate economic competition for private capital and industry, like that of the antebellum period, was going to be intense. State officials and boosters predicted

---

[6] Ibid; *Laws of the State of Missouri, Regular Session, 22nd General Assembly, 1862–1863*, 25–29, and *Laws of the State of Missouri, 1863–1864*, 25–26; Avery and Shoemaker, *Messages and Proclamations*, 3:470–71; 4:68, 151–52. The figure for accumulated debt includes an undetermined—but relatively small—amount acquired through loans and forced assessments upon banks.

terrible economic consequences if the state debt remained un-funded.[7]

Additionally, and just as important to many a mid–nineteenth-century American politician, payment of the debt was a matter of honor. States, according to Fletcher, needed to be "jealous of our character for keeping our faith with all men. . . ." Moreover, he added, "states, like individuals, must prove their intentions by exertions to pay honest debts. . . ." To Fletcher, the reduction of the debt was a "noble struggle to maintain the honor of the state." Governor Fletcher was certainly not alone in these sentiments. The legislature, meeting in 1866, matched Fletcher's rhetoric by proclaiming "it to be our fixed and unalterable purpose . . . that the faith of the State shall be preserved with all her creditors. . . ." Fletcher's gubernatorial successors shared these sentiments. Joseph McClurg, shortly after taking office in January 1869, continued the fiscal chorus by stating that "our promises must be strictly regarded" and that "the honor of the State is involved and every citizen should regard his own honor at stake." Five years later in January 1874, newly installed governor Silas Woodson emphasized that Missourians should "learn no such words as 'fail,' 'dishonor,' 'repudiation.'"[8]

The concerns of Missouri's public officials placed them squarely within the mainstream of the fiscal thinking of the period. On one level, their attitudes toward state debt were part of the larger contemporary debates on the relative honesty of governments issuing greenbacks and redeeming banknotes in silver. The purely financial aspects of these debates were often lost in the ethical issue of whether it was honest for government to traffic in either fiat money or currency redeemable in a less valuable specie. On another level, Missouri's political leadership reflected a general concern with an explosion in nationwide state debt. As total state indebtedness in the United States increased from $257 million in 1860 to $450 million by

---

[7] Fletcher quoted in Avery and Shoemaker, *Messages and Proclamations*, 4:61, 92. Further discussion of the debt and the popular reaction to it can be found in David Thelen, *Paths of Resistance: Tradition and Democracy in Industrializing Missouri* (Columbia: University of Missouri Press, 1986; paperback edition, 1991), 63–69. Some of the problems associated with state debt are examined in Keller, *Affairs of State*, 329. Harry Scheiber has also described this interstate economic competition as "state mercantilism" in his "Federalism and the American Economic Order," 97.

[8] Fletcher, the legislature, and McClurg are quoted in Avery and Shoemaker, *Messages and Proclamations*, 4:148, 214, 215, 358; 5:269.

1875, financial analysts and public officials became wary. In viewing a financial scene whereby a state like Virginia now stood responsible for a debt exceeding $45 million, financial editor Alexander Noyes wrote that "moral sense seemed for a time to have deteriorated." All levels of government had imitated the example of Washington in making the acquisition of debt "the order of the day." A sampling of opinion at the time revealed many who proclaimed the debt—among other things—"a tax," "an evil," "an incubus," "a source of corruption," and "a calamity." The attitudes of the financial analysts eventually set in as numerous states passed constitutional provisions barring the contraction of further debt.[9]

Nationwide, the immediate postwar period stood as a time of massive state fiscal restructuring. In many states this restructuring translated into drastic reductions of the levels of taxation and spending. According to C. K. Yearley, the postwar years thus inaugurated a virtual "fiscal starving time" for state governments. In other states, however, restructuring meant combining fiscal austerity with attempts to repudiate debts. Most prominent in the defeated states of the Confederacy, repudiation fever struck in waves. Reconstruction governments disallowed state debts incurred during the war, and post-Reconstruction "Redeemer" governments disallowed many of the debts incurred during the antebellum and Reconstruction periods. Although the political battles between "funders" and "repudiators" were not fought exclusively in the southern states, the issue of repudiation did not take firm hold elsewhere until after the depression beginning in 1873. Repudiation movements then occurred mostly in those states hardest hit by railroad overexpansion and gen-

---

[9] Paul Studenski and Herman E. Kross, *Financial History of the United States: Fiscal, Monetary, Banking, and Tariff* . . . (New York: McGraw-Hill, 1963), 194. Noyes quoted in Alexander D. Noyes, *Thirty Years of American Finance: A Short Financial History of the Government and People of the United States Since the Civil War 1865–1896* (New York: G. P. Putnam's Sons, 1900; reprint, New York: Greenwood Press, Publishers, 1969), 18. Other financial opinions quoted in C. K. Yearley, *The Money Machines: The Breakdown and Reform of Governmental and Party Finance, 1860–1920* (Albany: State University of New York Press, 1970), 14. Constitutional provisions in William A. Scott, *The Repudiation of State Debts: A Study of the Financial History of Mississippi, Florida, Alabama, North Carolina, South Carolina, Georgia,* . . (New York: Thomas Crowell, 1893), 242. A brief discussion of state attitudes toward debt can be found in Ballard Campbell, *The Growth of American Government,* 21–22.

eral financial collapse. Kansas, Missouri, Iowa, Minnesota, and Michigan all witnessed efforts to roll back the debt.[10]

Nonetheless, for the majority of states in the years immediately following the Civil War, default was to be avoided at all costs. A contemporary author, John F. Hume, expressed the thoughts of many when he warned against the "leprosy of repudiation." To Hume, the repudiation of public debts could only rub off on the private sector and lead to a decline of public morals. Hume's sentiments could be seen throughout the polity. In Kansas, that state's most widely read newspaper attacked repudiation as an evil that "ends in financial and moral bankruptcy." Ultimately, both major political parties reflected this judgment and denounced repudiation throughout the 1860s and 1870s. Given this political consensus, state officials sought other methods to liquidate their debts. In Missouri, the government turned not only to a virtual fire sale of the bankrupt railroads that fell into state ownership, but also to a full-pressure campaign to recoup the expenses of the Civil War.[11]

THE RISE OF THE STATE AGENT

Missouri did not stumble blindly into the claims process during the Gilded Age. Four years of war provided the state with numerous opportunities to try to recover its money. Though the opportunities generally disappeared quickly, state officials gathered a corporate knowledge of the best methods for extracting money from Washington. In a polity that saw Washington assume a greater presence and responsibility in governmental activity, Missouri's leaders realized the necessity of direct lobbying to press the state's agenda. To that

---

[10] Yearley quoted in Yearley, *The Money Machines*, 98. For more-detailed examinations of nineteenth-century repudiation controversies, see Keller, *Affairs of State*, 329; Scott, *Repudiation of State Debts*, passim; and Robert B. Jones, *Tennessee at the Crossroads: The State Debt Controversy, 1870–1883* (Knoxville: University of Tennessee Press, 1975).

[11] John F. Hume, "Responsibility for State Roguery," *North American Review* 139 (1884): 575. Kansas quote taken from *The Leavenworth (Kans.) Times and Conservative*, October 28, 1866. Republican and Democratic Party Platforms, 1856–1880, in Ira Hyde Collection, Western Historical Manuscripts Collection (WHMC), Columbia, Missouri. By the 1880s, the issue of repudiation had disappeared from the national platforms. See Hume, "Responsibility for State Roguery," 577.

end, the state turned initially to paid agents to provide the benefits the formal agents of federalism could not.

However, before reaching that conclusion, and for most of the Civil War, Missouri's leadership emphasized legislative action. Ever since the early months of 1862, Missouri's congressional delegation had worked earnestly to gain the bulk of the state's indemnification through special legislation. Congressional action was necessary because Missouri incurred the largest part of her military debt for troop operations that fell outside of Salmon Chase's interpretation of the original claims bill of July 27, 1861. Constant guerrilla warfare and repeated invasions of Missouri necessitated frequent emergency calls for state militia that never received the proper mobilization authority from Washington. According to Chase's rules, the expenses generated by such troops were not eligible for reimbursement. Thus, Missouri was constantly in the position of having to petition Congress for expenses that exceeded $7 million by the end of the war.

The Missouri congressional delegation was among the first to realize that Chase's rules did not cover the expenses of militia classified as having merely acted in concert with Union troops. The delegation quickly succeeded in ushering through Congress a special indemnification act in July 1862, Congress' first, reimbursing the expenses of certain militia called out in 1861. A good start, this bill did not begin to cover the state's costs. Prodded by the governor and the state legislature, the state's representatives and senators introduced indemnification legislation in Congress every session. On a number of occasions, such legislation passed in one house only to fail in the other. Despite its initial success, the delegation struggled—and failed—for the remainder of the war to gain any financial compensation.[12]

While Missouri waged a fruitless battle in Congress for money, the state tried other methods to open the lock on the treasury. It had just about the same amount of success. As has already been indicated by Governor Gamble's trips to Washington, Missouri's leaders realized early the necessity of maintaining someone in Washington, besides its elected officials, to represent the state's financial interests with

---

[12] Avery and Shoemaker, *Messages and Proclamations of the Governors*, 4:17; *Laws of Missouri, 1864–1865*, 458; *Congressional Globe*, 38th Cong., 2nd sess., 672–73, and its accompanying committee report, Senate Report, 38th Cong., 2nd sess., 1865, S. Doc. 107, serial 1211.

the federal executive. The reality that Gamble could not stay in Washington forever forced the governor to seek more permanent voices within the Lincoln administration. Consequently, Gamble turned to two Missourians, U.S. Attorney General Edward Bates and the solicitor general of the United States Court of Claims, Charles A. Gibson. Personal friends and political allies of Gamble, both men proved valuable assets during the initial chaotic months of the war. Bates gave the governor what he needed most—access to President Lincoln and his secretary of war. It would be in part through Bates's friendly intercession that Gamble succeeded in getting the previously mentioned $200,000 in August 1861.[13]

It would also be through Bates that Gamble secured the appointment of Gibson as the chief government litigator before the court of claims. The court of claims would not adjudicate any of the claims of states, but it was, nonetheless, an ideal position from which to help represent Missouri within the Lincoln administration. The solicitor general had little responsibility. Congress created the court of claims in 1855 solely to investigate the claims of individuals against the government. The court, therefore, possessed no judicial standing and could only recommend case dispositions to Congress. Charged with representing the government's interests before a court that lacked the power to settle its cases, Solicitor Gibson would have time to look to other tasks. Indeed, Gibson never even really saw himself as the solicitor general. As Gibson noted well after the war, he was in Washington to act primarily as "the representative of the state government of Missouri. . . ." Governor Gamble cemented Gibson's official relationship with the state when Gamble appointed him state agent in 1861. Solicitor Gibson's war years were thus spent primarily as a state agent roaming the executive offices of the Lincoln administration in search of military hardware and cash payments for the state government.[14]

Gibson confined his activities to the offices of the War and Treasury Departments. During a time when governors often corres-

---

[13] For the role of Bates, see William E. Parrish, *Turbulent Partnership*, 56; Edward Bates, *The Diary of Edward Bates, 1859–1866*, ed. Howard K. Beale (Washington: Government Printing Office, 1933), 201.

[14] Gibson quoted in Charles A. Gibson, "Autobiography of Gibson," typescript, 44, Gibson Papers, Missouri Historical Society (MHS), St. Louis. Gibson, "Autobiography," 51; Parrish, *Turbulent Partnership*, 56, 81, 92.

ponded and collaborated more closely with the president than with their own state legislatures, it was only natural that Gibson, the personal emissary of a state executive, gravitated to administrators in the federal executive branch. Moreover, and just as important, the wartime executive offices could provide some badly needed money, especially for those state volunteer regiments that ultimately mustered into permanent federal service. In the War and Treasury Departments, accounting and disbursing clerks could be presented with new, or missing, information. This information could then be the difference in obtaining claims that fit within the detailed parameters of the July 27, 1861, legislation authorizing the treasury to reimburse the states. It was also a place where departmental secretaries exercised broad discretionary control over money and supplies that had already been appropriated by the Congress for general wartime usage. Accordingly, by the end of the war, Charles Gibson had helped Governor Gamble secure a wide variety of military hardware and over $768,000 in cash payments.[15]

Despite this success, Gibson's efforts in the executive offices never came close to matching Missouri's estimated wartime expenditures, which totaled more than $7 million. The simple problem for Missouri was that too many of her claims fell outside the limits of the general claims indemnification bill of July 27, 1861. As a result, the treasury's accounting officers could not audit the state's claims without special congressional authorization. Agent Gibson, however, like most agents, seems to have had little interaction with either Congress or his own state's congressional delegation. Lacking a legislative appointment and thus serving as essentially the personal emissary of Missouri's governor, Gibson confined his operations to the executive agencies.

The limitations of Gibson's position presented a serious problem for a process of indemnification that demanded coordination and cooperation between state executive officials, legislators, and congressmen. At no point during the war did the state government coordinate the indemnification effort through one person or agency. Instead, a constantly shifting group of militia officers from the state adjutant's,

---

[15] For a discussion of the relationship between governors and the president, see Hesseltine, *Lincoln and the War Governors*, passim. Avery and Shoemaker, *Messages and Proclamations*, 3:469.

quartermaster's, and paymaster's offices tackled the subject, to little avail. With an ever-changing list of claims and supporting evidence being prepared by the state's different military agencies, confusion arose quickly in the congressional delegation over what exactly the state could, and should, be asking for. Two bills, for example, submitted during the same calendar year differed by over $2 million in the amount requested for reimbursement. Amid the confusion of numbers, the state's indemnification effort floundered.[16]

Immediately after the conclusion of the war in 1865, newly installed governor Thomas Fletcher sought to correct the problem by hiring a private agent to take complete charge of the state's claims. The decision met significant resistance. This resistance highlighted a degree of intragovernmental squabbling that distracted the indemnification effort. Despite Missouri's continual frustration with the claims process and the ever-increasing agitation of the issue within the legislature, factions in the legislature and the congressional delegation distrusted the use of an agent. Many legislators, in particular, looked warily upon the office of the governor and its assortment of powers and patronage that seemed to have grown uncontrollably during the war. More importantly, there was a backlash against industrialism in Missouri that refused to exalt the value of professionalism. According to the historian David Thelen, "Missourians rejected specialized knowledge as the basis for interpreting and treating their problems in favor of traditional values and controls." Once this was coupled with the equally popular and related demand for retrenchment, legislators found it easy to refuse Governor Fletcher the authority to hire an agent. Quite simply, many Democrats and Liberal Republicans thought the use of a state agent merely an added expense the state could ill afford, especially when the normal federal agents of the state—its governor and congressional delegation—served at no further cost. Adding to the difficulty of employing an agent was a measure of resistance within the congressional delegation. Some believed that an agent would steal congressional thunder—and the credit among constituents—for bringing home the much-needed money.[17]

---

[16] See the varying amounts requested in the bills submitted January 1865 and then in December 1865. Senate Report, 38th Cong., 2nd sess., 1865, S. Doc. 107, and Senate Report, 39th Cong, 1st sess., 1866, S. Doc. 12.

[17] Thelen, *Paths of Resistance*, 186; John B. Gray to Louis Benecke, February 27 and March 15, 1871, Benecke Papers, WHMC. For a brief description of the

Opposition to the use of an agent was strong enough to deny Governor Fletcher the needed legislative authorization to appoint one. Committed to reducing a state debt that then included $24 million in railroad bond issues, Fletcher chose to disregard the legislature. After consulting with some friendly members of the legislature and the congressional delegation, Fletcher believed that he had enough political backing to hire an agent. The expected success of the agent would, according to Fletcher's thinking, be enough to melt legislative opposition. Therefore, in September 1865 the governor selected John B. Gray to be his agent. Denied the authorization to pay an agent, Fletcher hired Gray on the premise that the legislature would later approve a commission of 1.5 percent of the total compensation Gray secured for Missouri. While Fletcher did indeed get Gray's services cheaply, as agents often charged commissions of 33 percent, Fletcher miscalculated the legislature's reaction. By the time Gray secured any of Missouri's claim, the legislature remained unwilling to provide Gray's compensation, and future governors would be wary of going against the legislative will.[18]

However, to those who supported the concept of an agent in 1865, Gray was a good choice. A former adjutant general of Missouri, Gray was intimately familiar with many of the circumstances behind the claims, having, in fact, spent time in Washington during the war determining what payroll credits the United States owed Missouri. More importantly, he was a man with many contacts. Most prominent radical politicians within the state knew him well. A lawyer, Gray also labored in a profession that spawned a large percentage of claims agents who, in turn, knew the methods and people crucial to moving claims through the bureaucracy. Gray himself had just opened up a business as a private claims agent, representing people with claims against both Missouri and the United States. Unlike his predecessor as state agent, Gray focused entirely upon the state's claim. With the support of Governor Fletcher, he then took complete control of the reimbursement effort, pushing aside those state officials who had in the past exercised control over separate portions of the claim. It was

administrative structure of Missouri during this period, consult Isidor Loeb's "The Development of Missouri's State Administrative Organization," *Missouri Historical Review* 23 (1928): 49–60.

[18] For this episode of intragovernmental controversy, and its ultimate closure, see *Journal of the Missouri House of Representatives, Adjourned Session, 1871*, 516–83. Hereafter cited as *MO HJ*.

an immense task. Vouchers, payrolls, and supporting evidence, all of which Gray had to present before the federal government, were scattered throughout the state among various commands and administrative offices. Working without any clerical assistance, he put together approximately 200,000 vouchers and 400,000 supporting documents totaling over $7.4 million in expenditures by December 6, 1865. No other state had contemplated, or would do so in the future, such a large claim.[19]

Having brought order to an unwieldy mass of paper in Missouri, Gray traveled to Washington. Once in the capital, Gray was faced with the state agent's principal tasks of coordinating and lobbying. He responded by establishing contact with the third auditor of the treasury, John Wilson, and sought his advice concerning the presentation of the claim before Congress. Wilson was not encouraging. To Wilson, the largest difficulty was Gray's attempt to settle all of Missouri's claims in one piece of legislation. Several states had already attempted this and failed. Undeterred, Gray pressed the claim, while smoothing tensions within the state's congressional delegation. Shortly after his arrival, Gray assembled most of the delegation at Willard's Hotel, the capital's most prominent political gathering place. As Gray later recalled, he then announced his mission, and even suggested that he might withdraw from active lobbying if any might see his presence as "an intrusion or an interference with their prerogatives." For the time being, Gray's handling of the meeting and his apparent forthcoming attitude mollified any resentment within the delegation. Senator B. Gratz Brown agreed to introduce the appropriate legislation in the Senate on December 13, 1865. Brown's formal introduction of the bill, however, would be just about all that the senator would do, in either House or Senate, to aid its passage. Brown suffered from a dyspepsia that forced him into bed for most of the session.[20]

---

[19] Ibid. Some sense of Gray's claims activities can also be seen in the following scattered correspondence: John B. Gray to John Bogy, July 30, 1866, Bogy Papers, MHS, and "Civil War Claims," Miscellaneous Manuscripts, WHMC. For totals, see *MO HJ, 1871*, 532.

[20] Gray quoted in John B. Gray to Louis Benecke, February 27, 1871, Benecke Papers, WHMC. *MO HJ, 1871*, 516–38. Brown's illness is somewhat mysterious and not really accounted for by his biographer. Brown's role in the indemnification effort is also absent. For background on Brown, consult Norma L. Peterson, *Freedom and Franchise: The Political Career of B. Gratz Brown* (Columbia: University of Missouri Press, 1965).

Thus lacking the assistance of the bill's sponsor in the Senate, Gray had to lobby tirelessly. According to Representative H. T. Blow of Missouri, Gray cornered "a very large majority of the House" and explained the bill in its particulars. Gray, rather than any member of the state's delegation, attended committee meetings and answered all questions raised. Gray was a clearinghouse of information dealing with the claim, as members of the state delegation referred the questions of other members to the state agent. By the time the legislation passed both houses on April 17, 1866, Gray had seen to it that most members were aware of the nature and necessity of a bill that he believed would settle a debt that "almost paralyzes the industrial recuperation of the State. . . ." To Representative R. T. Van Horn of Missouri, Gray's lobbying had been "indispensable to the successful presentation of the claim" and its passage in both houses of Congress.[21]

As Missouri's principal administrative point of contact, Gray's duties had just begun. Having shepherded the bill through the legislative branch of the government, he now had to do the same through the executive. As before, Gray's new labors required personal contact and constant attention. At issue was a bill that mandated an extensive, if not redundant, process of administrative accounting. It authorized the president to appoint a commission of three men to meet in Missouri and audit all claims incurred since August 24, 1861, for troops called out at the request of the departmental commander to serve "in concert" with United States troops. Following the commission's auditing, the claims were to be given to the third auditor for a complete reaudit. For those claims that survived the journey through the various levels of bureaucracy, the bill contained an appropriation of over $6.7 million.[22]

The provisions of this indemnification bill were somewhat unusual when compared to special antebellum claims legislation. Although most such enactments were detailed, carefully describing the circumstances and types of claims to be audited, antebellum legislation rarely dictated the formation of a special commission to screen the claims. Beginning with the Dakota Indian Claims of 1862, however, Congress

---

[21] Blow and Van Horn quoted in *MO HJ, 1871*, 518. Gray quoted in U.S. Congress, Senate Report, 39th Cong., 1st sess., 1866, S. Doc. 12.

[22] *U.S. Statutes at Large*, 14 (1866): 38–39.

turned often to ad hoc commissions to adjudicate claims disputes with
the states. To man such commissions, Congress looked to the War
Department and its Inspector General (IG) Corps. It was a reliance
that increased in the years following the Civil War as the inspectors
general became the virtual emissaries of Congress and the secretary
of war, especially in claims disputes. This usage of the IG served a
variety of purposes. For the Congress and the War Department, the
IG was a readily available source of claims adjusters whose historical
mission implied the enforcement of accountability, whether operational or fiscal, in military matters. For the IG, the claims mission
helped extend the institutional life of a corps that had to justify its
purpose, funding, and existence throughout the antebellum period.[23]

Because the Missouri commission would not come from the inspector general's office, the state hoped to deal with a more politically
malleable and friendly group. In this the state would not be disappointed. In the early summer of 1866, President Andrew Johnson
appointed a three-member commission that had close ties to Missouri, the military, and himself. Two men, J. Mosely and John D.
Stevenson, resided in Missouri, while the third, Alpheas S. Williams,
was a native of Michigan. All possessed certain qualifications, but in
terms of their future work with Missouri's claims, nothing may have
been as important as Stevenson's personal friendship with Gray that
dated back ten years. Not only did this friendship provide the state
agent with unlimited access to the commission, it also allowed Gray
to push Alpheas Williams to delay his acceptance of an ambassadorial
appointment, which President Johnson offered in October 1866.
Gray's ability to intervene was critical. As the president had soured
considerably on Missouri's radical political leadership over the issue
of Reconstruction, Missouri's Radical Republicans believed that
Johnson would not fill the vacancy in the commission, thus killing
indemnification for a state then identified as opposing the president.
Gray thus met with both Stevenson and Williams, arguing persua-
sively that any vacancy on the commission would be disastrous for
Missouri.[24]

<hr />

[23] For background on the inspector general's role in claims disputes, see David A.
Clary and Joseph W. A. Whitehorne, *The Inspectors General of the United States
Army 1777–1903* (Washington: Government Printing Office, 1987), 244–88.

[24] "Report of the Missouri Claims Commission," Rough Minutes and Abstract, vol.
16, 1–2, E. 759, RG 217, NA. Information on Stevenson can be found in *MO HJ,*

Having remained intact, the commission met in St. Louis at the end of July 1866, just three months after the passage of the enabling legislation. It then proceeded to hold hearings until the middle of December, though nothing substantial occurred throughout August. Stationery had to be ordered and advertisements placed in newspapers notifying the public of the commission's hours. More importantly, clerks had to be found to help sift through a mountain of papers. The bill of April 1866 authorized only one clerk, and it had become obvious to all concerned that one was not going to be enough. The solution to this problem came from the War Department. It detailed seventeen clerks from the Western Department paymaster general's office to assist in the preparation of payrolls and vouchers. Why the War Department provided these clerks is unknown, although it can be surmised that Alpheas Williams, a distinguished former general, exercised some personal influence with his former commander, William T. Sherman, who in 1866 also commanded the Military Division of Missouri.[25]

A crisis of manual labor thus averted, by the middle of August the commission settled into a routine and generally convened six days a week, six hours each day. The work was tedious, with John B. Gray shaping each day's agenda. Gray determined which claims to examine and presented each of the expenditures with its supporting evidence. Where the physical evidence was weak, especially in justifying the state's usage of the militia, the commission president, John Stevenson, frequently adjourned the proceedings to allow Gray to summon witnesses to provide verbal testimony. When the witnesses arrived before the commission, usually after substantial delays, Gray tended to dominate the question and answer sessions. On claim after claim, Gray carefully guided the witnesses through testimony that satisfied the commissioners as to the necessity of Missouri's expenditures. Little controversy arose. Whether it was claims for troop pay presented in August or claims for quartermaster supplies

---

1871, 532. For Alpheas Williams, see *Biographical Directory of the American Congress, 1774–1961* (Washington: Government Printing Office, 1961), 1818, and Stewart Sifakis, *Who Was Who in the Civil War* (New York: Facts on File Publications, 1988), 716–17. Some hint of the problem with President Johnson can be found in Avery and Shoemaker, *Messages and Proclamations*, 4:152.

[25] "Report of the Missouri Claims Commission," Rough Minutes and Abstract, vol. 16, 1–45, E. 759, RG 217, NA; *Missouri State Times* (Jefferson City), February 15, 1867.

presented in October, Gray continually provided reasonable answers to the occasional question posed by the commissioners.[26]

On December 14, 1866, the commission finished its labors, having allowed Missouri an unprecedented $6.48 million, which also included a deduction of $760,000 for Missouri's still unpaid direct tax from the war. The commission then forwarded the claims to Washington for similar examinations in the third auditor's and second comptroller's offices. Once again, Gray accompanied the claims to make his explanations. In both offices Gray's shepherding proved invaluable. He met daily with the chiefs of the examining offices and readily produced evidence from five large dry goods boxes he had brought with him from St. Louis. Gray also lobbied treasury officials successfully to assign clerks and expedite Missouri's claims within bureaucracies that were being subjected to the demands and pressures of other states and their agents. Gray's attention paid dividends. Not only did he successfully fend off an attempt by the army's quartermaster to deduct $1 million for unpaid wartime expenses, he managed to secure a rebate on the state's wartime direct tax, as well as several Missouri bond issues held in trust by the government. By the time Gray left Washington in April 1867, he had acquired almost $100,000 more than the original commission had allowed.[27]

The short-term effect of Gray's work was beneficial. Missouri wasted little time in disposing of the money and retiring a good portion of the debt. Governor Fletcher, who had pressed Gray into service and made the reduction of the state's debt a virtual crusade, immediately used most of the reimbursed dollars to pay off wartime bond issues. The rest he funneled into the permanent school fund and a seminary fund. Fletcher's distribution of the money provoked some measure of controversy, but he generally had little choice in the matter. On the one hand, legislation authorizing the bond issues had mandated that any future reimbursement be applied first to bond redemption. A subsequent state supreme court decision reinforced such a distribution. On the other hand, no legislation or great sympathy for public education bound Fletcher to the school fund; he placed

---

[26] Report of the Missouri Claims Commission," Rough Minutes and Abstract, vol. 16, 1–45, E. 759, RG 217, NA; *Missouri State Times*, February 15, 1867.
[27] *MO HJ*, 516–39.

some money there as matter of equity. At the beginning of the war, a different school fund had been raided to support the military effort. Fletcher merely replaced what had been taken.[28]

Having completed his distributions, Governor Fletcher thought the reimbursement an important milestone for the state. The indemnification, coupled with his other fiscal measures, had reduced the state debt significantly, meeting one of the chief goals of his administration. Writing on January 8, 1868, Fletcher proclaimed "our credit as a state has not only been restored, but raised to a standard" greater than ever. Dignity had been restored to Missourians, as they were "able with the just pride of honest men to rejoice in a financial standing in the money markets of the world equal to that of any of the states."[29]

Disregarding the inflated oratory of the period and that Missouri's securities were valued 10 percent less than several New England states, Fletcher's comments avoided other points. Missouri was indeed considerably better off, yet the state still carried an unwieldy debt in excess of $11 million. More troublesome, Fletcher's glowing financial assessment did not reveal the extent to which he, and his agent, had come under fire. At issue was Fletcher's use of an agent. When controversy erupted in the winter of 1867–68, the trouble symbolized what had become a major undercurrent of state politics in the immediate postwar period: a shifting of the balance of power between the legislatures and governors. Traditionally the weaker of the two branches, state executives experienced an increase in their function and power during the Civil War. The postwar period, however, witnessed a backlash as legislatures jealously guarded their prerogatives and rolled back the power of state executives. According to a contemporary observer of American government, Lord Bryce, by the 1880s the legislatures had succeeded in defining the executive as little more than a glorified clerk confined in responsibility to "various matters of routine." No governor who exceeded this role would be tolerated kindly, and it did not take long for the state war claims to produce such an example in Missouri. The resulting intragovernmen-

---

[28] *Missouri Statesman* (Columbia), May 10, 1867; Avery and Shoemaker, *Messages and Proclamations*, 4:112, 151–54.

[29] Fletcher quoted in Avery and Shoemaker, *Messages and Proclamations*, 4:108, 148.

tal bickering made future governors even less willing to propose employing an agent.[30]

The success of John B. Gray in guiding Missouri's claims through the treasury failed to impress a significant number of state politicians. Many legislators, representing an emerging alliance of Democrats and Liberal Republicans that had begun to coalesce over a variety of other issues, did not view the accomplishment as a testament to the tenacity and fiscal management of Governor Fletcher and his ruling faction of Radical Republicans. Indeed, the legislature pounced on Fletcher's indemnification crusade as an example of the high-handed behavior of the governor and the profligacy of the radical faction during a time of supposed fiscal retrenchment. Moreover, because the legislature never authorized the use, let alone the pay, of an agent in 1865, many legislators thought Fletcher's actions unconstitutional. Making matters worse for Fletcher was the amount of money that eventually found its way into the pockets of Agent Gray for his services. In accordance with Gray's agreement with Governor Fletcher, the agent deducted 1.5 percent of the total reimbursement, or $98,555, for his compensation. The size of this payment, which was $2,000 more than the president of the United States made in four years, provided partisan ammunition to legislative opponents, who then assailed Fletcher and the radicals. Opposition political organs proclaimed Gray a "seedy courtier" of Fletcher's and the whole episode either a "shame and disgrace" or "a Radical rascality." To many within the legislature, all Gray did was pick up the claim in Washington and bring it back to the capital in Jefferson City. The furor did not subside. The state house passed a resolution demanding an investigation of Fletcher's extralegal behavior, and Fletcher eventually caved to pressure that came both from within and without his party. He instructed his own attorney general to file suit against Gray for the return of the commission, plus interest, on the grounds that he, the governor, had entered into an unconstitutional arrangement.[31]

---

[30] Information on state securities can be found in Scott, *Repudiation of State Debts*, 214. Bryce quoted in James Bryce, *The American Commonwealth*, 2 vols. (Chicago: Charles H. Sergel and Co., 1891), 1:508.

[31] Quotes of political organs can be found in the *Liberty (Mo.) Tribune*, March 6, 1868, and *Weekly Peoples Tribune* (Jefferson City, Mo.), February 26, 1868. For legislative and executive activity, examine *MO HJ, 1868*, 378, 427, and *MO HJ, 1871*, 534; *Columbia (Missouri) Statesman*, May 19, 1871.

The case took three years to complete, with the courts ultimately deciding against Gray. Though partisan politics and concerns over the governing balance of power had fueled this controversy, the legislature eventually acted as Thomas Fletcher hoped it would. Soon after the court system rendered its judgment in the spring of 1871, a legislature dominated by the Liberal Republican and Democratic opponents of Fletcher and Gray convened in Jefferson City. Satisfied that it had put the state executive branch in its proper place, the legislature was then in a position to acknowledge the effectiveness of a state agent. It soon opened hearings to determine if Gray deserved any compensation after all.

The legislature thus left the door open for future governors to use an agent. But just as intragovernmental concerns and party politics had slowed down the acceptance of the use of an agent, so too would matters of individual political reputation. By 1871, Missouri had a new governor, Thomas Fletcher having left office in 1869. The new governor, former senator B. Gratz Brown, attacked the idea of any compensation for Gray. He did this for two reasons. First, Brown never saw the importance of an agent. When in the Senate, he had submitted the legislation that formed the basis for Missouri's reimbursement, but he had been too bedridden to notice Gray's work in leading the legislation through Congress and the subsequent commission meetings. Second, and just as important, Brown had assessed the politics of the compensation controversy and concluded that he was better off if Gray remained discredited. With Gray's role in reimbursement minimized, Brown stood as the primary champion of indemnification because of his initial introduction of the claims legislation. The political capital available to the person who could bring home more than $6 million was not a matter to be easily dismissed. Governor Brown thought such capital should not be shared. Nevertheless, the legislature persisted. It then held an extensive inquiry that pulled in numerous depositions and witnesses, including the somewhat hostile Governor Brown. In a period of Missouri's history known for virulent party clashes over test oaths and voting rights, partisanship disappeared from the subsequent hearings. Many legislators of both parties now testified to the absolute necessity of employing Gray, while others emphasized that Missouri got his services relatively cheaply anyway. After a number of observers noted that other claims agents, whether private or state, charged commis-

sions ranging from 5 to 15 percent, the legislature concluded that
Fletcher had acted wisely all along. One year later, the legislature
restored Gray's money, minus the additional 6 percent in interest it
charged Gray in May 1871. Governor Brown resisted to the end,
refusing either to approve or disapprove the measure. The bill had to
become law without an executive signature.[32]

THE AMBIGUITY OF AGENTS AND LOBBYING

The controversy over John B. Gray's compensation illustrated the
continued importance of local matters in the shaping of Missouri's
indemnification effort. Not only did it reveal competing governmental and personal interests that threatened the most effective means of
handling the claims, but the clamor involving Gray distracted the
state's leadership from handling new claims problems. Indeed, since
1867, when Gray secured more than $6 million for the state, Missou-
ri's claims situation became more muddled. The chief problem was
that the state had incurred war-related debts for many years after
Gray presented Missouri's accounts in 1866. In some cases, the muster records of militia units had been either lost or simply never presented to the state adjutant general. After Gray's initial settlement,
muster rolls and the attendant requests for back pay trickled into the
adjutant general. In other cases, a steady flow of claims from citizens
entered the state's quartermaster office requesting compensation for
a variety of items furnished, or taken by, the militia and entitled
"irregular claims." Heading the list were claims for food, supplies,
horses, rent, and transportation. By the end of 1870 there were 2,820
separate claims totaling $233,914.[33]

---

[32] Evidence of Brown's unwillingness to share political capital can be found in
John B. Gray to Louis Benecke, February 27 and March 15, 1871, Benecke Papers,
WHMC. Although Gray could have merely written two self-serving explanations of
the controversy, it would have been out of character. Other information on the difficulties between Gray and Brown can be seen in R. T. Wingate to B. Gratz Brown,
April 27, 1871, Governor Brown's Papers, R. 148, F. 14768, WHMC; W. Slayback
to Brown, May 11, 1871, Governor Brown's Papers, R. 148, F. 14768, WHMC;
Avery and Shoemaker, *Messages and Proclamations*, 5:127–29; *Laws of Missouri,
1871–1872*, Act of March 14, 1872. The long reach of the investigation can be seen
in W. H. Stone to Erastus Wells, March 29, 1871, Letters Received, Third Auditor,
vol. 4, E. 604, RG 217, NA. The legislative compensation of Gray is discussed in
MO HJ, Adjourned Session, 1871, 516–34.
[33] *MO HJ, Appendix, 1869–1870*, 10.

Inundated with war-related claims, the state again had to figure out just how to proceed. The next step would not be easy. Missouri had reached an awkward moment in its governmental history. Like so many other states, individuals, and interest groups, it had discovered the importance of agents in handling relations with the federal government. But almost simultaneously, it had also discovered that institutional competition between legislatures and governors could brake the ability of the state to operate successfully within the federal system. Yet, the greatest threat to the existence of state agents during this period did not come from jealous legislators. Of greater importance to the survival of state agents in Missouri was the negative popular perception of agents and lobbyists and their expanding role in American governance. This generated numerous concerns. Political theorists feared electoral unaccountability. State politicians and governing officials feared the cost of employing agents, whose commissions had been known to reach 33 percent of the returned claims. Congressmen feared the power and prestige that could accrue to the successful agent for doing what had traditionally been their jobs. And finally, the general population feared the potential of corrupting influence.[34]

Of all the fears, corruption had the greatest impact. In the popular imagination, most political scandals in the early Gilded Age seemed to involve lobbyists. Whether it was the failure of the United States Senate to convict President Andrew Johnson, the Credit Mobilier corruption, the Whiskey Ring, or the Gold Ring, the prominent scandals of the period could be easily tagged to "the lobby." The expansion of governmental authority at all levels during the war ushered in not only a new era of governmental power but also a new era of lobbyists to access that power. Encouraged by vaguely written laws that could be shaped and molded, lobbyists of all stripes descended on public officials. State legislators, being generally the most politically inexperienced, were particularly ripe for lobbyists. The list of

---

[34] For a general discussion of corruption and lobbying, see Summers, *The Era of Good Stealings*, passim, but especially 16–31, 107–21. Though concerned more with lobbying during the Progressive Era, Elisabeth S. Clemens's *The People's Lobby: Organizational Innovation and the Rise of Interest Group Politics in the United States, 1890–1925* (Chicago: University of Chicago Press, 1997) presents a strong overview of lobbying in the later part of the nineteenth century. Campbell, *The Growth of American Government*, 19 discusses the popular perception of the effect of lobbyists on government.

lobbyists and their clients was seemingly endless: manufacturers, insurance companies, real estate speculators, craft workers, railroads, coal miners, stone cutters, stock breeders, state historical societies, veterans, and even beekeepers. The sudden explosion in the numbers of lobbyists and their attendant power led many to fear for the safety of republican government. State governing officials were thus caught between the probability that employing agents meant administrative success and the growing popular sentiment that the influence of agents meant corruption and scandal. Missouri's leaders, in particular, would spend the remainder of the nineteenth century trying to balance these contradictory pressures in their handling of state claims.[35]

Following John B. Gray's successful reimbursement effort, Missouri turned to its state military officers to unlock any remaining claims mysteries. This situation developed at first as a matter of expedience rather than through any inordinate fear of lobbyists. After the widely reported work of Gray, the claims issue seemed settled. The state had received millions of dollars, and few people expressed concern over new claims. In such an atmosphere, a succession of legislatures assigned responsibility for the claims to the state's military hierarchy. It was a logical choice. State adjutants and quartermasters general were not without claims experience. Between 1861 and 1865, the adjutant general made some wartime trips to Washington to check on troop credits and pay status. Moreover, the Missouri adjutant served as the chief information collector for the wartime congressional delegation that then attempted to usher the state's claims through the bureaucracy. But more importantly for the reassignment of the claims responsibility, at war's end the militia was an institution in search of a mission. With neither Confederates nor Indians to fight

---

[35] Summers, *The Era of Good Stealings*, 16–31, 107–21; Campbell, *The Growth of American Government*, 19; Thompson, *In the "Spider's Web*," 56, 65. The ways in which vague laws encouraged the formation of claims agencies is discussed in W. A. Owens to James S. Rollins, March 28, 1865, Rollins Papers, F. 91, WHMC. For a general description of lobbyists working in and around state legislatures in the latter part of the Gilded Age, see Ballard Campbell, *Representative Democracy: Public Policy and Midwestern Legislatures in the Late Nineteenth Century* (Cambridge, Mass.: Harvard University Press, 1980), 152. For a detailed examination of lobbyists in another state legislature, see Robert Harrison, "The Hornets' Nest at Harrisburg: A Study of the Pennsylvania Legislature in the Late 1870s," *Pennsylvania Magazine of History and Biography* 103 (1979): 334–55.

in Missouri, it was a ready target for legislative budget cutters bent on either dismantling the force or abolishing the top military offices. When the claims issue reemerged as an important concern of state officials, legislators latched upon militia officers as the cure to their problem. Not only did members of the military hierarchy have some institutional experience in dealing with the claims, they served far more cheaply than state agents and appeared to have little else to do with their time.[36]

Missouri's state military offices soon bore a greater resemblance to claims agencies than to departments devoted to military readiness. Some indication of this can be seen in the personnel who worked in the offices. At the highest level it did not take long for the position of adjutant general to be seen as restricted entirely to claims. Consequently, the majority of applicants for the job were private claims agents, or lawyers, who had prosecuted citizens claims against the national and state governments. Some who therefore got the post used the office as a means to furthering their own private claims interests.[37]

The same situation developed among the clerical help. By 1873 three out of the four clerks who served in the office either worked as conduits of confidential information to preferred private agents or actually moonlighted as private agents representing claims against the state. The best example of the latter surfaced in the spring of 1872 when the adjutant general discovered that one clerk, E. S. Woog, had operated secretly as a claims agent. By the accounts of numerous people, Woog had removed numerous claims from the office, hid them in the back room of a Jefferson City grocery store, and then processed only the claims of those people who had commissioned him as their agent. Writing in late 1872, the adjutant general, Albert Sigel, believed that Woog had virtually "monopolized the claims business against the State. . . ."[38]

---

[36] Information concerning an attempt to abolish the militia hierarchy can be found in E. D. Townsend to Samuel Simpson, September 30, 1868, Missouri State Claims, E. 759, RG 217, NA.

[37] For the character of the men who sought the office, refer to B. B. Cahoon to B. Gratz Brown, December 30, 1870, Governor Brown's Papers, R.148, F. 14780, and Nathan C. Kouric to Hardin, January 5, 1875, Governor Hardin's Papers, R. 152, F. 15278, WHMC; J. D. Strother to Hardin, November 11, 1875, Governor Hardin's Papers, CFD-165, F. 15293, Missouri State Archives (MSA), Jefferson City.

[38] Chris Gundelfinger to Louis Benecke, July 7, 1874, Louis Benecke Papers,

As a postscript to his activities, E. S. Woog did not fade quietly
from the claims scene. Fired by Sigel in 1872, Woog reapplied for
his old position the following year when the governor appointed a
new adjutant general, J. D. Crafton. Rejected by Crafton, who had
become aware of the clerk's earlier dealings, Woog promised ven-
geance upon Missouri and disappeared for a little more than a year.
After vacationing in Europe, Woog turned up in Washington, where
he readily gained a clerical position in the Treasury Department.
From here he worked diligently to disrupt Missouri's attempts to
gain indemnification. As events later unfolded, the state did not need
any outside interference to sabotage its claims plans. It could do that
on its own.[39]

Between 1868 and 1874, the claims situation in Missouri was characterized by administrative chaos, as well as by the attempts of successive legislatures to minimize the liability of the state. At the outset
of this period the state determined that it would handle its irregular
and pay claims differently. Irregular claims, or those for supplies furnished, would be audited and settled where appropriate so that the
state could then petition the United States government for its own
indemnification. Using an "act to protect the State of Missouri against
illegal claims" passed during the war, the legislature authorized a
series of commissions to audit the irregular claims. The commissions,
and state military officials responsible for helping the commissioners,
were beset with difficulties. No one was quite certain as to the exact
types of claims that could be audited, or whether there was actually
any money to pay the claimants. When on rare occasions the commissioners were relatively certain of their actions, they often provided
little satisfaction to the claimants or their agents. Applying the standard of scrutiny used in Washington, the commissioners rejected far
more than they approved. For example, the commission meeting between August and September 1869 received 1,039 claims, worth over

---

WHMC; Dan Draper, et. al. to Brown, June 28, 1874, Governor Brown's Papers, R.
148, F. 14765, WHMC; Albert Sigel quoted in Sigel to Brown, April 11, 1872, Governor Brown's Papers, R. 148, F. 14765, WHMC.

[39] Woog to Brown, May 22, 1872, Dan Draper, et. al. to Brown, June 28, 1872,
Governor Brown's Papers, R. 148, F. 14765, WHMC; Affidavit of C. J. Gundelfinger,
January 26, 1874, Woog to John A. Logan, January 28, 1874, J. D. Crafton to George
Spencer, April 15, 1874, Albert Sigel to Crafton, April 20, 1874, and the accompany-
ing Senate Committee on Military Affairs' draft report on Senate Bill #330, all lo-
cated in Box 44, S. 43A-E10, RG 46, NA.

$85,000, of which they approved one claim worth thirty dollars. The commission either rejected outright the remaining claims or suspended them pending the presentation of more supporting evidence. Given the record-keeping practices of the various commissions, there is no way of determining the validity of either the rejected or suspended claims.[40]

Claims for pay suffered an even worse fate. Missouri's adjutants general, who were directly responsible for these claims, came and went quickly, and when they stayed for any appreciable amount of time, they were overburdened with a host of responsibilities that did not match the level of clerical help. Shortly following the war, the adjutant found himself bearing the additional titles of acting quartermaster general and acting paymaster general.

As a result of all such turmoil, most claims record keeping fell into disarray. Soon after John B. Gray had brought relative order to the records of the state, the adjutant general noted that, in many instances, there was no way to verify certain claims short of sending a clerk to Washington to copy the War Department's service records. Moreover, when the state could verify and then approve a payroll (or service) claim, the perennial problem of funding arose. But even if the state found the money, that did not always guarantee the reimbursement of a militia unit. For example, during Governor Fletcher's administration, Missouri received money from the United States to reimburse the services of the 81st and 82nd Enrolled Missouri Militia regiments without having to seek special legislation. A series of errors then occurred, leaving the majority of these soldiers without their pay. Even though the legislature never made an appropriation to disburse the money, the state treasury proceeded to indemnify individuals anyway. The problem, however, was that the treasury reimbursed the wrong people. Numerous men had presented forged powers of attorney and then walked away with the money. This episode only underscores the nagging persistence of claims-related problems. By 1874 there were still over $365,000 worth of service claims approved and left lying unpaid in the state adjutant general's office.[41]

---

[40] Samuel Simpson to Wilson, February 6, 1868, Letters Received, Third Auditor, E. 604, RG 217, NA; *MO HJ, Appendix, 1869–1870,* 10–13.

[41] Simpson to John Wilson, February 6, 1868, and George Childress to Wilson, December 13, 1869, Letters Received, Third Auditor, E. 604, RG 217, NA. See

The issue of settling these claims languished in the political forum prior to 1874. Neither Republicans nor Democrats carved out any particular stance on claims reimbursement, and popular dissatisfaction with the situation had not yet built to a point where the issue became a focus of political debate. Even more important, while the state's claims continued to face the same difficulties they had always faced in hostile Congresses, bigger problems lurked at the state level. There, the spirit of financial retrenchment threatened any payment that a state must first make to individual claimants before the state could then apply to Washington for reimbursement. The tenor of the time could be seen in Governor McClurg's message to the legislature in January 1870 when he proclaimed that "no extravagant legislation should be indulged in; no uncertain schemes, although they may appear plausible and deserve to be called 'liberal and progressive.' " Thus, repeatedly, the state government lacked the resources and the political will to pay off those few claims audited and actually approved by the varying commissions. The state continued to carry a significant debt, and conventional wisdom demanded restraint on an issue that, to most Missourians, had been supposedly resolved with Gray's settlement of 1866. Numerous attempts to have the state pay the claims were then, to one claims agent, easily "Tommahawked" amid the cries of what another agent derisively reported as "retrenchment."[42]

But the chief roadblock to solving the claims issue was an increasingly negative reaction against the agents. Just as lobbyists began to attract widespread notice for their activities in the nation's capital, so, too, did they attract attention in Missouri. Agents and lobbyists, representing constituencies ranging from claims to penitentiaries, descended annually upon the legislature in Jefferson City to promote their clienteles and draft the legislation that would be introduced. To many within the press and the electorate, this activity was a corrupting influence that subverted the governing process. A growing and politically vocal element, not confined by party affiliation, perceived

---

Missouri Statesman, March 10, 1871, for a defeated legislative measure to fund the state's claims. Avery and Shoemaker, *Messages and Proclamations,* 5:248–49; *Missouri Adjutant General's Report, 1874,* MHS.

[42] McClurg quoted in Avery and Shoemaker, *Messages and Proclamations,* 4:411. Claims agents quoted in John W. McClean to Louis Benecke, July 13, 1874, and Sennaca Hammack to Benecke, February 6, 1873, Benecke Papers, WHMC.

lobbyists as serving only to line their own pockets. Though difficult to measure, the growth of this popular attitude was enough to frighten a number of governors and legislators. Legislators began to proclaim their independence from the lobby, while also derailing legislation identified too closely with the lobby.[43]

The notoriety of the lobby placed those interested in the passage of claims legislation in a curious dilemma. Though claims legislation had frequently benefited from the efforts of lobbyists, those same efforts had created a backlash. The problem for claims legislation was that the lobbyists themselves benefited all too obviously from any enactment. Invariably, claims lobbyists were private agents who gained directly by the passage of any appropriation for claims, whether "irregular" or payroll. Because all agents charged a commission based upon a percentage of a client's successful claim, and some agents purchased the claims of impatient individuals at depreciated prices, it did not take a great stretch of popular and legislative imaginations to believe that all claims legislation was intended more for the greedy agent/lobbyist than for the needy claimant. Therefore, it should have come as no surprise that the state senate killed a claims appropriation in 1872 because, according to one interested observer, Sennaca Hammack, some senators thought the bill had been "brought up by Agents" who had speculated in the claims.[44]

In a political era often described as rife with politicians too receptive to the wiles and money of special interests, Missouri officials seemed especially immune to the overtures of claims agents. The unpopularity of agents in Missouri was such that even the label "agent," which in previous times had generated a more favorable reaction than "lobbyist," no longer softened the image and purpose of those interested in pushing claims legislation. By 1875 enough criticism had been generated to warrant talk of the legislature regulating the activities of claims agents. Agents and claimants eventually

---

[43] *Missouri Republican* (St. Louis), March 15, 1873; Unidentified and undated clipping (April–December 1873?), Clippings, Benecke Papers, WHMC. For a general analysis of legislatures and lobbyists in the Gilded Age, consult Campbell, *Representative Democracy*, 52. Although this work deals primarily with legislatures following the time period in question, it still contains pertinent information.

[44] Hammack quoted in Hammack to Louis Benecke, February 6, 1873, Benecke Papers, WHMC. By 1874, the state adjutant general believed this to be the only reason why the legislature had never acted. *Missouri Adjutant General's Report, 1874*, 25–26.

sensed and reacted to the hostile atmosphere in which they had to work. It soon became a virtual standard operating procedure among all those interested in the claims to deny first any connection to the claims lobby before then proceeding with the business at hand. Needless to say, a large number of agents and speculators constituted the self-proclaimed disinterested parties.[45]

Despite the growing resistance of some legislators to the best efforts of claimants, agents, and speculators, the lobby persisted. Letters flowed to Missouri's elected officials, and claims agents frequently rallied in Jefferson City to set their strategy. There, they targeted state legislators who were veterans, including Col. A. P. Richardson, a perennial supporter of claims legislation. The lobby also targeted legislators who were themselves claims agents. Agent and state senator Louis Benecke of Chariton County, in particular, served as a focal point for a claims lobby anxious to find an attractive champion. Benecke seemed the ideal choice. A veteran, Benecke moved easily among a legislative fraternity then made up of large numbers of veterans. An ethnic German, he had influence within the German population and with Missouri's prominent German-speaking United States senator, Carl Schurz. A successful and well-known claims agent, he also possessed strong connections among claims agents, including John B. Gray, and in the administrative agencies of the state government. By 1873 the claims lobby, Richardson, and Benecke began to gain some success. The state appointed an agent to act on behalf of the state. A. J. Neugent assumed these duties, collected the available information on the irregular and payroll expenditures, and in October presented a combined state claim for over $800,000 before the third auditor in Washington.[46]

---

[45] Summers, *The Era of Good Stealings*, passim, but especially 20–31, contains the best analysis of corruption and its popularly perceived linkage to lobbying. Thompson discusses the connotations of "lobbyists" and "agents" in *In the "Spider's Web*," 65. For reports of agent fraud, examine Brown and Wright to Third Auditor, January 25, 1871, H. Tritt to J. C. Parker, May 24, 1872, and Peter Hinter to Third Auditor, August 26, 1871, Letters Received, Third Auditor, vol. 2, E. 604, RG 217, NA. For talk of regulation, see Richard Everingham to George C. Bingham, March 1, 1875, Adjutant General's Office, Regular Service Claims, Box 211, RG 133, MSA. Agent attempts to distance themselves from their cause can be found in Sennaca Hammack to B. Gratz Brown, January 28, 1871, and E. F. Rogers to Brown, December 2, 1871, Governor Brown's Papers, R. 148, F. 14780, WHMC.

[46] Sennaca Hammack to Louis Benecke, February 6, 1873, and E. F. Rogers to Benecke, February 4, 1875, Benecke Papers, WHMC; U.S. Congress, Senate Report, 43rd Cong., 1st sess., 1874, S. Doc. 70, serial 1584.

The agent's early work revealed that he would have little success in pressing Missouri's interests with the government. As should have been anticipated by Neugent, who was a practicing private claims agent, the auditor quickly rejected the request. Of the expenditures presented for reimbursement, most were for items that the state itself had not yet paid. Neugent also attempted to justify reimbursement by requesting that the auditor pass the entire claim under the provisions of the April 1866 legislation shepherded by John B. Gray. Because the current claim also had not been first examined by a federally appointed commission, as had been mandated in Gray's 1866 bill, it was easy for the auditor to reject the claim. Undeterred, but apparently no wiser as to the precedents involved with pressing this type of claim, Neugent turned to Missouri's congressional delegation. Using the information and directions supplied by Neugent, the state's representatives and senators then introduced the appropriate legislation in early 1874. Failure came slowly because this claim lacked not only the justification evident in Gray's claim, but also Gray's organizational skill and personal contacts. Needing administrative help and preoccupied with other matters, the state's congressional delegation exerted little effort, and various bills entered committees from which they never reappeared. Hampering Neugent in his lobbying efforts were allegations of fraud in his own private practice that had filtered into Washington and the treasury's accounting offices.[47]

The defeat of Neugent's bills in Washington moved Missouri's claims to their most controversial stage. Pressure to do something mounted from many directions. Agents and claimants joined with the newly installed adjutant general, J. D. Crafton, in demanding action. While both Crafton and the claims lobby pushed for actual state payment of the claims, the legislature was not ready for that kind of assumption. Pinned between the need to do something and the fiscal reality of not being able to do anything substantive, the legislature would do the next best thing: it created a special commission that had absolutely no chance of solving the problem. The legislature empowered a commission to look into the situation and audit all claims

[47] Third Auditor to Second Comptroller, November 1, 1873, S. 43A-E10, Box 44, Committee on Military Affairs, RG 46, NA; *Congressional Record*, 43rd Cong., 1st sess., 744–45, 2372; U.S. Congress, Senate Report, 43rd Cong., 1st sess., 1874, S. Doc. 70, serial 1584.

and issue promissory notes, or certificates of indebtedness, for those it deemed valid. The state would, in turn, present these claims to the federal government for reimbursement. Missouri would in no way be obliged to redeem the certificates until Congress first paid the state. With Congress traditionally refusing payment until a state assumed the actual obligation, and with the state legislature now issuing promissory certificates, confusion and fraud would be the only results.[48]

As authorized by state law, a commission of three men convened on May 1, 1874, to begin auditing—and reauditing—all outstanding claims pending against the state. Very little time passed before agents swamped the commission with claims of all stripes. With the already overburdened Adjutant/Quartermaster/Paymaster General J. D. Crafton chairing, the commission struggled without any specially hired clerks. Scheduled to finish by August 1, 1874, after which all further claims against the state were to be forever barred, the commission continued through the early winter. When the commissioners completed their labors, they had processed 11,961 separate claims, approving 7,554. The total value of the certificates issued exceeded $2 million. Although the commission did not issue any certificates for those claims audited after the sanctioned closing date of August 1, the commission did approve over $800,000, believing that the legislature would eventually authorize the issuance of certificates.[49]

At first glance, the amount of activity before the commission is surprising. Most agents knew the provisions of the authorizing legislation, and they knew equally that the commission's certificates stood little chance of being redeemed by a United States indemnification bill. By this analysis the agents logically should have displayed little interest in the actions of the commission. Although the legislature's threat that this was the last opportunity to present the claims can account for some of the activity, a closer examination reveals that many agents believed they could still persuade the legislature to change its mind and authorize the redemption of the certificates without having to go to Congress first. Despite the reservations of at least one agent, J. A. McAllister, concerning what he thought would

---

[48] Sennaca Hammack to Benecke, March 2, 1874, Benecke Papers, WHMC; *Missouri Adjutant General's Report, 1874*, 25–26; *Laws of Missouri, 1874*, 102–5.

[49] *HJ MO, Appendix, 1875*, 3–12; Avery and Shoemaker, *Messages and Proclamations*, 5:279.

be "considerable opposition in some quarters to any appropriation," the majority of the state's agents believed their legislative influence strong enough to gain state payment. Consequently, an unprecedented number of claims flooded the commission.[50]

It is important to note that numerous individual claimants did not have the same faith as their agents in the ultimate redemption of the certificates. Indeed, agent confidence seemed inversely proportional to that of their clients. Throughout the summer of 1874 innumerable claimants sold their claims to agents at greatly depreciated prices, hoping to make whatever money possible from what appeared to be an all-around bad deal. Some claims agents readily bought the claims in the hopes of holding on to them until the face value would be redeemed by the state. Most wanted to turn around and sell the claims to brokers operating in the country's financial markets once the commission approved their claims and issued the appropriate certificates of indebtedness. In the uncertain financial world of a business built upon commission fees, speculation would be the primary means of survival for claims agents.

Much was now at stake for those agents speculating in the claims. This was especially true for William Hequembourg, owner of a large credit and claims agency in St. Louis. Having invested large sums in claims speculation, Hequembourg appealed to friends—including former agent John B. Gray—and state legislators with any ties to the claims commission to exert their influence on his behalf for quick audits and early issuances of certificates. The stakes were equally large for state senator and claims agent Louis Benecke, who stood to make, or lose, a great deal of money. He had purchased a number of claims from his clients and was in the process of brokering the certificates of a fellow state senator for his constituents. Benecke also cooperated closely with Hequembourg's agency in St. Louis in pushing claims before the commission. Thus involved, Benecke used his own contacts within the commission to better the odds of not only having his claims approved, but of also having the certificates issued early to better capitalize upon the prices in the speculator's markets. Benecke knew two clerks in the adjutant general's office, Charles

---

[50] Agent attitudes on the ultimate passage of congressional legislation can be found in John W. McLean to Benecke, July 13, 1874, Benecke Papers, WHMC. McAllister quoted in McAllister to Benecke, June 27, 1874, Benecke Papers, WHMC.

Bosse and Chris Delfsinger, who were then detailed to assist with the commission's work. They both monitored events for Benecke. Delfsinger ultimately promised Benecke that he would be the first to have the completed certificates when issued in October.[51]

The willingness to speculate in the claims grew throughout 1874 and the early part of 1875. Feeding this tendency were unwary customers in the financial markets looking to buy the certificates, little aware of the conditions placed upon their ultimate redemption. Because Missouri had regained its reputation for repaying debts in the Gilded Age, there was no reason to suspect the certificates. Amid this climate, W. A. Hequembourg encouraged Benecke in July 1874 to get as many claims as possible because it was not generally "known that the certificates will not be paid by the state until Congress acts." Hequembourg took care also to enclose a select list of claimants whom Benecke should contact.[52]

As speculation increased, so too did the campaign to gain redemption of the certificates. Claimants, agents, and speculators raised redemption as a prominent issue during the gubernatorial and legislative elections of 1874. In their battle these men would have an ally in the adjutant general, J. D. Crafton, who in December 1874 reported, incorrectly, to the governor that the "issuing of certificates . . . is to all intents and purposes a payment by the State of these claims." The agents also prepared themselves for the coming battle by drafting different pieces of legislation that would cover what seemed to be all possible contingencies. One bill aimed at redemption from the state, while a second aimed at indemnification from the federal government. The general strategy appears to have been that if one bill failed to get the state to pay first, the other would authorize the employment of yet another state agent to proceed to Washington and press Missouri's cause. The agents coupled the drafting of the latter legislation with a complementary campaign directed at the governor; its purpose was to persuade the governor to appoint a state agent regardless of the legislature's action. According to one peti-

[51] W. A. Hequembourg to Benecke, October 12, November 2 and December 10, 1874, Kinley to Benecke, n.d., Charles Bosse to Benecke, May 11, 1874, W. A. Hequembourg to Benecke, June 1 and June 9, 1874, Chris Delfsinger to Benecke, July 7, 1874, Benecke Papers, WHMC.

[52] Hequembourg quoted in W. A. Hequembourg to Benecke, July 17, 1874, Benecke Papers, WHMC.

tioner, R. H. Browne, Missouri could succeed only "if a state agent is appointed at once. . . . An agent is absolutely necessary as interested parties cannot in the present temper of public affairs work in what is known as the lobby without an agent."[53]

The climax of agent lobbying came in January 1875 when the legislature finally convened. At that time, the community of claims agents assembled in Jefferson City to achieve what agent E. F. Rogers called "a unison of action. . . ." A frenzy of activity followed, as various agents tried to pressure the legislature, governor, and congressional delegation into action throughout the winter and on into the spring. This concentrated campaign produced mixed results. In the legislature, both Liberal Republicans and Democrats refused to make the claims a partisan issue. The minority Liberal Republicans, for example, described the attempt to force state redemption as an "infamy" and an "abomination." For their part, the Democrats stalled all bills that aimed at state redemption. The only thing that they consented to do was instruct the state's U.S. senators to give high priority to national reimbursement.[54]

The state executive, at first, was no more responsive. Outgoing Democratic governor Silas Woodson repudiated his adjutant general and labeled the entire clamor the work of an agent and speculative industry that could "afford to employ a heavy lobby." Moreover, Woodson believed Missouri under "no legal or moral" obligation to redeem the certificates. In fact, to do so would be an "injustice to the great body of the people of the State," who would have to finance a scheme that benefited a minority and should be rightfully handled by the federal government. Woodson's successor and fellow Democrat, Charles Hardin, endorsed the tenor of this position upon his inaugu-

[53] Crafton quoted in MO HJ, Appendix, 1875, 5. John W. McClean to Benecke, July 13, 1874, Benecke Papers, WHMC; Jas. Craig to Charles Hardin, November 22, 1874, R. 152, F. 15278, and Silas Woodson to Hardin, January 16, 1875, Governor Hardin's Papers, R. 152, F. 15277, WHMC; Browne quoted in R. H. Browne to Hardin, February 14, 1875, Governor Hardin's Papers, R. 152, F. 15277, WHMC.

[54] Rogers quoted in E. F. Rogers to Benecke, January 1, 1875, Benecke Papers, WHMC. The extent of the lobbying can be seen in E. F. Rogers to Benecke, January 1, 1875, A. W. Meyers, January 8, 1875, E. F. Rogers to Benecke, February 4, 1875, and A. W. Meyers to Benecke, April 19, 1875, Benecke Papers, WHMC. Quotes taken from Booneville (Mo.) Weekly Eagle, December 11, 1874. A. W. Meyers to Louis Benecke, January 8, 1875, Benecke Papers; Memorial of the Missouri General Assembly, January 19, 1875, Governor Hardin's Papers, R. 152, F. 15277, WHMC; Congressional Record, 43rd Cong., 2nd sess., 961.

ration in early January 1875. Immediately after the inauguration, however, Hardin showed signs of wanting to resolve the issue. Deluged with letters demanding some action, the governor investigated what could be done. He consulted with members of the legislature and in February 1875 dispatched his newly appointed adjutant general, the famous artist George Caleb Bingham, to Washington to talk both with members of the Treasury Department and the Missouri congressional delegation. The results of this month-long inquiry were not favorable to any quick resolution of the claims difficulties. The legislature continued to refuse to do anything more than petition Congress for the passage of claims legislation, while the congressional delegation offered no encouragement at all. Watchful of its prerogatives, the delegation vehemently opposed using a state agent to coordinate federal affairs. According to Governor Hardin, the delegation believed an agent a "useless expenditure of money" because it was "unreasonable to suppose that Congress would have less confidence in the representation of its own members than in those of a mere lobbyist." The earlier success of John B. Gray—and other state agents—suggests that the delegation confused its institutional distrust of the "lobby" with the reality of an agent's effectiveness.[55]

The rising distrust of agents and lobbyists could not have come at a worse time. The Missouri claim was badly disorganized and opposition mounted in Congress to the passage of all special claims legislation. The biggest problem for Missouri was that no one really knew how much the state should seek in reimbursement. Throughout 1874, members of the congressional delegation had been busy trying to push special indemnification bills. They did not, however, wait or coordinate such efforts with the state adjutant general or his commission, which was then in the process of auditing over $2 million more in claims that the state would turn around and present to the government. When in December 1874 the adjutant did indeed present the claims for which he had issued certificates, congressional wariness mounted. To Missouri senator Louis V. Bogy, the late additions

[55] Woodson quoted in *Booneville Weekly Eagle,* January 15, 1875, and Avery and Shoemaker, *Messages and Proclamations,* 5:281. For information of Hardin's endorsement of the position see Avery and Shoemaker, *Messages and Proclamations,* 5:390. Hardin to G. C. Bingham, February 16, 1875, Governor Hardin's Papers, R. 152, F. 15277, WHMC. Hardin quoted in Avery and Shoemaker, *Messages and Proclamations,* 5:451.

raised the question of fraud, thus rendering "the task hopeless, especially with the present complexion and disposition" of a Congress already watchful for large claims that might also unlock the treasury for other states. Because the possibility still existed that an additional $800,000 in certificates might be issued for claims audited by Crafton, Bogy recommended that Missouri postpone all action until someone could figure what the federal government really owed the state.[56]

Bogy's analysis of the situation was essentially correct. Missouri's claims were in disarray, and Congress would therefore pay little attention to them. But Bogy recommended one other thing to Governor Hardin while Missouri put its claim in order: the state must publicize the situation so that false hope did not lead to rampant speculation in the scrip. Here, too, Bogy identified a key aspect of the ongoing claims drama, an aspect that in many ways drove the interest and pressure to get reimbursement. Speculation in the scrip issued by the Crafton Commission had continued unabated during the winter of 1874 and 1875. By early January 1875, the value of the scrip reached its highest point, as some brokers sold at a profit of 12.5 cents per each dollar invested. Brokers in St. Louis could not get enough of the scrip to meet demand. But this boom in scrip lasted only a short time further. Senator Bogy's pessimistic outlook for reimbursement in Congress helped create a panic in the markets that killed the demand for scrip in late February.[57]

The market continued in that condition for the next few months as the agents tried to pump life into both the redemption effort and the speculative trade. Although news of possible redemption would have been of great benefit for the value of scrip, it was not absolutely vital. Indeed, in the spring many agents wearied of gaining redemption and looked to other means to reenergize the market. The idea settled upon was to make sure that the state issued certificates for all those

---

[56] *MO HJ, Appendix, 1875,* 10; J. D. Crafton to the Third Auditor, December 11, 1874, Missouri Claims, Abstract Crafton Service Claims, vol. 17, E.759, RG 217, NA; Bogy quoted in Lewis V. Bogy to Hardin, February 19, 1875, Governor Hardin's Papers, R. 152, F. 15277. For congressional wariness, examine Bingham to Hardin, February 20, 1875, Governor Hardin's Papers, R. 152, F. 15277, WHMC. Bogy's reaction can be found in Bogy to G. C. Bingham, January 30, 1875, Governor Hardin's Papers, R. 152, F. 15277, WHMC.

[57] Avery and Shoemaker, *Messages and Proclamations,* 5:451; John S. Mellon to Benecke, January 4 and February 25, 1875, Benecke Papers, WHMC.

claims audited by the Crafton Commission after its authorized closing date of August 1, 1874. According to commission member and agent A. W. Meyers, the release of these certificates would generate confidence throughout the market, and the "value of other certificates would be appreciated." The only way to achieve this release, Meyers believed, was through the legal system. Though not quite sure how, or indeed under what pretense, the governor and adjutant general might be legally forced to issue the certificates, Meyers tried to rally support for a suit. He mounted an extensive letter-writing campaign among the agents and called for a meeting in Jefferson City to coordinate his vaguely defined legal action. Meyers's intended lawsuit never got past this early stage of development.[58]

While Meyers tried to mobilize a legal campaign, revelations of fraud in the operations of the Crafton Commission undermined the entire Missouri claims and speculative industries. Beginning in early February, allegations flowed into the new adjutant general's and governor's offices that the service claims audits of the Crafton Commission were riddled with fraud. Initially, the charges focused on two conspiracies to deceive the commissioners. The first implicated a prominent agent, E. F. Rogers, and former adjutant A. G. Neugent, who had also served for a period of time as the state agent. The connection between Rogers and Neugent had been long lasting. Rogers had served during the war as an officer in Neugent's regiment of Cass County Union Home Guards. According to the allegations, after the war, Rogers and Neugent had forged powers of attorney for over one-half of a militia company seeking back pay. As a consequence, when the Crafton Commission audited the muster roll and issued certificates for this military service, the forgers—Rogers and Neugent—received the certificates. They were then free to sell the certificates in the speculative markets, keeping all profits.[59]

In another emerging scandal, it appeared that several muster rolls had been submitted, and approved, for companies that had only tech-

---

[58] Meyers quoted in A. W. Meyers to Benecke, April 19, 1875, Benecke Papers, WHMC.

[59] Richard Everingham to Bingham, February 4, 1875, Adjutant General's Office, Fraud Service Claims, 1875, Box 211, RG 133, MSA. The long-standing connection between Rogers and Neugent is described in Wiley Britton's *The Aftermath of the Civil War* (Kansas City, Mo.: Smith, Grieves, and Co., 1924), 251.

nically enrolled for service. They had not actually performed any active service, whether in concert with Union troops or by command of the governor. Here, too, forgery allowed for people to sign for an entire unit's certificates and then sell the scrip as fast as possible. These scandals burst upon the state, forcing Governor Hardin to order Adjutant Bingham to review the entire operation of the Crafton Commission. Bingham's investigation, which lasted the next two years, spread quickly in scope. Starting with an inquiry directed against Agent Rogers, Bingham expanded his search to include all members of the Crafton Commission and former governor Silas Woodson, who had cosigned all certificates issued by the commission and personally owned $198,045 worth. Although Bingham quickly exonerated Woodson, by July the adjutant uncovered a process by which John D. Crafton collaborated with certain speculators to defraud the state. Not only did it appear that Crafton knowingly approved defective muster rolls, such as those forwarded by Rogers and Neugent, but that he also issued $112,761 worth of certificates for nonexistent service by forging the signature of Governor Woodson.[60]

By October of that same year Bingham concluded that all of Crafton's work touching upon service claims was tainted either by clerical sloppiness or by fraudulent intentions. One year later, the state had indicted seven men, including John D. Crafton. Commissioner A. W. Meyers, who had tried to force the governor to allow the issuance of more certificates to appreciate the value of all certificates, was not implicated. From the outset of the commission's work, Crafton had divided responsibilities among the three members. Crafton worked exclusively on those for services rendered, while Meyers and H. Clay Taylor waded through those for supplies and transportation. When Bingham finished his investigation in 1877, he had determined that all certificates issued for services—$1.42 million worth—were in some way fraudulent. He also believed that Crafton had paid $25,000

---

[60] Avery and Shoemaker, *Messages and Proclamations*, 5:423–35, 460–61; M. C. Jacobs to Bingham, February 25, 1875, Bingham to D. K. Stockton, February 26, 1876, and Hardin to Bingham, March 18, 1875, Adjutant General's Office, Fraud Service Claims, 1875, Box 211, RG 133, MSA; Bingham to E. F. Rogers, July 7, 1875, Adjutant General's Office, 3rd Quarter Miscellaneous, 1875, Box 210, RG 133, MSA; Silas Woodson to Bingham, July 10 and 24, 1875, Adjutant General's Office, Fraud Service Claims, 1875, and Silas Woodson to Bingham, September 20, 1875, Adjutant General's Office, Regular Service Claims, 1875, Box 211, RG 133, MSA.

in scrip to at least one person who had threatened to expose the fraud in its early stages.[61]

The scandal involving the Crafton Commission had an immediate effect on Missouri's ongoing claims situation. Although the affair quickly destroyed speculation in the certificates for services, the public disclosure that fraud only touched service claims revitalized interest in the certificates for "irregular" claims related to supplies and transportation furnished to state troops. Between July 1875 and early February 1876, demand boomed again for these certificates. Speculation increased the value of the certificates between 5 and 7.5 cents per dollar. Thus inflated in value, the certificates became an increasingly acceptable medium of financial exchange. Living in a still relatively cash-starved state, Missourians often substituted the certificates for currency. The "irregular certificates," like the service certificates before them, proved especially popular in direct swaps for real estate.[62]

But, yet again, the boom was only temporary. As time passed, more information came to light about the operations of the Crafton Commission. Among the new information was a charge by one of the indicted men, Heyman Levin, that the commission rarely required any evidence of a claimant's loyalty to the Union. Most people connected with the state's claim then realized that there would be little chance of the United States government reimbursing even the "irregular claims" for supplies and transportation furnished. In all reimbursement proceedings, Congress and the treasury were sensitive to

---

[61] Fraud and sloppiness revealed in Third Auditor to Bingham, October 6, 1875, Adjutant General's Office, 4th Quarter Miscellaneous, 1875, Box 210, RG 133, MSA. A good summary of the Crafton frauds can be found in *Report of the Adjutant General of Missouri Upon Certificates Issued by the Missouri War Claims Commission of 1874* (Jefferson City, Mo.: Stephens Printing Co., n.d., 1907 likely), 1–21. For information following the indictments, see J. A. McCallister to Benecke, October 14, 1875, and Charles A. Winslow to Benecke, September 20, 1876, Benecke Papers, WHMC; Avery and Shoemaker, *Messages and Proclamations*, 5:423–25; Bingham to Rollins, March 25, 1876, Rollins Papers, R. 6, F. 124, WHMC.

[62] This paragraph was based upon correspondence contained primarily in the Benecke Papers at the WHMC. See, for example: J. A. McCallister to Benecke, October 14, 1875; Chris J. Gundelfinger to Benecke, February 3, 7, 10, 16, 1876; Charles Bennett to Benecke, February 18, 25, March 1, 10, 20, May 18, 1876; and John Cox to Benecke, February 26, 1876. For further evidence of the usage of the scrip as currency, consult Hugh Allen to Bingham, August 25, 1875, Adjutant General's Office, Regular Service Claims, and Edward R. Kilbourne to Bingham, September 18, 1875, Adjutant General's Office, General Correspondence, Box 211, RG 133, MSA.

the idea of paying rebels for property lost during the war. News of this leaked, and scrip flooded the financial markets as many people tried to unload their certificates. The resulting panic flattened claims speculation by March 1876.[63]

Another effect of the scandal was to reorient claims agents and holders of scrip on congressional indemnification. Abandoning their attempts to have the state redeem any of the Crafton claims scrip, interested parties intensified efforts to have the state pursue other outstanding claims with Congress. Once again, letters flooded the governor demanding that a state agent be hired to bring order out of the chaos. A seemingly equal number of letters recommended individuals for the job. Former governor Thomas C. Reynolds and Missouri political power broker Montgomery Blair put forward a candidate for state agent, as did a leader of the politically energized state agricultural Grange. Even three members of the previously recalcitrant congressional delegation joined the call for an agent. For these members, an agent would remove from their shoulders the burden of having to deal with complex claims questions.[64]

As much as state officials might have desired that the whole issue of indemnification just disappear, it showed little sign of doing that throughout 1875 and into 1876. The scandal involving the Crafton Commission touched vast numbers of people, including many outside the state who had come into possession of the scrip. For some within Missouri, such as agent J. A. McCallister, the federal government's reimbursement was vital to stave off personal financial difficulty due to ill-advised speculation. For others, such as Edward

---

[63] J. A. McCallister to Benecke, October 14, 1875; Chris J. Gundelfinger to Benecke, February 3, 7, 10, 16, 1876; Charles Bennett to Benecke, February 18, 25, March 1, 10, 20, May 18, 1876; and John Cox to Benecke, February 26, 1876, Benecke Papers, WHMC. For the discrediting of the scrip for "irregular claims," consult Bingham to Hardin, February 12, 1876, Governor Hardin's Papers, R. 151, F. 15221, MSA. Though related only tangentially, Frank W. Klingberg's *The Southern Claims Commission* (Berkeley: University of California Press, 1955) conveys just how sensitive the government was about indemnifying anyone who might have pro-southern sympathies.

[64] Governor Hardin's Papers, R. 152, F. 15278 at the WHMC contain numerous letters pertaining to the hiring of an agent. Included are James H. Lay to Hardin, March 23, 1875; Walter King to Hardin, March 25, 1875; Thomas C. Reynolds, January 3, 6, 7, 1876; J. W. Trimble to Hardin, January 6, 1876; Representatives Aylett H. Buckner, Robert A. Hatcher, and Charles H. Morgan to Hardin, January 14, 1876; Representative Charles H. Morgan to Hardin, January 15, 1876; T. R. Allen to Hardin, January 24, 1876.

Kilborne, some reasonable assurance of indemnification was needed in order for Missourians to continue substituting the scrip for currency in their debt payments. This type of debt servicing was not confined by state lines. Although the United States had moved steadily to a uniform money supply of bank notes, alternative currencies still floated around the country. Throughout the Northeast, in particular, people and businesses trusted one such alternative that had escaped the government's punitive taxes—the Missouri scrip—to pay off loans and services.[65]

If the interstate implications of the scrip problem did not provide enough impetus to Missouri's leaders to try resolve the situation, Crafton's certificates spread well outside the United States. One man in Canada had purchased $30,000 in scrip, while another had secured $100,000 worth. Consequently, a number of such scrip holders held the United States government directly responsible, and they then mistakenly submitted their scrip to the Treasury Department for reimbursement. However, most scrip holders sought varying types of relief from the Missouri executive offices. Some demanded the hiring of an agent, while others sought to determine if their scrip was valid. Still others wrote to describe distress and plead the necessity of reimbursement. No one communicated the reality of the problem caused by the Crafton Commission better than Susanna Shelton, who simply informed Governor Hardin that "i never got my husband militia money[.] it is thirty dollars. . . . i am in great need of it at the present time and if you can git the money why i will pay you for your trouble." Financially and politically it made little immediate sense for the state to quit the claims business just yet.[66]

---

[65] Much of this paragraph is based upon dozens of letters in the General Correspondence file, Adjutant General's Office, Box 211, RG 133, MSA. See, for example: Edward R. Kilborne to Bingham, September 18, 1875, Third Auditor of the United States to Bingham, November 6, 1875, W. S. Field to Bingham, March 9, 1876, and J. M. Ward to Bingham, December 30, 1875. Similar information can be found in Edward R. Kilborne to Bingham, September 2, 1875, Correspondence 3rd Quarter, 1875, J. A. McCallister to Bingham, August 5, 1875, and Hugh Allen to Bingham, August 25, 1875, Regular Service Claims, Adjutant General's Office, Box 211, RG 133, MSA; J. A. McCallister to Benecke, August 26, 1876, Benecke Papers, WHMC; Alex Paddock to Hardin, March 18, 1875, and J. A. McCallister to Hardin, March 27, 1876, Governor Hardin's Papers, R. 151, F. 15221, WHMC. For a general discussion of monetary affairs and the availability of alternative currencies in the Gilded Age, see Milton Friedman and Anna J. Schwartz, *A Monetary History of the United States, 1867–1960* (Princeton, N.J.: Princeton University Press, 1963), 16–25.

[66] Edward R. Kilborne to Bingham, September 18, 1875, Third Auditor of the United States to Bingham, November 6, 1875, W. S. Field to Bingham, March 9,

Thus unable to escape the claims issue, Governor Hardin decided to act. He would not, however, appoint a state agent. Legislative fears of extending the governor's patronage, fiscal retrenchment, and—despite the willingness of three congressmen—fragile egos in the congressional delegation all weighed heavily on Hardin, as they did with his predecessors. Consequently, he would have his adjutant general, and personal friend, attempt to take care of the problem. In early February 1876, Hardin ordered Bingham to Washington to secure reimbursement for the state. By any measure, Bingham had just become the unofficial state agent. The appointment was entirely logical given the local concerns that so drove Missouri's indemnification effort. Bingham served more cheaply than any agent. He represented no expansion of gubernatorial patronage power. And he possessed the sterling reputation needed to help dissociate the claims from the widely perceived corrupting influences of agents and lobbyists.[67]

However, Bingham would have no luck in securing reimbursement. Here too, matters related to Missouri politics joined with events controlled in Washington to undermine any potential reimbursement. While some members of Missouri's fifteen-man congressional delegation eagerly awaited the arrival of Bingham so that he could take charge of the claims process, other members were not so anxious to hand control to the popular Bingham. In what amounted to a repeat of B. Gratz Brown's treatment of John Gray in 1871, an undetermined number of members feared the credit that the adjutant might receive if any claims legislation should pass. This was particularly true of some ambitious members because it had been rumored that Bingham might soon run for either governor or some congressional seat. According to Bingham, these congressmen hedged their cooperation because they were "under the apprehension that it may

1876, and J. M. Ward to Bingham, December 30, 1875, Adjutant General's Office, Box 211, RG 133, MSA; Edward R. Kilborne to Bingham, September 2, 1875, Correspondence 3rd Quarter, 1875, J. A. McCallister to Bingham, August 5, 1875, and Hugh Allen to Bingham, August 25, 1875, Regular Service Claims, Adjutant General's Office, Box 211, RG 133, MSA; J. A. McCallister to Benecke, August 26, 1876, Benecke Papers, WHMC; Alex Paddock to Hardin, March 18, 1875, J. A. McCallister to Hardin, March 27, 1876, and Shelton to Hardin, April 19, 1876, Governor Hardin's Papers, R. 151, F. 15221, WHMC. For inquiries directed to the federal treasury, see Letters Received, Third Auditor, vol. 3, E. 604, RG 217, NA.

[67] Special Order #20, February 4, 1876, Adjutant's Office, Service Claims, 1875–1877, Box 211, RG 133, MSA.

give me a political standing to the detriment of themselves or some of their especial friends."[68]

Nonetheless, Bingham pressed ahead. He had become inured to internal political resistance. Ever since his assumption of the adjutant's duties, political enemies angered by Bingham's Democratic leanings and anticorruption pronouncements had sought to curb his influence. Many of the enemies were in the legislature, where they tried first to abolish the position of adjutant. Having failed, the legislators then pushed to stop funding Bingham's salary. With political opposition in Jefferson City and Washington, Bingham focused on the claims. For the adjutant, the cause became something of a crusade, involving, he later noted, making the United States fulfill "one of its most sacred obligations."[69]

Once in Washington, Bingham initiated a number of discussions. He first consulted with the secretary of the treasury and several men within the state delegation. Of particular interest to Bingham were Senators Bogy and Francis Cockrell and Representative Erastus Wells. Bogy had taken a strong interest in the claims since the beginning of his term in March 1873. He was also a personal friend of both Bingham and Governor Hardin. Cockrell, an ex-Confederate general, was a member of the Senate's committee on claims, which might have to investigate and report on Missouri's indemnification bill. Wells would be in charge of submitting claims legislation in the House. The early consultations were not encouraging. This was especially true regarding the claims produced by the Crafton Commission. Most thought Crafton's work too tainted to press for legislation. Consequently, they believed it necessary to keep the state's claims separate, pushing legislation only for those claims that had been actually paid by the state and originally submitted before Crafton became the adjutant. To Secretary of the Treasury Benjamin H. Bristow this seemed the only possible solution "as by asking too much [Missouri] may lose all."[70]

---

[68] Congressmen Aylett H. Buckner and David Rear to Bingham, February 6, 1876, Adjutant's Office, Miscellaneous, 1st quarter, 1876, Box 210, RG 133, MSA; Bingham to James S. Rollins, March 16, 1876, Rollins Papers, R.6, F. 124, WHMC.

[69] Legislative opposition to Bingham is discussed in M. D. Morgan to Bingham, March 19, 1875, Adjutants Office, Miscellaneous, 1st quarter, 1875, Box 210, RG 133, MSA. Bingham quoted in Bingham to Hardin, March 16, 1876, Rollins Papers, R. 6, R. 124, WHMC.

[70] Bristow quoted in Bingham to Hardin, February 12, 1876, Hardin's Papers, R. 151, F. 15221, MSA.

Bingham took few chances. On February 28, three weeks after his arrival in Washington, he drafted a bill for presentation in the Senate. The proposed legislation authorized the third auditor to examine $319,876.11 in service claims that Missouri had paid after the closing of the war. Bingham made sure that these claims had nothing to do with Crafton's ill-fated commission. Somewhat bewildered by the complexity of the claims situation and unsure of their ability to shepherd the state's case through Congress, Senators Bogy and Cockrell looked to Bingham to stay in Washington and lobby.[71]

The fate of Missouri's bill, like most such legislation, depended upon personal contact and influence. Some evidence of this came shortly after Bingham had Bogy introduce the bill into the Senate. Of basic importance was getting the bill assigned to a committee over which Missouri could exercise some influence. Congress had traditionally channeled state war claims into the Committee on Military Affairs, but Cockrell worked diligently to steer the bill into the Committee on Claims, where he happened to sit. After some initial confusion, Cockrell succeeded. With the bill in a somewhat friendly committee, the next steps in the process depended upon access to the appropriate committee members. Just as for any state agent or lobbyist, such access could be gained either through a personal interview or a formal hearing. At first, Bingham chose to establish his contacts and try to present Missouri's case through a hearing. In this he would be disappointed. The glacial pace of the congressional process surprised him, and he grew impatient when a hearing did not quickly materialize. For Bingham the reason for delay was obvious. Electoral politics had squeezed the legislators' attentions. Though only the spring of 1876, Bingham believed that the excitement of the presidential canvass ground the governing process to a halt. Because both parties were trying to make "political capital for the presidential campaign," Bingham noted to his friend James S. Rollins, "they are not disposed to do anything else."[72]

---

[71] Bingham to Hardin, February 28, 1876, Governor Hardin's Papers, R. 151, F. 15221, MSA; Bingham to Rollins, March 9, 1876, Rollins Papers, WHMC; *Congressional Record*, 44th Cong., 1st sess., 1329; Bingham to Hardin, February, 28, 1876, Governor Hardin's Papers, R. 151, F. 15221, WHMC.

[72] Bingham first quoted in Bingham to Hardin, March 13, 1876, Governor Hardin's Papers, R. 151, F. 15221. The second quoted passage is taken from Bingham to Rollins, March 16, 1876, Rollins Papers, R.6, F. 124, WHMC.

While perhaps true to some extent, the influence of electoral politics did not account completely for whatever delays frustrated Bingham. Indeed, more importantly, Adjutant Bingham simply overestimated the ability of the standing committees to digest their business. Committees met only twice weekly and rarely allowed petitioners to appear before them.

When Bingham finally got his hearing on March 22, he thought the presentation went well. Not a dissenting word came from the committee members, who then referred the bill to a subcommittee of three headed by Cockrell. The Missouri senator guaranteed a safe report within the next few days. Bingham, however, took few chances. He circulated more widely, consulting with what he later described as "our leading friends." Throughout late March he lobbied selected House members while also drafting and submitting to the House an indemnification bill identical to the one under consideration in the Senate. Here too he angled for a committee hearing, but while waiting for the opportunity, he did not fail to corner committee representatives and present the state's case ahead of time. It was a wise decision because the adjutant never got his anticipated hearing. The bill's sponsor, Erastus Wells, unlike Senator Cockrell, was not a member of the committee to which the legislation had been assigned. Nevertheless, Bingham believed his personal lobbying paid dividends. Several representatives assured him that Missouri's bill would be reported favorably to the House before the session ended that August.[73]

Such optimism proved false. The House Committee on Claims joined the Senate committee in not reporting the Missouri bill at all. Like so many other state claims, this attempt died in committee. The explanation for failure was complex. To a considerable extent, the Missouri bill got swallowed up in the Kentucky delegation's attempt to pass expansive claims legislation. The Kentucky bill would have allowed the third auditor to audit all outstanding state claims for services rendered without specific state-by-state authorization from Congress. Not only did the Kentucky plan have the virtue of aiming to simplify the claims process, it also avoided the perception of being

---

[73] Bingham to Rollins, March 25, 1875, Rollins Papers, WHMC; Bingham quoted in Bingham to Hardin, March 23, 1876; Bingham to Hardin, April 3, 1876, Governor Hardin's Papers, R. 151, F. 15221, WHMC.

pork-barrel politics. Even as Bingham lobbied and testified before the Congress, he believed that the Kentucky plan was "framed in the interest of *all* the states . . . , [and therefore] it will likely receive a more general support than would be given to our bill which looks only to the reimbursement of our own State."[74]

Though important, Kentucky's broad legislation alone did not kill the Missouri bill. At least one other factor contributed to its demise. Other claims business intruded upon Bingham. Ever since his arrival in Washington, Bingham divided his attention between the present legislation before Congress, the continuing investigation of the Crafton Commission within the Treasury Department, and his own long-standing personal claim against the government for the destruction of his home during the war. Pulled in different directions, Bingham devoted a decreasing amount of attention to lobbying during a period when the Kentucky plan began to attract the precious time of lawmakers. In fact, Bingham's responsibility for the Crafton Commission investigation ultimately ended his ability to shepherd the claim at all. In early May, the adjutant left for Jefferson City in order to participate in the trial of John Crafton.[75]

A final setback for the Missouri claim developed in the fall of 1876. This too came out of the Crafton Commission. Charges began to flow in New York and Chicago newspapers tied to the Republican Party that the ruling Missouri Democrats had indeed made it a practice of approving the claims of ex-Confederates, issuing them scrip, and then seeking reimbursement from the United States. In the charged atmosphere of a presidential election, the allegations made good editorial copy. A Republican Party that still enthusiastically embraced "waving the bloody shirt" made the most of the charges by directing them toward the Democratic nominee for president, Samuel Tilden, on the eve of the election. In the tightly fought campaign, much of which still centered on the Democratic Party's attempts to dissociate

---

[74] An early discussion of the Kentucky bill is in Bingham to Hardin, March 13, 1876, Hardin's Papers, R. 151, F. 15221, WHMC. Bingham's quote can be found in the same file in Bingham to Hardin, April 3, 1876.

[75] Bingham to Hardin, April 20 and 25, 1876, Governor's Papers, Hardin, CFD-165, F. 15294, MSA. For some information on Bingham's personal claim against the government, see Nancy Rash, *The Paintings and Politics of George Caleb Bingham* (New Haven, Conn.: Yale University Press, 1991), 212–13. For official allusion to the "pressure of other business," see Governor Hardin's message of January 5, 1877, in Avery and Shoemaker, *Messages and Proclamations*, 5:425.

itself from wartime charges of Copperheadism and disloyalty, these particular allegations caught the Democratic Party off guard. The charges were particularly hard to deal with because Missouri seemed to represent perfectly the Republican assertions that while the Confederacy may have lost the war, it had won the peace. Senator Cockrell had been a general in the Confederate army and Senator George Vest had served in the secessionist congress. Vest, in particular, was a lightning rod of trouble for the Democrats. Prone to making controversial statements on veterans' pensions, Vest had also been an early candidate for the Democratic presidential nomination.

As late as November 4, Samuel Tilden's campaign workers scrambled to explain the Missouri claims situation. One such worker in New York, Thomas L. Snead, nervously telegraphed Governor Hardin that "Republican falsehoods about the scrip are injuring Tilden." Snead carried no small amount of political baggage in this situation as he, too, had a long list of service in the Confederate army and congress. Still, Hardin passed Snead's message on to Bingham for him to explain. Bingham, worn out and soon to resign, eventually replied that the legislation before Congress contained claims paid only to people having had proof of loyalty. While technically true, Bingham's reply did not note that the Crafton Commission had, indeed, issued scrip without making the corresponding loyalty test. Moreover, in December 1874, Crafton did attempt to have the third auditor redeem all such scrip. Despite this, Bingham sputtered against the charges, especially those in the *Chicago Inter-Ocean,* all of which he labeled "a base fabrication, invented to press a cause too rotten to be supported by truth."[76]

Even in an election as close as that of 1876, which had to be resolved by a special election commission, it is doubtful that the Missouri claims controversy played any significant role in the outcome. The last-minute nature of the dispute, and it being but a small part of a larger campaign issue, decreased its electoral significance. The larger importance of this episode was that it gave national exposure to the corruption of the Crafton Commission. A public relations disaster, the episode ruined any chance that Missouri could receive

---

[76] The charges are discussed in Dowell Lawson to Hardin, November 4, 1876, Hardin's Papers, R. 151, F. 15221, WHMC. Snead and Bingham quoted in same file: Thomas L. Snead to Hardin, November 4, 1876, and Bingham to Lawson, no date.

reimbursement for the claims associated with Crafton. It also made it that much more difficult to gain reimbursement on other claims that had never been processed by the Crafton Commission. The publicity surrounding the Crafton Commission tainted all of the state's claims in the eyes of Congress and the treasury. No amount of congressional goodwill or cooperation could overcome this.[77]

Immediate fallout to the succession of claims debacles would be registered in the state government. As early as the summer of 1875, Missouri's newly convened constitutional convention adopted a provision barring the legislature from ever paying a Crafton claim without the United States Treasury first providing reimbursement. The legislature did not treat the claims any better. Faced with the airing of a long parade of corruption and newspaper charges that state offices had been turned into a "claims factory," the legislature quickly eliminated clerks who had long been authorized to work exclusively on the claims. Almost simultaneously the legislature directed that all claims and supporting vouchers deposited in Washington be returned to the state paymaster general's office. These claims, including Crafton's and all others, could then be picked up by the original individual claimants. By the end of 1877, the legislature had apparently washed its hands of all matters pertaining to reimbursement.[78]

The issue was, however, still not dead. Hundreds of dissatisfied claimants remained, who then wrote their congressmen, the state adjutant's office, and the United States Treasury. Although the legislature and governor had effectively opted out of the claims business, the congressional delegation did not. One year later in 1878, Senator Cockrell used his influence as chairman of the Committee on Military Affairs to shepherd a bill through Congress that directed the treasury to examine all of Missouri's claims for services, excluding Crafton's, that the state had actually paid since Gray's settlement of 1866. Because the legislation appropriated no money, Cockrell pushed the bill easily to passage in the House and Senate in February 1879. Cockrell's

---

[77] For the impact of the Crafton claims on the disposition of other claims, see newspaper clipping, no identification, no date (November 13, 1879?), Benecke Papers, WHMC.

[78] For constitutional prohibition, see Missouri Constitution, (1875), sec. 52. Quote taken from the *Booneville Weekly Eagle*, January 21, 1876. Remainder of paragraph is based upon *Booneville Weekly Eagle*, March 17, 1876, and *Missouri Laws, 1877*, 297, 310.

action had the effect of blocking the legislature's attempt to return all claims-related material to the state and ultimately from there to the individual claimant. This blocking of legislative intent ruffled few political feathers. The legislature and congressional delegation were apparently unaware of what the other was doing in regard to the claims.[79]

At this point arose the age-old problem of how best for the state to proceed. Who would collect Missouri's claim and present it to the army of clerks that awaited it in Washington? Faced now with the opportunity to reenter the claims arena, the legislature continued to hesitate to employ an agent. Consequently, it first directed the governor to use the adjutant general. This did not work, although much of the difficulty was beyond the adjutant general. The treasury had long allowed the substitution of certified copies of supporting documentation for long-destroyed originals, but it now refused any such copies that the adjutant, E. Y. Mitchell, tried to provide. On a similar note, Mitchell could persuade neither clerks nor cabinet officials to release supporting information that had been stored in Washington. For his troubles, Mitchell succeeded only in formally presenting Missouri's claim for $319,876.11 to the third auditor by April 1880.[80]

Even before Mitchell had tried to usher the claim, scattered sentiment grew in some newspapers for the state to employ an agent. This attitude was, however, more than balanced by a chorus of opinion that still rejected the use of an agent. Nonetheless, by the following year the legislature moved to authorize an agent. In the absence of any known explanation for this change, the move seemed inspired by two conditions. First, as the *Missouri Statesman* pointed out, the job had become too complicated for the state's representatives and senators, let alone the state adjutant. The disaster of the Crafton Commission and Bingham's inability to make headway in Washington had made this point clear. Second, the legislature checked what had concerned it since the end of the war: the power of the governor and his

---

[79] *Congressional Record*, 45th Cong., 2nd sess., 1627, 2404, 2913, 3211; 45th Cong., 3rd sess., 1879, 405, 754; *Missouri Statesman*, February, 7, 1879.

[80] *Missouri Adjutant General's, Acting Quartermaster and Paymaster General's Report, 1877 and 1878*, 7–9; Special Orders #5, State of Missouri, July 25, 1880, Missouri State Claims, Box 368, E. 759, RG 217, NA; Avery and Shoemaker, *Messages and Proclamations*, 6:90–91; John T. Heard, *Report of the Honorable John T. Heard, Agent for the State Claims to the Fund Commissioners* (Jefferson City, Mo.: State Journal Co., 1883), 1–9.

ability to use either the claims or the agent to his benefit. Accordingly, the legislature removed the claims from the isolated, and theoretically unchecked, hands of the governor. In his place, the legislature appointed a "Fund Commission" whereby the independently elected state auditor shared authority over the claims with the governor and his political appointee, the state adjutant. Having thus weakened the power of the governor in this matter, the legislature finally authorized the commission to appoint an agent.[81]

In July 1881, John T. Heard received his appointment as state agent. Heard, a lawyer and sometime Democratic state representative, signed a contract that previous agents Gibson, Gray, and Neugent would have envied. Serving with complete legislative approval to work with Congress and executive branch officials concerning all state claims, Heard would receive the generous compensation of a 5 percent commission on all reimbursed money. Heard wasted little time in his pursuit of indemnification, showing much of the same determination and efficiency that had marked the earlier efforts of John B. Gray. Putting aside anything having to do with the Crafton claims, Heard concentrated on what Adjutant Mitchell had presented in 1880. He familiarized himself with the claim, gathered vouchers and documentation not made available to the state adjutant, and consulted with members of Congress over strategy. Within one year, he presented a revised claim for almost $295,000 to the auditor, who then whittled the figure down to $234,594.10. Heard did not quibble over the reduction, preferring instead to agree with the auditor that the state lacked the appropriate evidence. Satisfied, Heard pushed legislation that passed Congress on April 22, 1882. In August, Missouri received its money.[82]

The quick pace of this indemnification owed much to Heard's willingness to travel frequently and to accept evidence from the most unlikely of places. He rode about the state and made repeated trips to Washington, collecting payrolls and military orders documenting

[81] *Missouri Statesman*, February 7, 1879; *Missouri Laws, 1881*, 163–65.

[82] *Missouri Laws, 1881*, 163–65; *Missouri Statesman*, July 15, 1881; Power of Attorney, July 22, 1881, Missouri State Claims, Box 368, E. 759, RG 217, NA. Avery and Shoemaker, *Messages and Proclamations*, 6:295–98; Deputy Third Auditor to Heard, March 6, 1883, Missouri State Claim, Box 59, E. 759, RG 217, NA; John T. Heard, *Report of the Honorable John T. Heard*, 1–21; *Congressional Record*, 47th Cong., 1st sess., 3272; *People's Tribune* (Jefferson City, Mo.), August 11, 1882.

service and state payment. In Missouri, Heard got special assistance from Heyman Levin, a private claims agent who had been indicted, but not convicted, in the Crafton conspiracy. Levin maintained a master list of most Missouri soldiers who had served in the war, complete with their addresses. Heard then used this list to solicit receipts from the soldiers, documenting the state's disbursement. Once in Washington, Heard found help from the long-silent E. S. Woog, the onetime state claims clerk who had promised to wreck Missouri's claim for all time. Then a clerk in the Indian Affairs Bureau, Woog worked diligently to shape the claim so as to pass the investigations of the auditor. Woog provided no public explanation as to his philosophical change of heart, and Heard left no record of having paid Woog, but Heard's large—and vague—expense account of over $2,000 hints at what might have been funneled to Woog.[83]

Claims-related issues remained in the public eye for the next two decades. During that time, the Crafton claims continued to be agitated and manipulated. With no scrip actually having been redeemed in legal tender currency or specie, over $1.4 million in scrip remained in the hands of anxious citizens. This was particularly so among some investors who owned large blocks of scrip in excess of $100,000. Their persistence in lobbying all types of state officials for action kept the Crafton claims readily visible. Consequently, state adjutants, attorneys general, governors, and the congressional delegation frequently sought indemnification. By the turn of the century, however, these officials had concluded that Missouri needed to find some way to bypass Congress and get the issue before the United States Court of Claims. That court, the state believed, would see the justice of the claims and then direct the treasury to initiate a detailed audit. If done through the court of claims, Missouri would also be spared the agony of trying to get an actual appropriation for any claims allowed by the treasury. The court of claims maintained its own reimbursement fund and could then pay the state.[84]

---

[83] Avery and Shoemaker, *Messages and Proclamations*, 6:295–98; Deputy Third Auditor to Heard, March 6, 1883, Missouri State Claim, Box 59, E. 759, RG 217, NA; John T. Heard, *Report of the Honorable John T. Heard*, 1–21; *Congressional Record*, 47th Cong., 1st sess., 3272; *People's Tribune*, August 11, 1882.

[84] *The Evening Star*, November 1904; clipping, scrapbook, vol. 6, Francis Cockrell Collection, WHMC; *Kansas City Times*, February, 3, 1906, clipping, Benecke Papers, WHMC; *Report of the Adjutant General of Missouri Upon Certificates Issued by the Missouri War Claims Commission of 1874*, 1–21; *Daily Tribune*, July 4 and September 20, 1907, April 7, 1908.

The route to the court of claims would be filled with frustration. Initially, the state went directly to the court of claims, which promptly threw out the case, asserting that it had no jurisdiction. Missouri then petitioned Congress to provide that jurisdiction. This failed too, prompting the state attorney general to sue in the federal court system to have the jurisdiction changed. In 1907, the Supreme Court quashed the attorney general's plans. It did not authorize the change. The state's failure in 1907 was indicative of its larger experience with the claims. In 1862 and 1866, Missouri had set early precedents both in terms of the type of legislation that circumvented Chase's rules and the size of the reimbursement. But from 1866 forward, the state struggled to duplicate its success. Burdened by numerous claims tainted by scandal, Missouri's indemnification effort floundered. Making matters more difficult, aside from George C. Bingham and John T. Heard, few dynamic officials rose to guide the claims along the informal administrative paths of federalism. Such specially designated officials had become necessary because there would be little concrete cooperation on the part of the national government. Instead, both Congress and the treasury remained firmly wedded to traditional precedents that protected its purse. While thus not providing behind-the-scenes cooperation to further any related goal or objective, such as either education or railroad capitalization, the government did not plant new obstacles to Missouri's indemnification.[85]

Reimbursement thus depended upon an individual state's initiative. Precedents existed for all parties to study. Effective methods, such as the use of an agent, for administering the claims were well known. But in the end, Missouri failed to capitalize further on this knowledge because of issues generated closer to home. Conflicts between governors and legislatures, a clamor for bureaucratic retrenchment, and the popular fear of the corrupting influence of agents all degraded the indemnification effort. Within such a climate, Missouri then lurched from one claims crisis to another after 1866. If there was some comfort for Missouri to draw from this experience, it was that local concerns overwhelmingly shaped the indemnification efforts of other states. The issues would not always be the same, and the relative success of a claims operation would not always be so barren.

---

[85] Ibid.

3

Memory and Claims in Kentucky

THE DEGREES TO which either local circumstances or the public demand for retrenchment determined administrative action varied from state to state. Indeed, even within any given state, the relative importance of these issues generally changed over time. In Missouri, economic urgency, and the attendant demand for retrenchment, eventually gave way to concern over corruption. In Kentucky, although matters of retrenchment consistently shaped structures and methods, the state's broader political relationship with Washington cast a far greater shadow over the claims proceedings.

In contrast to Missouri, Kentucky's public finances were in remarkably good shape. In 1865, Kentucky's debt posed no great threat to economic expansion in the postwar era. Unlike Missouri, the antebellum railroads had not overexpanded in Kentucky. Few roads had come into the state, and even fewer had to be capitalized by state bond issues. Kentucky thus avoided the necessity of having to assume the debts of bankrupted companies. Kentucky's good fiscal fortune continued into the 1860s as the war itself did little to increase the state's debt. Ironically, the war proved a small boon to the state's finances as the public debt dropped from $5,698,000 in 1859 to $5,254,000 in 1865. Revenues had remained fairly constant throughout the war, while increases in military spending were offset by decreases in other spending categories. Financial stability continued for much of the Gilded Age as the public debt dwindled to little more than $1 million by 1871, leaving State Auditor Howard Smith to proclaim that there were "few states, if any, in the Union whose finances are in as sound and healthy a condition as those of Kentucky. . . ."[1]

But general financial stability in the early Gilded Age did not mean a lack of problems. Inconsistencies in county property valuations deprived the state treasury of millions in tax dollars. Proving that few

---

[1] For public debt, see E. Merton Coulter, *The Civil War and Readjustment in Kentucky* (Chapel Hill: University of North Carolina Press, 1926), 252. Howard Smith quoted in same, 383.

men could be trusted with large amounts of public dollars, sheriffs embezzled over $500,000 from the state in 1872. Perhaps worst of all, Kentucky's stock investments yielded few dividends. These types of problems were disconcerting and cause for much controversy as governors and legislatures embarked on popular campaigns to clean up the corruption. In spite of all this, the problems were both relatively minor and typical of state governance in the Gilded Age. Kentucky's postwar era offered the promise of economic expansion unfettered by a crushing public debt. In terms of war indemnification, there was relatively little economic need for the urgency that so controlled Missouri's efforts to secure reimbursement.[2]

Nonetheless, Kentucky's claims operation did not lack for either urgency or fervor. In 1865 the state estimated that it had spent over $3 million in support of the Union, and it had small desire to lose any portion of a potential reimbursement. Indemnification also became wrapped in Kentucky's larger, and volatile, political relationship with Washington. Overwhelmingly Democratic and states' rights in its orientation, Kentucky presented the only legitimately constituted southern opposition to the national administration during most of Reconstruction. Kentuckians spilled much venom upon a perceived radical republicanism that they believed destroyed the constitution and any semblance of state autonomy. In such a climate, Kentucky's governing leaders viewed any difficulty in gaining reimbursement as reflecting the vindictiveness of a federal government controlled by radical Republicans.[3]

A logical conclusion given the passions of the period, this analysis of the claims situation was incorrect. To a large extent, Kentucky thought its claims experience unique. Every delay in reimbursement and every rejected claim seemed part of a Republican plan to punish a nonconforming state. Not only was this a short-sighted view that failed to consider the difficulties of other states, but it was also a misreading of evidence that showed Kentucky to have been quite successful. Like most states, Kentucky conducted its intergovernmental operations with a selective sense of what other states were

---

[2] Hambleton Tapp and James C. Klotter, *Kentucky: Decades of Discord, 1865–1900* (Frankfort: Kentucky State Historical Society, 1977), 124–28.

[3] Thomas L. Connelly has developed Kentucky's sense of persecution in his "New-Confederatism or Power Vacuum: Post-War Kentucky Politics Reappraised," *Register of the Kentucky Historical Society* 64 (1966): 257–69.

doing. During the postwar era Kentucky was acutely aware of the reimbursement successes of most other states. They were also equally unaware of, or paid little attention to, the failures of these same states. For at least the first fifteen years after the Civil War, Kentucky's claims experience occurred in a vacuum of perception that further distorted its more general relations with the federal government.

INTERGOVERNMENTAL TENSIONS AND ADMINISTRATIVE INNOVATIONS

Kentucky's postwar difficulties with the federal government descended directly from the war itself. During the entire sectional crisis, the state had been torn between conflicting impulses. Politically moderate and generally desirous of preserving the Union, Kentucky also possessed a southern cultural heritage that made the state sympathetic to the Confederacy and the cause of states' rights. After much initial waffling, Kentucky remained in the Union, but the state was too divided in its sentiments to enjoy a close relationship with the federal government. Kentucky's resulting intergovernmental relations, according to the historian E. Merton Coulter, were thus characterized "by mutual distrusts, suspicions, and misunderstandings."[4]

Historians have well documented Kentucky's wartime difficulties with the federal government. Early controversies over troop recruitment led quickly to problems associated with a large Union military presence in the state. To many Kentuckians, the state quickly became an occupied territory of the Republican-led federal government. The suspension of habeas corpus, the arrest or banishment of political candidates, and the military's intimidation of voters all readily disillusioned many of the most ardent Unionists in the state.[5]

Discontent with the federal government and the Republican Party

---

[4] Coulter, *The Civil War and Readjustment in Kentucky*, 189.

[5] The writing on Kentucky's difficulties with federal authority is voluminous. See particularly William B. Hesseltine, *Lincoln and the War Governors*, 209–11, 244–46; Coulter, *The Civil War and Readjustment in Kentucky*, 189–214; Thomas L. Connelly, "New-Confederatism or Power Vacuum: Post-War Kentucky Politics Reappraised," 257–69; Betty Gibson, "'Reconstruction' and 'Readjustment': Some Comparisons and Contrasts," *The Filson Club History Quarterly* 35 (1961): 167–73.

became critical near the end of the war upon the military's freeing of slaves and the subsequent debate and passage of the 13th Amendment. The amendment's elimination of slavery nullified all that many white Kentuckians believed they had been promised, before and during the war, concerning their own ability to determine the future of their social and economic institutions. Further Republican talk of racial equality, the Freedmen's Bureau, and limiting the civil and political rights of ex-Confederates ruined any chance of creating a political or governing environment sympathetic to Washington. The political and social rift with the federal government was deep. But it had developed slowly and did not stop more than 90,000 Kentuckians from serving in Northern armies. The rift likewise did not stop the flow of Union money during the war to help pay for Kentucky's costs in raising and equipping these men. Kentucky's wartime ability to get compensation can be explained generally by the federal government's willingness to advance money based upon an estimate of a state's future claims. However, this policy provided nothing unless a state was organized enough to petition for the cash advance in Washington.

For Kentucky, the requirement of organization posed a potentially insurmountable problem. The state's military mobilization had been chaotic. During the early months of the war few people really knew what units were being raised, or, for that matter, on which side of the conflict they would fight. Kentucky's early official policy of neutrality resulted in the fact that both the Union and Confederacy raised troops in the state. Matters cleared only slightly when on May 24, 1861, the state legislature stripped the state's pro-Confederate governor, Beriah Magoffin, of his military authority and transferred it to a Military Board of five men. The legislature allowed Magoffin to sit as one member of the Military Board, yet the pro-Union leanings of the board were unmistakable.

For the remainder of 1861, Kentucky developed a clear military chain of command loyal to the Union, but it was still a chain of command that did not know the details of its mobilization. Few state officers kept proper records of their expenditures. Many officers created units without keeping copies of their payrolls. Moreover, the War Department failed to establish a mustering agency within the state, which then led to regiments joining the army before actually mustering into Union service. Revealed many years later, even the final act of induction was not without problems. Numerous Kentucky regiments were actually mustered into the army by officials unauthorized to do so. Despite this confusion, the state tried to get advances from Washington. After some initial delay and despite what should have been a tortuous process, Kentucky got most of what it asked for. In May 1862, the state received $315,000. The next month it gained $436,000. In 1864, Kentucky collected an additional $300,000. By any measure, the state had been very successful. It had garnered a total wartime advance of $1,051,000 when the average total advance for the loyal states had been $352,938.[6]

Kentucky's ability to get advances helps suggest the level of Washington's concern over the state's possible secession. Next to the recruiting and arming of troops, pumping money into the Bluegrass region was the best way to prop up the Unionist movement. The federal government took few chances with any of these activities. Immediately after the fall of Fort Sumter in April 1861, Abraham Lincoln selected his longtime friend Joshua Speed to operate within the state as an agent of the administration. Speed had wide powers. He could recruit troops and provide weapons, while also creating a network of civilian leadership loyal to the Lincoln administration. A Kentuckian, and widely known within the Unionist movement, Speed easily ingratiated himself with Kentucky's Military Board. By late 1861, Speed worked closely with the board as a self-styled "attorney in fact for the State of Kentucky." The title itself revealed the power behind Speed. Lacking any legislative appointment or executive power-of-attorney to represent the state, Speed became Kentucky's official agent merely because Lincoln, with the Military Board's cooperation, made him so. Only in 1862, when it became pointless to further deny Speed his formal recognition, did Beriah Magoffin appoint him a state agent. In that position, Speed provided

---

[6] "Adjutant General's Report," December 1, 1865, Doc. #9, *Kentucky Documents, 1865*, vol. 1, 4 describes the condition of early mobilization. Figures for Kentucky's advances can be found in a number of areas, but see particularly C. D. Pennebaker to Thomas Bramlette, October 18, 1865, Governor's Papers, Thomas Bramlette, Militia Correspondence, Box 5, F. 105, Kentucky State Archives (KSA), Frankfort. Figures for the advances of other states can be found in U.S. Congress, Senate Report, 50th Cong., 1st sess., 1888, S. Doc., 1286. Nevada, West Virginia, and Virginia were excluded from computations because these states contributed, and claimed, an insignificant amount of manpower and material to the Union war effort.

Lincoln with a trusted liaison and the Union cause in Kentucky with plenty of money.[7]

Speed's ability to get money for Kentucky never went beyond the cash advances that began in May 1862. His status as Lincoln's friend and personal emissary counted little toward actual reimbursement under the congressional act of July 27, 1861. Cash advances were a wartime expedient with few documentary strings attached. Actual indemnification of expenses was another matter, and here Speed, like all other state agents or representatives, eventually ran into the wall of the treasury bureaucracy. Throughout 1862, Speed floundered within that distinctly uncooperative bureaucracy, trying to find various forms of authorization and voucher documentation. No one in Kentucky seemed to have any supporting information on the state's claims. The state had purchased military equipment, but what was then done with that equipment was unknown. Most important, the third auditor of the United States speculated that few Unionist Kentucky troops got the material, let alone Kentucky troops operating under the authorization of Secretary Chase's rules. The third auditor would not process Kentucky's claims until Speed produced some documentation.[8]

Speed never produced that documentation. In fact, by the end of 1862, he was no longer Kentucky's agent. In August, the state's internal politics had changed when Beriah Magoffin resigned, allowing James F. Robinson to serve out the remainder of his term. Described by the president of the state Military Board as "a distinguished and loyal citizen," Robinson paved the way for an initial loosening of the national grip on Kentucky. The War Department returned military

---

[7] Lincoln to Robert Anderson, May 14, 1861, Abraham Lincoln, *The Collected Works*, ed. Roy P. Basler, 9 vols. (New Brunswick, N.J.: Rutgers University Press, 1953–1955), 4:368–69, 559. Information on Speed's activities can be found in a variety of correspondence. See Magoffin to Speed, February 28, 1862, Third Auditor to Speed, March 29 and December 22, 1862, Third Auditor to L. B Temple (president of the Military Board), August 4 and September 27, 1862, Letter Books, Third Auditor, vol. 1, Speed to Third Auditor, May 3 and 29, 1862, Letters Received, vol. 1, Speed to Third Auditor, May 26 and 29, 1862, Letters Received, Third Auditor, vol. 4, E. 604, RG 217, NA.

[8] Magoffin to Speed, February 28, 1862, Third Auditor to Speed, March 29 and December 22, 1862, Third Auditor to L. B Temple (president of the Military Board), August 4 and September 27, 1862, Letter Books, Third Auditor, vol. 1, Speed to Third Auditor, May 3 and 29, 1862, Letters Received, vol. 1, Speed to Third Auditor, May 26 and 29, 1862, Letters Received, Third Auditor, vol. 4, E. 604, RG 217, NA.

recruiting and the handling of military affairs in the state to the governor's office. The Military Board soon faded from view, as did Joshua Speed.[9]

The future of Kentucky's intergovernmental relations looked somewhat bright. Robinson was a noted Union man, and, although he did not seek reelection in November 1863, he was succeeded by a man no less devoted to the Union, Thomas F. Bramlette. Indeed, Lincoln's administration went to great lengths to insure Bramlette's election by declaring martial law, removing rival candidates from the ballot, and intimidating dissenting voters. Bramlette's love of the Union never waned, but his goodwill toward the Lincoln administration evaporated quickly. Content with the intervention that made him governor, Bramlette rebelled when that intervention continued after his inauguration. Over Bramlette's objections, the administration turned slaves into soldiers and arrested state officers critical of the policy. When the government later denied Bramlette's attempt to raise state troops, the governor moved decidedly toward those who had opposed Lincoln from the outset of the war.[10]

The status of the state's war claims fueled many Unionists' growing antipathy toward Lincoln and the radicals. Though the recipient of over $1 million in cash advances, the state had not had any of its actual claims adjusted by 1864. There was also little indication that the government would, in the near future, move on any of the state's claims. This hesitancy was of particular concern to Bramlette and the legislature on a series of claims emanating from John Hunt Morgan's raid of 1863. Kentucky's dissatisfaction grew with news that both Indiana and Ohio, which had also suffered Morgan's raid, had succeeded in introducing special indemnification legislation in Congress. Resolving that Kentucky was "as loyal as any state within the Union," the legislature demanded equal treatment before the United States government.[11]

Kentucky's indignation was misplaced. Indiana and Ohio had

---

[9] J. B. Temple quoted in J. B. Temple to Lincoln, August 17, 1862, OR, 3:2:401. The transfer of military authority is noted in Edwin Stanton to Robinson, August 24, 1862, OR, 3:2:451.

[10] Coulter, The Civil War and Readjustment in Kentucky, 170–79.

[11] Information on the Morgan claims can be found in Third Auditor to W. S. Ketchum, May 29, 1863, Letter Books, Third Auditor, vol. 1, E. 617, RG 217, NA, and Resolution of January 20, 1864, Acts of the General Assembly of the Commonwealth of Kentucky, 1863–1864 (hereafter referred to as Kentucky Acts).

merely proposed legislation that the government reimburse its costs. There was no indication that Congress would approve any such thing. More importantly, Kentucky was hardly alone in having its claims unexamined. At the time of Kentucky's resolution demanding equal treatment, only three other states had received claims indemnification. Still, these more general circumstances mattered little. Few Kentuckians knew the status of all state claims, and they were not predisposed to search hard for explanations. The government was responsible for a host of perceived infamies forced upon the state, and a claims conspiracy only made sense. It was an attitude that lived on for the next two decades.[12]

Convinced that Congress and the Lincoln administration had conspired against Kentucky, the state government tried repeatedly to pry money from Washington. The effort was broadly conceived. Not only did the legislature and governor attempt to expedite all of Kentucky's claims against the United States, but they also moved to assist individuals who possessed claims directly against the government. In the first area, the state acted in accordance with the tried methods of the antebellum past. The legislature authorized the governor to appoint an agent, and it also directed Kentucky's United States senators to get claims legislation favorable to the state. In the second area, the state moved in a more pragmatic direction. Dissatisfied with the pace of reimbursement to its individual citizens and the apparent discrimination, the legislature proposed an alternative method of claims adjudication. To that point in early 1864, individuals had two options in their pursuit of indemnification. They could either deal directly with government agents working with the army quartermaster or they could file claims with the court of claims in Washington. Both methods offered small hope of quick action. Kentuckians did not trust army quartermasters, and the court of claims promised great expense in legal fees and transportation.[13]

The solution, the legislature thought, was twofold. First, the legislature reauthorized the post of state agent and then expanded its responsibilities. In the past, a state agent had only handled the state's claims against the government. Now the state authorized him to prosecute individual claims, which included claims for property damages,

---

[12] U.S. Congress, Senate Report, 50th Cong., 1st sess., 1888, S. Doc., 1286.
[13] *Kentucky Acts, 1863–1864*, 109–11, 391.

back pay, enlistment bounties, and pensions. However, the system would not be free for the claimant. For all claims less than $1,000, the legislature authorized the agent to charge a commission of 10 percent. Second, the legislature proposed that Washington adopt at least one of a series of temporary devices to handle individual claims. One recommendation was to form a special branch of the court of claims in Kentucky. Another recommendation proposed giving claims jurisdiction to the United States District Court operating in Kentucky. Yet another idea was simply to let the state adjudicate claims against the United States and provide money out of a general appropriation. Although the quartermaster general of the army would, in the future, agree with the spirit of these proposals and recommend the creation of independent commissions in every state, all such suggestions met with silence in Washington. There would be no changes in procedure.[14]

The above list of solutions all originated with the legislature. Governor Bramlette remained strangely removed from the process of making the administration of the federal system work. Unlike his counterpart in Missouri, Thomas Fletcher, Bramlette slipped quietly into a role of intermediary between his executive appointees and the legislature. But perhaps more importantly, the legislature's reaction to a lack of reimbursement reflected the misconception that all, or certainly most, claims problems originated with the federal government and its Republican officials. The detailed record left by the state agent and quartermaster tell a different story. Soon after the legislature spurred the state executive branch to action, three officials traveled to Washington: the newly appointed state agent, Charles Pennebaker; the quartermaster, S. G. Suddarth; and the adjutant general, Van Winkle. At different times, each of these men met with the third auditor, R. W. Atkinson. Both Pennebaker and Suddarth then left with mixed impressions. They were satisfied that the auditor and his staff had, and would in the future, cooperate fully, treating Kentucky like all other states. However, Atkinson had also convinced them that Kentucky's claims were a mess. What Joshua Speed had found to be the case two years earlier remained the same. Documen-

---

[14] Ibid; *Kentucky Acts, 1863–1864,* 388, and resolution dated January 20, 1864; Bramlette Memorial to Congress, January 25, 1864, Governor's Papers, Thomas Bramlette, Box 1, F. 2, KSA. The quartermaster's proposal was found in the *Frankfort Commonwealth,* February 12, 1867.

tation for Kentucky's claims of over $3 million did not exist. The problem was particularly acute in reimbursement for service. Unit payrolls had disappeared.[15]

By late spring, the fate of the state's claims was primarily in the hands of Agent Pennebaker. A lawyer and onetime Union army colonel, Pennebaker concentrated most of his efforts in the auditor's office. Congress was in session, but he believed it pointless to deal with either House or Senate. According to Pennebaker, members were too involved with pension, bounty, and old claims disputes to bother with Kentucky or any other state. In the broader universe of governing responsibilities, constituent service counted far more than the corporate interest of an individual state. Lacking what he believed to be a receptive audience to lobby, Pennebaker concentrated on the purely administrative feature of his position: he tried to find documentation for the auditor. Pennebaker left Washington to visit all of Kentucky's military units in the field. Once in the camps, he compiled lists of casualties and discharges from imperfect records that dated to the beginning of the war. As payrolls, vouchers, and other supporting evidence accumulated throughout 1864, the agent forwarded it to Washington and the third auditor's office.[16]

Pennebaker's diligence produced no tangible result in 1864. He had no experience with the claims and never properly organized his evidence into the standard forms of ledgers and abstracts used in the auditor's office. Making matters more difficult, Pennebaker did not yet have a hold on any of the state's expenditures for equipment and supplies. Auditor Atkinson simply refused to look at these claims, pronouncing them impossible to understand. But Pennebaker's problems were most exacerbated by his dual responsibilities of representing the claims of the state government and the claims of individual citizens. The agent was overburdened. His greatest workload came from individual claimants because a citizenry irate from governmental abuses, perceived and real, constantly petitioned his services. Between April and December 1864 alone, Pennebaker received

[15] "Quartermaster Report," December 1, 1864, Doc. #12, *Kentucky Documents, 1863–1864*, 7–11.

[16] "Report of the State Agent," January 1, 1865, *Kentucky House Journal, 1865*, 129–30. For Pennebaker's efforts to accumulate evidence and then ship it to Washington, see a variety of correspondence in Letter Books, Third Auditor, vol. 2, 48, 142, 143, 149, 155, 156, 170, and 180, E. 617, RG 217, NA.

approximately 3,000 letters, which then produced more than 1,000 individual claims to represent against the United States.[17]

Pennebaker's expanded duties were revelatory. Kentucky, like all states, was not hesitant to experiment with the mechanics of the federal system to try to make it work. The idea of a paid state agent representing a private citizen before the federal government had been a seldom-used innovation. But at the same time, it was merely a temporary device to get past the immediate difficulty. Furthermore, Pennebaker's activities demonstrate the difficulties of the state intervening on behalf of individuals. Pennebaker was swamped with claims and driven quickly to reassess his situation. He concluded that he could not do it alone. In numerous letters and reports, Pennebaker documented the need for help. When not tracking down errant military payrolls in the field, his office routine left little time to eat or sleep. Between 9:00 A.M. and 3:00 P.M. daily, Pennebaker made the rounds of the administrative departments in Washington. He spent the daylight hours before and after those rounds catering to the demands of the crowds of soldiers and officials who came to the office. Only at night was he able to answer the thousands of letters and claims that came from Kentucky. In a job that required a great deal of personal contact, Pennebaker was reduced to providing general information and blank claims forms for publication in the state's newspapers. Short of giving up, Pennebaker concluded that he needed a raise and two new clerks.[18]

Over the next few years, Kentucky adjusted its assistance to individual claimants. Pennebaker got his sought-after raise and one additional clerk. The state also established three local agents in Bowling Green, Franklin, and Louisville. Their task was to put each claim in proper order before sending it on to Pennebaker in Washington. But the fine-tuning did not alleviate Pennebaker's workload. Despite the additional help, he became increasingly bogged down with individual

---

[17] Pennebaker to Bramlette, December 15, 1864, Governor's Papers, Bramlette, Militia Correspondence, Box 5, F. 101, KSA and *Kentucky House Journal, 1865,* 129–33.

[18] Pennebaker to Bramlette, December 15, 1864, Governor's Papers, Bramlette, Militia Correspondence, Box 5, F. 101, KSA and *Kentucky House Journal, 1865,* 129–33. The newspapers remained Pennebaker's best means of getting out information and advice for as long as he handled individual claims. See *Tri-Weekly Kentucky Yeoman* (Frankfort), January 9, 1866, and *Frankfort Commonwealth,* January 20, 1866.

claims. Difficulties mounted in 1866 when Congress passed pension and bounty legislation that allowed greater numbers of people to press claims in Washington. The next year, over 15,000 letters containing 2,476 claims rolled into his office. Pennebaker soon found himself in the unenviable position of having to use his own money to hire an additional clerk and purchase office stationery.[19]

Kentucky's, and Pennebaker's, experience with individual claims was similar to that seen in other states. In 1864 the Missouri legislature developed a claims system for individuals totally separated from its state claims efforts. Subagents, appointed by the county courts, collected claims and then transferred them to a chief agent, who resided in St. Louis. Neither Missouri nor Kentucky met great success. In Missouri, the system suffered because the chief agent was rooted in the state, with few opportunities to travel to Washington. In Kentucky, the opposite was true. The chief agent remained in Washington, with little flexibility to return to Kentucky. Of further disadvantage for Pennebaker, he had a far greater workload. At that time, Missouri had yet to authorize its agent to handle the state government's claims. Despite these handicaps, state attempts to mediate individual claims owed their greatest difficulty to simple competition.[20]

Large numbers of claims produced large numbers of private agents anxious to serve and profit. Each private agent offered the promise of personal attention and a web of connections all the way to the treasury. Likewise, private agents were not the only competition. Near the end of the war, the privately funded United States Sanitary Commission paid agents to assist individuals for all war-related claims. Faced with these options, prospective claimants grew disenchanted with the representation offered by the states. Despite offers

---

[19] Pay, clerk, and other financial matters described in *Kentucky Acts, 1865*, vol. 1, 59–61, and notation in Executive Journal, Thomas Bramlette, Governor's Papers, Microfilm 993702, KSA. The Kentucky system is described in the *Frankfort Commonwealth*, July 14, September 29, and November 5, 1865. Other information in this paragraph can be found in Pennebaker to Bramlette, "Report of the State Agent," January 1, 1867, Legislative Doc. #8, 4, and "Report of the State Agent," January 1, 1868, Doc. #18, *Kentucky Documents, 1867*, vol. 2, 1–12.

[20] The beginnings, performance, and end of Missouri's program can be found in Avery and Shoemaker, *Messages and Proclamations*, 4: 133–34, 169; *Laws of Missouri, 1869*, 88; *MO HJ, Appendix, 1869–1870*; and Civil War Claims Record Books, vols. 1–9, Francis Minor Collection, MHS.

of free services, state-subsidized agents slipped into irrelevancy. In Pennsylvania, the governor publicly bemoaned the fact that claimants increasingly disregarded his state agents. In Kentucky, newspapers recommended that state agents be ignored, and by 1869 the state-sponsored systems began to disappear for a lack of use and efficiency.[21]

As Kentucky's efforts to push the settlement of the claims of its citizens faltered, so too did the state's attempts to master its own claim against the government. Military units continued to maintain poor records of service and expenditure, prompting the state adjutant to describe Kentucky's bookkeeping as a "serious embarrassment." Of equal trouble to ever gaining a proper accounting of state expenditures was the state's internal auditing procedure that paid few claims against the state and caused occasional cries of public outrage. Just as was the case with the commissions established by Missouri to audit claims against the state, Kentucky formed numerous commissions to pay off claims that would then be added to the state's total claim in Washington. The commissions, run by the quartermaster, maintained strict standards of inspection through what many commonly perceived as a Byzantine system of forms and documentation. By 1866, one observer believed the whole system discriminated against "poor people" who did not know the "forms of red-tapeism." Worst of all, he charged, poor claimants met rejection "because they do not come in a sort of court dress, suitable to be presented to flunkeyism. . . ."[22]

Kentucky's internal claims commissions resembled those commissions already seen operating in Missouri. They demanded the types of documentation that would be needed when the quartermaster gen-

---

[21] Avery and Shoemaker, *Messages and Proclamations,* 4: 133–34, 169; *Laws of Missouri, 1869,* 88; *MO HJ, Appendix, 1869–1870;* and Civil War Claims Record Books, vols. 1–9, Francis Minor Collection, MHS. For the work of the Sanitary Commission in Kentucky, consult the *Frankfort Commonwealth,* July 14, 1865. See also "Report of the State Agent," for Kentucky, January 1, 1869, Doc. #15, *Kentucky Documents, 1868,* vol. 2, 6. For similar problems in another state, see Governor's Message, Andrew J. Curtin of Pennsylvania, January 30, 1866, in Governor's Papers, Thomas Bramlette, Box 1, F. 8, KSA.

[22] The state's ongoing efforts to maintain its records, and the corresponding quote, can be found in General Order #2, February 9, 1865, General Orders Kentucky Volunteers, 1865, Military Records and Research Division, Frankfort. See also General Order #3 in same. An example of the commission authorizations can be found in *Kentucky Acts, 1865–1866,* 61–62. Quotes taken from the *Daily Kentucky Yeoman,* February 16, 1866.

eral forwarded the claim to the state agent in Washington. Similarly, both Missouri and Kentucky made only infrequent appropriations to cover the amounts authorized by the auditing boards. Yet there was a clear distinction between the efforts of the two states. Where Missouri often chose to make its payments in scrip redeemable only after the federal government reimbursed the state, Kentucky always paid approved claims in some form of legal tender. This policy removed from Kentucky's claims experience factors that so often dominated Missouri's indemnification efforts. Kentucky never had to wage a losing battle with the government over the nature of the scrip and whether it counted as a bona fide state expenditure. Better yet, not having issued scrip, Kentucky avoided the wild flames of speculation that engulfed the scrip in Missouri and then led to episodes of public corruption and Washington's wariness of the state's claim.[23]

The absence of these problems made it easy for Kentuckians to see a linkage between claims difficulties and the state's increasingly strained relationship with Washington. In August 1865, statewide elections produced a legislature that was decidedly pro-Confederate in its sympathies. That legislature, with the support of Governor Bramlette, then repealed all wartime acts that had restricted the civil liberties of Confederate sympathizers. Just as the state moved in this political direction, information about the state's claim in Washington seemed to confirm the idea that the Republican administration would try to penalize Kentucky.[24]

Despite the treasury's vague assurances to Agent Pennebaker and Governor Bramlette that progress was being made in auditing the claims, the process seemed to hit a roadblock in March 1866. After the auditor had approved a number of expenditures, he then forwarded a group of claims amounting to $34,000 to the secretary of war for verification that the expenditures had occurred under actual Union army service. According to State Quartermaster George Monroe, the transfer of the claims into a War Department notable for its radicalism meant a delay that could only be measured in years. Monroe was incensed. He charged the secretary of war with "foolish delay," noting further that "this treatment is perfectly outrageous,

---

[23] Delays in appropriations can be seen in "Report of the Quartermaster General," January 1, 1869, Doc. #5, *Kentucky Documents, 1868*, vol. 1, 5–7; *Kentucky Acts, 1869*, vol. 1, 100–101; *Kentucky Acts, 1872*, vol. 1, 87.

[24] Tapp and Klotter, *Kentucky: Decades of Discord, 1865–1900*, 12–13.

and I am almost forced to believe . . . that the action of our recent Legislature in certain respects has caused them to pursue this course toward Kentucky."[25]

Monroe had little cause for concern. Despite the fact that $34,000 in claims had been transferred to the War Department, that figure was but a fraction of the state's total claim of over $3.3 million then under consideration. Regardless, Kentucky's perception of the situation had to be filtered through the lens of its broader relationship with Washington and the dominant Republican Party. The majority of people concerned with indemnification thus saw federal discrimination. Quartermaster Monroe believed that the secretary of the treasury had abetted the War Department in its attempt to ruin Kentucky's claims. Agent Pennebaker concluded that all officials involved in the auditing process were disposed "to postpone Kentucky to other states. . . ." Governor Bramlette asserted that the government rejected Kentucky's claims for "no good reason," and that the state must trust "to an abatement of any unjust prejudice." Among the state's newspapers, the pro-Democratic *Tri-Weekly Kentucky Yeoman* was especially prone to see discrimination. Sectional bias, after all, was easy to find in what it called a "Sham Congress" only too ready to shower money upon northern states while denying the claims of loyal Kentuckians. The paper's editor concluded ultimately that all of the state's claims were being held hostage to Kentucky's next election in the fall of 1866, which many observers believed would be the Republican Party's last real opportunity to influence state politics.[26]

Although the above statements were no doubt deeply believed, they also reflected the pressure that Kentucky placed upon its officials to produce results. Quartermaster Monroe believed public censure likely if some progress was not made. Likewise, by December 1866, Agent Pennebaker had been employed for three years without having completely settled any of the state's claims. Legislative autho-

[25] Third Auditor to Pennebaker, March 5, 1866, and Monroe to Bramlette, March 6, 1866, Governor's Papers, Thomas Bramlette, Militia Correspondence, Box 5, F. 106, KSA.

[26] "Report of the Quartermaster General," December 1, 1866, Doc. #9, *Kentucky Documents, 1866*, vol. 2, 4–7; "Report of the State Agent," January 1, 1867, Legislative Document #8, 3; Governor's Message, January 4, 1867, *Kentucky House Journal, 1867*, 16; *Tri-Weekly Kentucky Yeoman*, April 14 and July 26, 1866.

rization for his job expired in February 1867, so the necessity of finding some explanations was probably even more apparent to him. Governor Bramlette, a moderate in a conservative state, pondered a senatorial run in 1867. The benefits of castigating the federal government could not have escaped him, especially after the state Democratic Party produced a platform in the summer of 1866 that denounced Washington's usurpations in Kentucky and the South.[27]

Although 1866 had been marked by unexpected delay, the year had not been a complete failure for the indemnification enterprise. In fact, progress occurred that belied the complaints of state officials. Beginning in May, Kentucky's congressional delegation successfully produced legislation that authorized the treasury to audit claims for state troops called into action in May 1862 but subsequently never mustered into the Union army. On another issue, the third auditor recommended that Kentucky receive a $500,000 advance on its yet to be approved claims. Finally, by December, Pennebaker managed to get over $1.8 million in claims approved by the third auditor without the paperwork being transferred to the War Department for review. Some time then had to elapse before the second comptroller conducted his own standard review, but there was nothing that would prevent Kentucky from receiving a large portion of this money in 1867.[28]

The hurdles that Kentucky had to pass in 1866 were no different from those experienced by other states. The state quartermaster and agent had to coordinate their activities and constantly pass relevant information between each other. Pennebaker, in particular, needed to immerse himself in the detail of each expenditure, justify it, and then prepare it in a format suitable to the treasury's accounting clerks. Once all of this had been done, Pennebaker had to appear before the auditor to try to explain any discrepancies that had been

---

[27] For Monroe's belief in impending censure, see his "Report of the Quartermaster General," December 1, 1866, Doc. #9, *Kentucky Documents, 1866*, vol. 2, 4–7. For the party platform, see Tapp and Klotter, *Kentucky: Decades of Discord, 1865–1900*, 15.

[28] Kentucky's claims legislation can be tracked in the *Congressional Globe*, 39th Cong., 1st sess., 2612, 2888–89, 2927, 3440; 39th Cong., 2nd sess., 971, 976, 1116; and *United States Statutes at Large* 14 (1867): 565. Recommendation for the advance seen in "Report of the Quartermaster General," December 1, 1866, Doc. #9, *Kentucky Documents, 1866*, vol. 2, 4–7. Figure for approved claims found in "Report of the State Agent," January 1, 1867, Legislative Document #8, 7.

found. In some cases, this would be difficult, as when Pennebaker struggled to explain enlistment payments to men whose names did not appear on Union army muster rolls. In other cases, explanations could be easy, as when Pennebaker discovered that documentation for over $1 million in expenses had been misplaced within the auditor's office. The bottom line was that Kentucky's administrative officials had to do the same things as other states' officials for an equal probability of success.[29]

Pennebaker's work in 1866 brought visible dividends in 1867. Throughout the year, Kentucky received indemnification checks totaling $1,005,865, which then led both the state agent and quartermaster to note proudly that, of all the states in the Union, Kentucky had been reimbursed the largest percentage of its claims. Despite the financial windfall, Kentucky's leaders continued to wonder about the cause of the state's outstanding claims. Over $1.5 million remained disallowed because, in large part, Kentucky's military payrolls were littered with soldiers who never mustered into the Union army. Consternation only increased when the War Department issued its final judgment that these claims fell outside of Secretary Chase's rules and needed, therefore, to be settled by special congressional legislation. Pennebaker had tried repeatedly to plead the state's case before the War Department and the second comptroller. He had even suggested to Secretary of War Ulysses S. Grant that some state troops be accepted retroactively into the army. His special pleadings did not work. Chase's rules clearly barred payment to troops who lacked proof of national service, and no one within the claims bureaucracy had displayed any willingness to break a precedent that might loosen the doors of the treasury. The presence of claims similar to those of Kentucky, such as New Jersey's, served as an almost constant reminder of what could happen if the treasury did make a special allowance. Perhaps the only surprise concerning this set of claims was that Pennebaker persisted as long as he did in trying to have it audited without legislation. His time, and the state's money, would have been better spent had he shifted his energies to acquiring special legislation much earlier in the process.[30]

---

[29] "Report of the State Agent," January 1, 1867, Legislative Document #8.

[30] "Quartermaster General's Report," November 30, 1867, Doc. #4, *Kentucky Documents, 1867*, vol. 1; Report of the Kentucky State Agent, January 1, 1868, Doc. 18, *Kentucky Documents, 1867*, vol. 2, 12–20, 23. See also J. M. Broadhead (second

Of greater embarrassment to Kentucky—and hence the source of its continuing distrust of the Republicans—the outstanding claims drained the state's financial coffers. Despite Kentucky's lack of a large public debt, most of its outstanding war expenses had not been paid off. At the beginning of 1867, Kentucky carried a war-related debt that cost the state approximately $90,000 in interest payments each year. Washington's indemnification payments in 1867 reduced that annual indebtedness only a small amount, to almost $78,000 per year. Administrative delay over any part of the state's claims increased Kentucky's total debt and its ability to locate Republican misdeeds in Washington. Writing on December 3, Kentucky's new governor, John W. Stephenson, spoke for many when he decried the "technical and specious objections [that] are interposed at Washington to the payment of this claim, so sacredly due."[31]

Despite the rhetoric, good fortune in Kentucky's claims collection continued throughout 1868. By the end of the year, Pennebaker received over $105,000, which he then deposited in Kentucky's sinking fund of debt retirement. In keeping with the previous few years, the receipt of the money did not mollify the state. The money was substantially less than in 1867, and Pennebaker immediately pinned the blame on treasury officials, who, he claimed, unfairly placed other states ahead of Kentucky. According to Pennebaker, Kentucky's success in 1867 resulted from the simple fact that few other states had filed any claims during that year. Unable to prioritize Kentucky behind any other states, accounting officials had no choice but to work on the state's claims in 1867. Pennebaker believed that the presence of other state claims in 1868 would make it easy for vindictive Republicans in Washington to discriminate against Kentucky.[32]

Beginning in 1869, Kentucky's method of dealing with the govern-

---

comptroller) to Pennebaker, December 7, 1866, in "Report of the State Agent," Legislative Document #8, January 1, 1867, 9–10. New Jersey possessed similar claims that met a similar fate. See L. Perrine to R. W. Clarke, October 18, 1869, Letters Received, Third Auditor, vol. 2, E. 604, RG 217, NA.

[31] First interest figure found in "Report of the State Agent," January 1, 1867, Legislative Document #8, 8. Second figure in "Report of the Kentucky State Agent," January 1, 1868, Doc. #18, *Kentucky Documents, 1867*, vol. 2, 15–16. Quote taken from Stevenson message to state assembly, December 3, 1867, *House Journal, 1867–1868*, 12.

[32] "Report of the State Agent" for Kentucky, January 1, 1869, Doc. #15, *Kentucky Documents, 1868*, vol. 2, 6.

ment on its claims began to change. At that time, the state shifted the primary claims responsibility from its agent to its permanent militia staff. The idea for change developed slowly. With over one-half of the state's claim still outstanding, Kentucky's leadership methods did not change because of a sense that reimbursement was now a matter of simple formality. Previously audited claims needed to be presented again, vouchers explained, and, most important, difficult claims for bonded interest needed to be organized and presented to a government that had never previously recognized such claims.

Instead, the most prominent reason for removing the agent appears to be that Pennebaker produced fewer and fewer results. Frequently sick, Pennebaker managed to push through the auditor's office in 1869 only $14,000 in claims out of a possible claim of $1.3 million. His work in Washington languished, while most collection, documentation, and presentation duties fell into the hands of either the state adjutant or the quartermaster general, a situation that both officers noted prominently. Governor Stevenson was made painfully aware of the reality of Pennebaker's absence when in July both he and the quartermaster, Fayette Hewitt, had to travel to Washington to review the state's claim. Another problem contributing to the demise of Pennebaker was Stevenson's growing sense that the agent had failed through simple inefficiency and a clash of personalities. According to reports, Pennebaker had become an annoyance in the treasury's offices, leading some clerks to delay Kentucky's claims as a basic matter of spite. One other matter not helping Pennebaker was a decline in individual claimants seeking his services. The state agent's backlog of claims and the rise of competing private agencies had siphoned off many citizens otherwise interested in his services. His unpopularity within the treasury had also somehow become known, which led to even more claims being transferred to other agents. Absent the individual claims, a state-employed agent to represent individual citizens in Washington was a luxury.[33]

---

[33] "Report of the Adjutant General for Kentucky," November 30, 1868, Doc. #4, *Kentucky Documents, 1868*, vol. 1, doc. #4, passim; "Report of the Quartermaster for Kentucky," December 1, 1869, Doc. #12, *Kentucky Documents, 1869*, vol. 2, 5–9; Governor Stevenson's message, December 6, 1869, in *Kentucky House Journal, 1869–1870*, 12–14. For reports of Pennebaker's inefficiency and personality clashes, see Hewitt to Stevenson, April 12, 1870, and April 16, 1870, Stevenson Family Papers, vol. 29, LC; H. P. Helm to Benjamin Bristow, November 22, 1870, Bristow Papers, LC.

The decision to remove Pennebaker started out as part of an effort to restructure the duties of the state agent. In March 1870, the legislature eliminated the agency as it had been configured since 1864. The legislature then authorized the governor, through his Sinking Fund commissioners, to appoint a nonsalaried agent for state claims. Like most other state agents across the country, this new agent would represent only state claims for some agreed-upon commission percentage.[34]

The legislature's authorization of an agent sparked more interest among the profession of agents than it did among the governor or his Sinking Fund commissioners. Realizing the magnitude of Kentucky's outstanding claim, and the attendant possibility for profit, agents and agencies sent their applications and letters of recommendation to the governor. The applications revealed that the competition among agents had become fierce. To one applicant, most of his fellow agents could be classified as "Shysters . . . who scarcely know the difference between an execution and a bill of lading." The applications showed also that the majority of the agents pursuing Kentucky had no direct personal link with the state. They retained multiple state clients, while also conducting a large business among individual claimants. Finally, the applicants all emphasized their greatest asset—the ability to break down all bureaucratic walls and rules in Washington.[35]

The treasury had become a particularly antagonistic foe for agents and lobbyists representing all states. Just as Congress entertained legislation requiring that lobbyists and agents register with the executive departments, the new secretary of the treasury, George Boutwell, made matters worse. In March, he issued official rules effectively prohibiting clerks from revealing any information about claims "under pain of instant dismissal." He also closed off the offices of the

---

[34] Stevenson's recommendation contained in *Kentucky House Journal, 1869–1870,* 12–14. For legislative directions, consult act of March 10, 1870, *Kentucky Acts, 1869—1870,* vol. 1, 40.

[35] Sample letter of recommendation seen in Congressmen George Adams and L. Trimble to Stevenson, April 12, 1870, Stevenson Family Papers, vol. 29, LC. Quotes can be found in William Brown to Stevenson, March 31, 1870, Governor's Papers, Stevenson, Box 1, F. 3, KSA, and George Evans and John Trimble to Stevenson, April 22, 1870, in F. 3 above. This paragraph is based also upon Pennebaker to Stevenson, April 19, 1870, and General Order of the Secretary of the Treasury, March 1, 1870, Governor's Papers, Stevenson, Box 1, F. 3; Pennebaker to Stevenson, April 7, 1870, Pennebaker to Third Auditor, April 1870, and John Trimble to Hewitt, April 22, 1870, in F. 4 above.

treasury to all agents who interfered with the conduct of business. There is some measure of irony in Boutwell's clamping down upon the agents. In the first tumultuous months of the Civil War, he had been among the very first state agents to appear in Washington. Governor John Andrew of Massachusetts wanted Boutwell especially for his "information, influence, and acquaintance with the Cabinet. . . ."[36]

To claimants, the government's hostility clearly indicated the need for agents and lobbyists who could bypass such inconveniences. However, in the end, their arguments mattered little to Governor Stevenson. He rejected the necessity of an agent, trusting instead the judgment of the state quartermaster general, Fayette Hewitt. The quartermaster had not only investigated the dealings of Pennebaker, but had also volunteered to handle the claims himself. A militia officer already employed by the state, Hewitt satisfied Stevenson that he was able to deliver indemnification without the added expense of a commission. As in such midwestern states as Missouri and Indiana, the appointment of the quartermaster also served unconsciously to ensure the institutional survival of a militia position frequently the target of legislative budget cutters.[37]

THE PERCEPTION OF CONSPIRACY AND THE REALITY OF SUCCESS

Over the next five years, the controversy and importance of the claims in Kentucky did not abate. The problem of accounting for defective payrolls continued, but the state had also to lurch from one additional claims crisis to another. At first, the primary crisis became ordering the state's claim before the expiration of authorization to prosecute claims under the act of July 27, 1861. Beginning June 30, 1871, all claims not allowed by the treasury had to receive special legislation. In 1870, Congress refused to pass annual appropriations

---

[36] Pennebaker to Stevenson, April 19, 1870, and General Order of the Secretary of the Treasury, March 1, 1870, Governor's Papers, Stevenson, Box 1, F. 3; Pennebaker to Stevenson, April 7, 1870, Pennebaker to Third Auditor, April 1870, and John Trimble to Hewitt, April 22, 1870, in F. 4, above. For Boutwell's appointment as Massachusetts' state agent, see *OR*, 3:1:99–100. Boutwell quoted in Thomas H. Brown, "George Sewall Boutwell: Public Servant (1818–1905)" (Ph.D. diss., New York University, 1979), 107.

[37] On qualifications of Hewitt and reason for not using an agent, see Stevenson's message, January 5, 1871, *Kentucky House Journal, 1871*, 13–14.

for reimbursements allowed by the auditor's offices. As a result of this legislation, Kentucky took on its greatest claims challenge. Beginning roughly in 1872, the state tried actively through the offices of the treasury, the halls of Congress, and the bench of the Supreme Court to receive indemnification for interest payments on its bonded war debt. There was no precedent for this during the Civil War era, and Kentucky tried to break new ground.[38]

Regardless of either the new deadline or the new types of claims that the state had to pursue, one remaining salient issue governed all claims activity. Kentucky's frosty relations with the federal government continued and worsened. Reconstruction politics served as a persistent irritant to the conservative state and the Republican-led Congress. Threats of martial law could frequently be heard from Washington. The claims issue could not be severed from such rhetoric given the background of Fayette Hewitt. The new recipient of all claims responsibility for Kentucky, State Quartermaster Hewitt was a meticulous man who had dabbled in the law. He reveled in the mental gymnastics of the claims and, later in his career, the auditing of state finances. Though important to the unfolding claims activity, these attributes mattered less than Hewitt's fiery personality and his previous service with the Confederacy. At the outset of the Civil War, Hewitt helped establish the Confederacy's postal system. Desiring military action, Hewitt left the postal service in December 1861 for the first of a number of staff positions in the army. For the next two years, he bounced around a number of unit commands before finally settling in as the adjutant of the Kentucky, or "Orphan," Brigade. According to all available accounts, Hewitt was a distinguished officer. Brave in battle and skilled in administration, Hewitt was an ideal staff officer with a passionate love of Kentucky and the Confederate cause.[39]

Of those within the Kentucky government, there would be no man as predisposed as Hewitt to believe that the United States acted unjustly toward the state. As he entered into his duties with the claims, Hewitt was convinced that the government applied its rules unevenly

---

[38] *United States Statutes at Large* 16 (1870): 250.

[39] W. H. Perrin, et. al., eds., *Kentucky: A History of the State*, 5th ed. (Louisville: F. A. Battle and Co., 1887), 744–45; William C. Davis, *The Orphan Brigade: The Kentucky Confederates Who Couldn't Go Home* (Garden City, N.Y.: Doubleday and Co., 1980), passim.

and that the rules themselves, although "proper and just" when used for the Northern states, harmed Kentucky because of its unique wartime situation as a border state. The irony of Hewitt as a former Confederate officer pursuing the Union claims of Kentucky could not have been lost on other key figures. One such person was the secretary of the treasury, George Boutwell. Described by one observer as "sallow, short-faced, and bright-eyed," Boutwell had been a shopkeeper turned governor of Massachusetts before the war. Tied closely to the prewar antislavery movement and wartime radical politics, Boutwell would be a natural suspect in any perceived attempt to harm Kentucky's financial interests. Another important person in Kentucky's unfolding claims drama was the government's new chief legal officer, Solicitor General Benjamin Bristow. As Hewitt steered the claims into litigious waters during the 1870s, he met the adverse opinions of Bristow. The solicitor was in no different a position than Secretary Boutwell. A Kentuckian, Bristow had been a vocal wartime supporter of the Republicans and, thus, effectively barred from holding any important office in the state. Like some other prominent Kentucky Republicans, such as John Marshall Harlan, Bristow found new political life in the federal government through Republican patronage. It would be no great stretch of the imagination for Hewitt, and most like-minded Kentuckians, to see Bristow as a more than willing accomplice to undermine and embarrass the state Democratic Party's efforts to secure reimbursement.[40]

Energetic and sensitive to any slight of Kentucky, Hewitt threw himself into his claims duties, trying to beat the June 30, 1871, deadline, after which all claims required congressional legislation. He worked well with his immediate supervisors, the commissioners of the Sinking Fund, and the accounting clerks in Washington. By the end of 1870, and despite the long sickness of one clerk in the auditor's office, he pushed through claims amounting to approximately $174,000. His work was a significant improvement over that seen in Pennebaker's last year as agent, but over $1,193,761 in claims remained outstanding. With the June 30 deadline fast approaching,

---

[40] "Report of the Quartermaster of Kentucky," December 1, 1869, Doc. #12, *Kentucky Documents, 1869*, vol. 2, 5–9, contains Hewitt's beliefs and quote concerning the state's claims. Boutwell described in P. J. Staudenraus, ed., *Mr. Lincoln's Washington*, 36. Ross A. Webb, *Benjamin Helm Bristow: Border State Politician* (Lexington: University Press of Kentucky, 1969).

Hewitt worked exclusively on one particular class of claims valued at close to $600,000. Hewitt's subsequent efforts proved Herculean, involving considerable time and the coordination of resources within the legislature, the Sinking Fund Commission, and the state military offices. But the efforts were also the state's most controversial, seeming to justify all of Hewitt's preconceptions regarding the discrimination of the United States.[41]

The class of claims in question came out of William T. Sherman's military campaigns in 1864 and 1865. Following Sherman's capture and reduction of Atlanta, Georgia, in September 1864, he cut his lines of supply and reinforcement to head deep into Confederate Georgia. This was his "March to the Sea" that did so much to destroy Confederate supplies, communications, and morale. Sherman's march was daring because it disregarded the security of the operational rear of his army in the hostile territory of Tennessee and Kentucky. Absent this protection, Thomas Bramlette's Unionist government in Kentucky called out all available militia to cover the state and Sherman's rear. The Capital Guards, Home Guards, and ordinary infantry all responded for the duration of the war, while Sherman marched first to Savannah, Georgia, and then north through the Carolinas. When the war had ended, the state had spent $582,692 in this final exercise of home defense.[42]

Technically labeled the Tenth Installment of Kentucky's War Claim, this set of claims had been presented once before by Agent Pennebaker. The auditor's office denied the claim, leaving no extant reason for the rejection. Hewitt revived the claim and hammered it through the War Department and the treasury, losing only $57,433 in disallowed expenditures. The claim had carried great risk of complete rejection. Neither the president nor the secretary of war had asked that these troops be called out, which former secretary of the treasury Chase's indemnification rules specifically mandated. Never-

---

[41] "Report of the Kentucky Quartermaster," January 2, 1871, Doc. #6, *Kentucky Documents, 1870*, 5–9. Governor Stevenson's message, January 5, 1871, *Kentucky House Journal, 1871*, 13–14, has information on total claims still due the state. "An Act to expedite the collection of the War Claims of the State of Kentucky," March 22, 1871, *Kentucky Acts, 1871*, vol. 1, 88–89, reveals the extent to which Kentucky tried to coordinate her resources in the final countdown to June 30.

[42] Figure is the amount first claimed in 1871. See "Report of the Kentucky Quartermaster," December 1, 1871, Doc. # 8, *Kentucky Documents, 1871*, vol. 1, 3–5, and *Observer and Reporter*, July 22, 1871.

theless, the secretary of war, William W. Belknap, gave his approval, followed eventually by the second comptroller's in the middle of June 1871. All that Hewitt needed at that point was the signatory approval of the secretary of the treasury so that Hewitt could draw the actual pay warrants for the state. It never happened.[43]

Delay and eventual rejection for Kentucky began with the fact that Secretary of the Treasury Boutwell was out of Washington for most of the final days of June 1870. The acting secretary hesitated to approve such a large sum for a claim of, to him, questionable merit. Because Boutwell was not expected back in his office before the passage of the expiration deadline, Hewitt insisted that the acting secretary take charge and issue the pay warrants. This he would not do, deciding on July 29 that the secretary of war should verify again that Kentucky's troops met the test of actual national service. Realizing the time demands set upon the claim, Belknap perfunctorily verified the troops' service the next day. Still wary of the claim and unwilling to issue the warrants, the acting secretary did the next best thing. Late in the evening of June 30, he signed the warrants and informed Hewitt that the signature was only legal if Boutwell approved. All possibility of Hewitt ever receiving the reimbursement without special legislation had vanished. Boutwell returned to the treasury's offices in the middle of July and refused to sign the warrants.[44]

Boutwell later explained his decision as a simple matter of precedent and obedience to Chase's rules. To Boutwell, Kentucky's troops never mustered into the Union army, and they never received a call to arms from the appropriate authority. Boutwell went on to note that succeeding secretaries approved Chase's interpretations by repeatedly following precedent. He also noted that Congress codified the rules into law when it provided Missouri special legislation in 1862 and 1866 for claims that the treasury refused to allow—all in accordance with Chase's rules. Boutwell went on to remark that Kentucky's government should have been aware of Chase's rules. The rules, after all, had been prepared and "made known to the country before any considerable expenses were incurred by the several states, and long before the expenses" of Kentucky's current claim. Boutwell

---

[43] "Report of the Kentucky Quartermaster," December 1, 1871, Doc. # 8, *Kentucky Documents, 1871*, vol. 1, 3–5.

[44] Ibid., 3–20; *Commonwealth v. Boutwell*, 13 Wallace 526 (1871).

further justified his last-minute intervention as a part of his accepted duties: every secretary, "as I am informed, has practically recognized it to be his duty to pass upon all claims. . . ."[45]

Though Boutwell was entirely correct that it had become custom for the secretary to pass a final judgment on state indemnifications, his adherence to the customs of the department was selective. It had also been the custom of treasury secretaries to accept the screening judgment of the War Department as to the conditions of militia service. Many people concluded immediately that Boutwell acted out of spite toward Kentucky, yet there is perhaps a more logical explanation; that is, Boutwell was gradually trying to remove the War Department from the claims process. Historians have hardly identified Boutwell with the civil service reform movement, but he did believe strongly in bureaucratic rationalization in both civil service hiring and organization. Indeed, he became a leading crusader within the administration of President Ulysses S. Grant to clean up fraud-encrusted customs procedures. Frequently reviled as a mere politician and radical crony of President Grant, Boutwell was ultimately the first department head to implement bureaucratic reforms before Congress legislated them thirteen years later in the Pendleton Act of 1883. Such thinking placed him squarely at odds with Secretary Belknap, a more orthodox patronage spoilsman and administrator who thought little of contemporary attempts to rationalize the executive department.[46]

Reaction from Kentucky was predictable and fit well within the tone of its intergovernmental relations of the preceding ten years. Outrage bubbled over at this most recent example of governmental arrogance and Republican conspiracies. According to one editorial, "as long as Kentucky is a nullity in National politics, . . . so long will

---

[45] "Report of the Kentucky Quartermaster," December 1, 1871, Doc. # 8, *Kentucky Documents, 1871*, vol. 1, 27–32; *Commonwealth v. Boutwell*, 13 Wallace 526 (1871).

[46] "Report of the Kentucky Quartermaster," December 1, 1871, Doc. # 8, *Kentucky Documents, 1871*, vol. 1, 27–32. This analysis extends also from Ari Hoogenboom's discussion of Boutwell's little-known career as a civil service reformer. See *Outlawing the Spoils: A History of the Civil Service Reform Movement, 1865–1883* (Urbana: University of Illinois Press, 1961), 68–69. A brief explanation of Boutwell's career as customs crusader can be found in White, *The Republican Era*, 123–26. The more orthodox portrayal of Boutwell can be found in John G. Sproat, *"The Best Men": Liberal Reformers in the Gilded Age* (Chicago: University of Chicago Press, 1982), 191–92.

she be a target for the shafts of Radical malice." The same editorial went on to proclaim: "the fact is, Kentucky is the victim of a gigantic diddling operation which is none the less contemptible for being puritanically elaborate." Few Kentuckians would have argued with the conclusion that "the present political complexion of the State weighs with the Secretary more than its [actual] record in the War."[47]

The state's official reaction became the most coherent attack upon the structure of the claims system offered by any state. It was also perhaps the most futile, rearguing issues long settled by the acquiescence of the other loyal states. Led by the indefatigable Fayette Hewitt, Kentucky's resistance centered on Chase's rules. With no apparent legal assistance, Hewitt prepared a detailed brief against the rules. In the brief, Hewitt disputed not only the application of the rules toward Kentucky, but also the constitutional ability of any executive official to restrict congressional legislation by the creation of rules. Hewitt issued his legal reasonings in a number of directions. First, they met a popular clamor for explanations in Kentucky. Second, they served as a device to get Secretary Boutwell to relent. Third, and failing a revision by Boutwell, Hewitt crafted his analysis of Kentucky's position as a basis for the first legal action against Chase's rules since their creation in 1861.[48]

Hewitt's basic premise was that Chase's rules "mutilate[d]" the original reimbursement legislation in the July 27, 1861, act. As reiterated by Hewitt, the bill spoke of reimbursement for troops "employed, engaged, or aiding" the suppression of the rebellion. Nowhere did the legislation note, as did Chase, an actual mustering of state troops into the Union army. Similarly, Hewitt reminded all concerned that the act implied nothing of Chase's other restriction that troops be "called out, and the expenditures incurred, at the request or under the authority of the President or . . . Secretary of War." Hewitt went on to state that all subsequent special reimbursement legislation was irrelevant to codifying Chase's rules into law. Missouri's congressional reimbursement in 1862 and 1866 merely exemplified remedies that expedited the processing of a state's claims. Those pieces of legislation, Hewitt concluded, did not mean

---

[47] Quotes taken from the *Observer and Reporter*, August 9, 1871.

[48] "Report of the Kentucky Quartermaster," December 1, 1871, Doc. # 8, *Kentucky Documents, 1871*, vol. 1, 1–25. Hewitt's report was read, and cited frequently, by a number of newspapers throughout Kentucky.

that all other states had to meet a test of actually mustering troops into the army. Hewitt shifted the final portion of his analysis to Boutwell's actual intervention in the processing of Kentucky's claim. Important to the fanning of Kentucky's outrage had been the element of Boutwell's last-minute refusal to sign pay warrants. Boutwell based this intervention on what he thought were the customs of his office. Hewitt disagreed sharply, noting that the secretary's involvement, or signature, was actually "unwarranted by law or practice."[49]

Hewitt's discussion of this aspect of the situation opened up just one of the internal divisions within President Ulysses S. Grant's administration. Boutwell's rejection of the claim explicitly overturned Secretary of War Belknap's judgment that Kentucky's militia had indeed actually performed national service. In what was perhaps the strongest point that could be made for Kentucky, Belknap had originally remarked that there was no other type of service possible at the time. State service could not have occurred even if the governor and legislature desired it. At the time of the militia's call to arms, Kentucky was under the martial law of the United States government. Hewitt scored well. Not only did Hewitt rub some already sore relations between Boutwell and Belknap, but he also addressed the legality of one cabinet secretary reversing the decision of another cabinet secretary. Belknap had been insulted by Boutwell's meddling in what the secretary of war believed was his area of operations, and relations between the two men never really recovered. The following year, tensions flared again over another state's claim when Belknap sensed, correctly, that Boutwell was gradually attempting to remove the War Department from the claims process. That Boutwell would eventually succeed in this is suggested by Hewitt's observation in December 1875 that the War Department had become a place "of little importance" in the claims process that "just consumes time."[50]

But in 1872, Kentucky's official and publicly expressed outrage was but the beginning of the state's attempts to get the money denied by Boutwell. The state was not unwilling to use the more accustomed political operations. While Hewitt and the press blasted Boutwell,

---

[49] Ibid.

[50] Ibid. Agitation between Boutwell and Belknap can be glimpsed in Belknap to Boutwell, April 6, 1872, Letters Received, Third Auditor, vol. 2, E. 604, RG 217, NA. Other information on Belknap's feelings can be found in the *Observer and Reporter*, July 29, 1871.

Kentucky's new governor, Phillip H. Leslie, tried to soothe Bout-well's feelings in behind-the-scenes maneuvering. Working through a mutual acquaintance, A. G. Hodges, Leslie contacted Solicitor General Benjamin Bristow. Believing that only Bristow's "cooperation" could sway Boutwell, Leslie offered to meet Secretary Boutwell with Hodges to discuss the matter. According to Hodges, he and the governor would travel to Washington by secret and separate routes "so that our purpose shall not be suspected" by other parties. Hodges went on to inform Bristow that Kentucky would "compensate me handsomely for the part I may take in accomplishing what I honestly believe is due from the General government to our state."[51]

Hodges's efforts at mediation were fruitless. In early October 1871, Bristow, a man who prided himself as a civil service reformer, rejected the offer as an insult to both Secretary Boutwell and himself. Having failed to sway Bristow to intervene, Hodges could only note that if Kentucky had to go through Congress for its indemnification, "much of the money will have to be used in securing a sufficient number of votes to accomplish it."[52]

It is not known whether the other important figures in Kentucky's battle for indemnification thought the same way about buying votes. What is known, however, is that Fayette Hewitt and Governor Leslie continued to do everything within their power to avoid having to petition Congress for the reimbursement. Their next, and last, recourse was legal. Soon after the failure of Hodges to initiate back-room negotiations, Fayette Hewitt hired a law firm to represent the state formally in all proceedings. Although Hewitt left no explanation of the formulation of a legal strategy, he plainly desired the United States Supreme Court, in its exercise of original jurisdiction over the executive agencies, to issue a mandamus forcing Boutwell to deliver the pay warrants already signed by the acting secretary of the treasury. Quartermaster Hewitt and his lawyers reasoned simply that Boutwell had no legal standing to withhold something already signed by the delegated authority. Kentucky's legal team wanted also to get the Court to pass judgment on problems not directly related to the issuance of the mandamus. The record is not clear, but it is most

---

[51] Hodges quoted in A. G. Hodges to Bristow, September 7, 1871, Bristow Papers, LC. Hewitt quoted in "Quartermaster Report," December 31, 1875, Doc. #14, *Kentucky Documents, 1875*, vol. 2, 5–7.

[52] Hodges quoted in Hodges to Bristow, October 4, 1871, Bristow Papers, LC.

likely that Hewitt wanted to get the Court to overthrow Salmon Chase's restrictive interpretation of the indemnification act.[53]

In both parts of the legal strategy, the Supreme Court ruled against Kentucky in December 1871, choosing instead to stand by the treasury's arguments as briefed by Solicitor Bristow. On the primary issue, the Court refused the mandamus, writing that the acting secretary had signed the pay warrants conditionally. Although he may well have had the authority to issue the warrants without Boutwell's approval, the acting secretary clearly, and legally, attached a condition to his signature. On the issue of Chase's rules, the Court chose not to pass judgment, preferring to wait for a case that was more applicable. It was also a case that the high court never got. For the remainder of the century, most claims litigation that made its way into the federal court system concerned statutes of limitation and the liability of the government for the accrual of a state's bonded war debt.[54]

The setbacks notwithstanding, Fayette Hewitt remained determined to get Kentucky its reimbursement. In this task, Hewitt was the recipient of some simple political good fortune. In the most recent election cycle, Kentucky elected John White Stevenson senator. A former governor, and the man who had originally turned Kentucky's claim over to Hewitt, Stevenson was a popular politician who possessed none of the rough edges of his state's quartermaster. Where Hewitt tended to antagonize, White smoothed relations between adversaries. A solid Democrat, White also managed to maintain personal friendships with members of Kentucky's outcast Republican Party. This was particularly true with Benjamin Bristow, a man whose popularity and reputation had sunk to its lowest level with his role in defeating Kentucky before the Supreme Court. To one newspaper in Kentucky, Bristow was a "presumptious functionary," who had sold out the Bluegrass State for Republican favors and who had "failed to learn the important lesson that it is both graceful and politic to be self-respecting and sincere." John White Stevenson, in other words, was a Democrat whom many Kentuckians thought would have the most influence in Republican Washington, especially

---

[53] Assembly of the legal team is found in a power of attorney for George R. McKee and Joseph Casey, October 3, 1871, Kentucky State Claims, Box 33, E. 759, RG 217, NA.

[54] *Commonwealth v. Boutwell,* 13 Wallace 526 (1871). For another relevant federal court case, consult *United States v. New York,* 160 U.S. Reports 598 (1895).

with a Kentuckian like Bristow, who still desired political power in his native state.[55]

To a considerable extent, this conventional wisdom was correct. It also bore testament to a still-decentralized federal system that could continue to function administratively while bitter partisan rhetoric filled the pages of newspapers. Following his legal defeat in December, Hewitt was therefore content to let Stevenson initiate legislation in the Senate authorizing the treasury to examine the claims. After some early failures to introduce such legislation in January, Stevenson succeeded, and pushed to passage a bill in May that allowed the treasury to audit Kentucky's claims for militia "acting in concert" with United States forces. Attached was an authorization for $1 million that would cover all outstanding claims except about $300,000 worth. Shortly thereafter the bill passed the House with little lobbying activity on the part of Fayette Hewitt. Here, too, Kentucky and Hewitt were probably fortunate. Hewitt came down with an undisclosed illness and could not interject his caustic presence into the proceedings. He thus left the bill in the hands of Kentucky's House delegation and, more specifically, Representative Henry D. McHenry, who then shepherded the bill to passage with little partisan distraction.[56]

The political process that Quartermaster Hewitt so feared, and one that he later protested he had never feared, had worked. The ease with which Kentucky got its special reimbursement was remarkable, and there is little information available to explain its passage. The only apparent opposition to Stevenson's and McHenry's efforts came from Republican Senator George Edmunds of Vermont.[57]

Edmunds's efforts were hardly partisan, or sectional, in nature. Edmunds was loyal to the Republican Party, but it was a loyalty that he did not let interfere with a different loyalty to fiscal conservatism,

---

[55] For Stevenson's friendship with Bristow, examine, for example, Bristow to Stevenson, August 31, 1874, vol. 31, Stevenson Collection, LC. Quote found in *Observer and Reporter*, November 29, 1871. For Stevenson's reputed influence, see H. T. Stanton to Stevenson, December 23, 1873, vol. 30 in same.

[56] *Congressional Globe*, 42nd Cong., 2nd sess., 205, 425, 498, 2909, 3056, 3763, 3890, 4324, 4504; *United States Statutes at Large* 17 (1872): 346. For Hewitt's role, see "Quartermaster Report," January 7, 1873, Doc. #8, *Kentucky Documents, 1872*, vol. 2, 3–4.

[57] For Hewitt's claim that he always wanted to go first to Congress, see his official report dated January 7, 1873.

improved labor conditions, and the expansion of American markets overseas. He was, in short, the prototypical Republican "Half Breed" reformer of the era who saw his party not only as a foil to Democrats but as a device to create legislation. Nevertheless, Edmunds managed to mute his beliefs and retain friends within the opposing and more orthodox Stalwart faction of the party. Indeed, this ability to play both sides of the Republican Party is best illustrated by his contemporary title, "The Stalwart Sweetheart of the Reformers." Pertaining more to the claims, Edmunds was also a part of a group of senators and congressmen including John Sherman, James A. Garfield, George F. Hoar, and William B. Allison, who all focused intently upon budgetary matters. None of these men would ever be hurried into allowing spending legislation to come up for a vote without what they considered ample time to review the specifics of the bill. Of these men, Edmunds in particular rejoiced in scuttling what he thought were frivolous pieces of legislation. Edmunds reveled in this role so much that Senator Hoar encouraged him to run for the presidency in 1880 because "of the fun you would have vetoing bills." For Edmunds, state claims legislation provoked particular heartburn. Aside from what might be considered to be deep-seated misgivings about state claims legislation, Edmunds's parliamentary interference with most claims legislation can also be explained by him having little to lose in terms of legislative give and take. All of Vermont's claims had already been well provided for by wartime legislation and an additional act in 1866. Although an inveterate opponent of state claims and a champion of fiscal restraint, Edmunds sought, as late as 1875, to maneuver the private claims of his individual constituents ahead of any state claim.[58]

Edmunds's opposition to Stevenson's indemnification resembled

---

[58] Edmunds lacks a complete biography. For a treatment of his role as Half-Breed reformer, consult Richard E. Welch Jr., "George Edmunds of Vermont: Republican Half-Breed," *Vermont History* 36 (1968): 64–73. Matthew Josephson describes George Edmunds briefly in *The Politicos, 1865–1896* (New York: Harcourt, Brace and World, 1938), 179. Hoar quoted in H. Wayne Morgan, *From Hayes to McKinley: National Party Politics, 1877–1896* (Syracuse, N.Y.: Syracuse University Press, 1969), 73. Hewitt makes mention of Edmunds's opposition in the same report cited above. Edmunds's contrasting behavior toward state and private claims can be glimpsed in his arguments in a congressional debate of March 3, 1875. See *Congressional Globe*, 43rd Cong., 2nd sess., 2193–96. Edmunds's continuing interest in state claims can be noticed in Third Auditor to John Sherman, February 14, 1879, Letter Press Books, Third Auditor, vol. 6, 145, E. 618, RG 217, NA.

that of most Liberal Republican budget watchdogs. They were committed to slowing the legislative wheels long enough so that Congress had a chance to examine bills that might have been pushed through the committee system a bit too fast. Just as important, and in the case of Kentucky's bill, Edmunds was determined that some safeguards be applied to the auditing process. Logically, he turned for guidance to the first special congressional reimbursement bill, which had indemnified Missouri in 1866. Edmunds dropped his opposition, allowing Stevenson's bill to proceed through the Senate provided it carried with it amendments that spoke vaguely of the treasury auditing Kentucky's accounts in accordance with the principles of Missouri's bill.[59]

Senator Edmunds almost succeeded in stalling Kentucky's reimbursement. The third auditor initially balked at reviewing the state's claim when Fayette Hewitt arrived at his accounting offices in the fall to present Kentucky's expenses. According to the auditor, the principles referred to in the bill meant that the claim would have to be reviewed first by a special commission, just as Missouri had in 1867. If this indeed were the case, Kentucky would be delayed at least one more year. Fortunately for the state, and once again counter to Boutwell's image as a radical determined to punish Kentucky, the secretary of the treasury accepted the legal advice of a departmental solicitor who deemed the commission superfluous. Hewitt then presented his documentation and readily procured more than $525,000 in reimbursement before the end of the year.[60]

Over the next three years, Hewitt continued to have success in pushing claims before the treasury's accounting officers. By 1875 he had secured almost $200,000 for the state, leaving an estimated $261,000 worth of claims still outstanding. Despite the large amount still left, Kentucky had been successful, and no other official would receive as much credit for that success as Hewitt. Praise flowed from many directions as the governor, legislators, and newspapermen portrayed Hewitt as the man who had slain the recalcitrant monster of the federal government and gotten Kentucky its just dues.[61]

Much of the praise focused on what had become the uniqueness

[59] Hewitt's "Quartermaster Report," January 7, 1873, Doc. #8, *Kentucky Documents, 1872*, vol. 2, 3–4 has hints of this chain of events.

[60] Ibid., 4–13.

[61] Governor Leslie's Message, January 8, 1873, *Kentucky House Journal, 1873*, 13; *Daily Kentucky Yeoman*, February 3, 1873.

of Hewitt's position. To his supporters, Hewitt stood apart as a militia officer who handled virtually all of his state's intergovernmental operations. Yet other states, including Missouri, had experienced periods when their military hierarchies exclusively handled the claims, but those operations had not provided results on the same scale as Hewitt's. To at least some of his supporters, the quartermaster's activities represented the triumph of a simplified intergovernmental operation that had avoided the perceived inherent graft of state agents. With reference to one of Hewitt's victories, the *Daily Kentucky Yeoman* trumpeted that "the Sharks [state agents] in Washington said that it could not be gotten through without employing them [and] giving them half" of the reimbursement. While this type of praise for Hewitt tended to ignore the critical role of Senator Stevenson in the most recent rounds of reimbursement, the broad-based outpouring of gratitude correctly noted the pittance at which Kentucky had gotten the quartermaster's services. Hewitt received no commission, which contrasted significantly with the 33 percent received by the state agents of New Jersey and Maryland. Similarly, Kentucky had not paid a $10,000 gratuity, as New Jersey had done with its quartermaster. For some champions of Hewitt, the cost analysis was sufficiently striking to justify proposals of a cash award.[62]

However, befitting the circumstances that led Kentucky to fire Agent Pennebaker and employ Hewitt in the first place, the state's political and newspaper leaders were not all so generous. Concern for bureaucratic retrenchment had led, in part, to Hewitt's assumption of the claims duties, and beginning in 1873 it also led some members of the legislature to wonder just how much Hewitt had actually saved the state—if indeed he had saved the state any money at all. House members wondered enough to appoint a special commission to investigate the matter. After meeting for a short time in April 1873, the commission concluded that the state had invested wisely in the quartermaster. According to their computations, Hewitt's expenses and compensation had cost the state only 7 percent of the total amount of money he had gained for Kentucky through reimbursement. The commissioners compared this cost throughout the federal system and

---

[62] Governor Leslie's Message, January 8, 1873, *Kentucky House Journal, 1873,* 13; *Daily Kentucky Yeoman,* February 3, 1873. Quote taken from the February 18 edition of the *Yeoman.*

determined that all other states had exceeded at least 10 percent in compensation.[63]

To the members of the commission and, by extension, the legislature, the significance of the investigation lay in the vindication of an administrative exercise that aimed to avoid unnecessary expenditures and the creation of an unresponsive bureaucracy. Although the commission used sketchy information and overestimated other states' administrative costs, including Missouri's, its conclusions were generally correct. Hewitt had been remarkably efficient, and Kentucky had managed just fine without a full-time agent. But perhaps more importantly, the commission's investigation highlighted the fact that Kentucky's claims operation and its broader relationship with the United States were in a transitional phase.

In some ways, this transition in the early 1870s would be marked by age-old claims frustrations. Very simply, Kentucky's leaders would never accustom themselves to Chase's rules and Washington's adherence to precedent. As late as 1875, Hewitt still fulminated that the treasury regarded Chase's rules "as being superior to the law itself. . . ."[64]

Consequently, the state mounted charge after charge to revise the regulations. In one example, this effort challenged the very idea that an executive department could issue interpretive rules for a congressional enactment. The challenge was premature and never evolved to actual litigation within the court system. Instead, Kentucky tried to bluff the treasury into relaxing its standards. But that was to no avail. Here Kentucky ran into one of its more formidable enemies, Benjamin H. Bristow, who was also the newly installed secretary of the treasury. Relying heavily upon the research of the treasury solicitor and citing legal precedents ranging from Lord Coke to Roger B. Taney, Bristow snuffed out the notion that executive officials could not interpret legislative enactments.[65]

In another example of the state's attack upon Chase's rules, Quartermaster Hewitt attempted to enlist members of the War Department as allies against a treasury that had in recent years muscled

---

[63] *Daily Kentucky Yeoman,* April 19, 1873.

[64] "Quartermaster Report," December 31, 1875, Doc. #14, *Kentucky Documents, 1875,* vol. 2, 6.

[65] Actions with Bristow are covered in the report of agents Pike and Johnson, July 24, 1875, Governor's Papers, Thomas McCreary, Box 1, F. 2, 1–14, KSA.

the army out of the review process. Here, too, Kentucky met little success. Secretary of War Belknap was in the midst of a fraud and corruption scandal and was apparently too busy, or preoccupied, to join Kentucky's efforts in the summer of 1875. The matter thus fell into the hands of Adjutant General E. D. Townsend, who then proclaimed that "this office, by its experience, from day to day, has become fixed in the view that the public interest demands the positive and rigid adherence to the regulations. . . ." To depart from precedent would defeat "the healthful checks [that] protect the public interest."[66]

Although a longtime staff officer with his tenure as adjutant general dating to the Civil War, Townsend engaged in little territorial protection of administrative responsibilities. Townsend's willingness to cede much of the War Department's role in state claims was properly couched in the language of fiscal restraint and precedent, but the adjutant could afford to be acquiescent. By the 1870s the War Department still struggled under an avalanche of war-related claims that individual citizens had filed against the army. State claims would not be necessary to accomplish any type of administrative empire building, or maintenance, in the War Department.

The obstacle of Chase's rules remained a feature of Kentucky's claims operation well into the 1870s. Nevertheless, the nature of that operation began also to show signs of change. First among these changes was what might be considered the beginnings of interstate cooperation that Kentucky, and other states, had heretofore ignored. Ironically, some of the early hints of this cooperation occurred in the legislature's investigation of the cost-effectiveness of its reliance upon Fayette Hewitt. The investigation was hardly systematic. The committee lacked sufficient information to know that other states, including Missouri and Kansas, had also received reimbursement at a cost of less than 10 percent of their total claims. But more important, the legislature had demonstrated an interest in the actual methods and claims of other states. By 1875, Hewitt himself was no longer oblivious to the problems of other states. He was also willing to acknowledge officially for the first time that they experienced the same administrative difficulties as Kentucky. After meeting with a number

---

[66] Townsend quoted in "Quartermaster Report," February 12, 1873, Doc. #14, *Kentucky Documents, 1873*, vol. 1, 20, 21.

of other state agents in Washington that fall, Hewitt finally concluded that it would be best for Kentucky to "make common cause in seeking from Congress the necessary relief."[67]

While Kentucky therefore displayed some interest in the possibilities of broader interstate cooperation in the early 1870s, that cooperation would be restricted. During this time, Hewitt limited his "common cause" to long-standing issues that affected all states with outstanding claims. Foremost among these issues were Chase's rules, which stood between most states and final reimbursement. Hewitt was decidedly less active on the issue of having the federal government assume Kentucky's interest on its war debt, which by that time still exceeded $60,000 per year. Although Hewitt was generally less energetic than a number of state agents in crafting legislation and lobbying before Congress, his inactivity on this issue was a simple function of being consumed with his crusade against Boutwell. When New York and Ohio started to beat the drums of interest reimbursement in the fall of 1871, Hewitt displayed little enthusiasm for the struggle that would then take place in Congress concerning authorizing legislation. After informing the governor that the proposed legislation had the possibility of reimbursing Kentucky more than $750,000, Hewitt turned matter of factly to preparing Kentucky's standard claim for its submission before the June 1872 deadline. Absent any other information or communication from Hewitt, the state's congressional delegation remained quiet during the subsequent battle for a bill that would reimburse the state's interest payments.[68]

Of the many controversies over state war claims in the postbellum period, the debate over interest became the most protracted. It was also, in some ways, the most telling explanation of congressional attitudes toward the appropriation of money to the states. At the heart of the debate in 1871 was legislation proposed by Senator Oliver P. Morton of Indiana that would reimburse all states for any interest incurred on bonds issued to pay for war costs. Unpopular from the beginning, Morton's legislation gained little momentum after its initial proposal. Part of the problem was Morton's creation of a bill that

---

[67] "Quartermaster Report," December 31, 1875, Doc. #14, *Kentucky Documents, 1875*, vol. 2, 7.

[68] "Quartermaster Report," January 2, 1871, Doc. #6, *Kentucky Documents, 1870*, 5–9; Governor Stevenson's message, January 5, 1871, *Kentucky House Journal, 1871*, 13–14.

applied only to bonded interest, which was the chief concern of Indiana. Despite language that encompassed all states, Morton had avoided mention of a variety of interest types and debt-servicing costs that concerned other states. Some delegations amended the bill to cover such costs, but for some important states, such as New York, the bill was too imperfect to receive their support.[69]

Aside from this difficulty, Morton's bill ran into a storm of opposition. In the debates that followed, the senators made little mention of either Chase's infamous rules or the fact that Indiana did indeed continue to accumulate war-related expenses. Instead, the several antagonists used the bill as a backdrop for a discussion that contained two of the more traditional elements of a claims debate. On the one hand, there was a complex discussion of the equitable obligations of government. On the other hand, a number of senators concentrated on the evil consequences of establishing a precedent that would throw the door of the treasury wide open.

In the abstract, the debate revealed the fluidity of the definition of equity. For Oliver P. Morton, equity was a simple concept. The government had an obligation that, although clearly outside the limits of relevant statutes, was just as clearly a matter of justice. Indiana and other states had spilled precious blood and treasure for the Union, and it seemed only fitting that the Union bear the cost. According to Morton, there was no doubt that "this is a debt due the States just as honestly as the money borrowed from individuals upon bonds. . . ."[70]

Morton's conception of equity was nothing new. Not only had the idea of equity appeared regularly in most arguments favoring special claims legislation, but the concept embodied a concrete purpose of Anglo-Saxon justice that grew up alongside the more familiar common and statute laws. After independence, while some states abolished separate courts of equity, others continued the English practice of establishing separate courts of equity, and still others incorporated equity courts into the common-law courts. The latter hybrid existed also in the federal government after Congress rolled courts of equity into the federal common-law courts. But what is most important is the fact that no matter the form, the judiciary, at either the state or

---

[69] The legislative history of this bill is in *Congressional Globe*, 41st Cong., 1st sess., 29; 41st Cong., 2nd sess., 1076; 41st Cong., 3rd sess., 115, 509, 549–53, 599.

[70] Morton quoted in *Congressional Globe*, 41st Cong., 3rd sess., 549.

national level, never became noted for its dispensation of equity justice until at least *Brown v. Board of Education* in 1954. Though legal and constitutional historians have noted this point either in argument or in general avoidance of the topic, they have not stressed that equity remained a viable concept administered outside the judiciary. For most of the nineteenth century, legislative bodies handled and dispensed the majority of equity cases.[71]

All of this certainly applied to federalism where matters of equity ultimately rested in the hands of Congress. In general, the judiciary in the nineteenth century rarely intervened in intergovernmental operations. In matters of equity involving the states and the federal government, the court system was even more prone to let the political system handle petitions for compensation. Precedents, especially in state war claims, thus accumulated rapidly, allowing Congress and the executive departments final disposition over matters. As has been noted repeatedly, Congress was then loath to surrender any such precedent involving claims to the judiciary. Even in the final decades of the nineteenth century, as Congress broadened the jurisdiction of the court of claims it made sure that final adjudication of war claims remained with either of the elected branches of government. The Bowman Act of 1883 and the Tucker Act of 1889 simply reinforced the rule that the decisions of the court of claims were only advisory, pending final approval of Congress. Moreover, the Tucker Act went even further when it barred the court from hearing any case related to war claims.[72]

Oliver Morton thus possessed the proper forum to argue for justice through equity, but his comments fell on deaf ears. For several senators, the concept of equity was a double-edged sword. To them, the problem was less one of the government assuming responsibilities for war-related expenses than one of equality in taxation. Where, in

---

[71] Lord Bryce discusses the development of equity courts in his *The American Commonwealth*, 1:480–81. For more detailed information on the constitutional development of equity, see Peter C. Hoffer, *The Law's Conscience: Equitable Constitutionalism in America* (Chapel Hill: University of North Carolina Press, 1990), 47–137. Lawrence M. Friedman, *A History of American Law* (New York: Simon and Schuster, 1973), and Kermit Hall, *The Magic Mirror: Law in American History* (New York: Oxford University Press, 1989), the two most recent and important general histories of law in the United States, generally skirt the issue of equity.

[72] A discussion of the Bowman and Tucker Acts can be found in *United States v. New York*, 160 U.S. Reports 598 (1895): 606–13.

other words, was the equity for states that had chosen to pay for the war by increasing taxes rather than issuing bonds that were often discounted more than 10 percent? The most articulate spokesman for this position was William Buckingham. Having served as governor of Connecticut throughout the war, Buckingham stressed that states such as Connecticut had repeatedly made the tough, yet proper, choice to tax. "Suppose [an] adjoining state," Buckingham argued, "has taxed its citizens and paid all its war debt. What propriety, what justice is there in imposing an additional tax upon that adjoining state to pay the present indebtedness of the one by its side?" Justin Morrill of Vermont seconded Buckingham when he asked why a state that taxed and maintained its credit should be liable for a state that "has been laggard in voting taxes."[73]

Thus almost isolated in his support for the bill, Morton rejected the applicability of Buckingham's and Morrill's use of equity. In an impassioned speech during a debate on January 20, 1872, Morton exclaimed that "this is not a question of equality of taxation among the states; but it is a question of contract, of strongly implied contract. A question of absolute justice." The United States, he asserted, had "sacred obligations" and "cannot deal with the states upon technical principles of law."[74]

The difficulty of Morton's position was magnified by the inescapable fact that few legislators in 1871 wanted to pass a broad enactment that might burden the treasury—no matter how equitable the claim as understood by Morton. Both Roscoe Conkling of New York and Finance Committee chairman John Sherman of Illinois injected powerful voices in opposition along these lines. The actions of Sherman and Conkling are significant for reasons other than their elemental concern for the integrity of the treasury. In Sherman's case, his position makes perfect sense. A decision to shield the treasury was in keeping with his history of speaking often about the utility of legislation, sound money, and tight congressional control over the budget. As a leading member of the emerging liberal faction of the Republican Party, Sherman also reflected the cautious fiscal voices of men such as George Edmunds, who prided himself in delaying state

---

[73] Buckingham and Morrill quoted in *Congressional Globe*, 41st Cong., 3rd sess., 551.

[74] Buckingham quoted in ibid., 624.

claims legislation. Sherman ultimately channeled Morton's legislation away from the standard destination of the Military Affairs Committee and into his own Finance Committee. Sherman then quickly killed the measure, although he did make vague guarantees of submitting legislation that offered interest indemnification on a state-by-state basis.[75]

But it is with Conkling that one can get a sense of just how deeply the idea of fiscal retrenchment had become established in the early Gilded Age. At first glance, Conkling's opposition to the interest bill is curious. Most obviously, Conkling had much to gain by its passage. His own state, New York, had accumulated interest-related debts that Morton's bill would both directly benefit and indirectly set precedents for more general legislation that could liquidate the state's debt. Just as curious, Conkling's opposition to Morton came at a time when both men were becoming tight allies, and prominent leaders, in the Stalwart faction of the Republican Party. However, regardless of these pulls of state- and self-interest, Conkling stayed well within the larger fiscal culture of the period. He would stand as a forthright defender of the integrity of the public treasury. Conkling then turned his back on his friend and ally, Oliver Morton, and dismissed the interest legislation as an undisguised "application for charity."[76]

As Indiana's chance for interest indemnification slipped away in 1871, so too did Kentucky's. Quartermaster Hewitt's awakening sense that Kentucky was not the only state with legitimate claims difficulties had not, at that time, enabled him to see past his most pressing problem. While Morton carried on his lonely crusade in the Senate, Hewitt remained fixated on the necessity of getting Kentucky's largest claim through the treasury before the statute of limitations expired. Despite Hewitt's single-minded determination over the next few years, he siphoned ever smaller amounts of money into

[75] For Sherman's role and statement of principles, see ibid., 625. Theodore Burton reveals the essence of Sherman's political and fiscal beliefs in his *John Sherman* (New York: Houghton, Mifflin and Co., 1906), 224–25. Final disposition of the bill is noted in *Congressional Globe*, 41st Cong., 3rd sess., 664–65, 689.

[76] Josephson, *The Politicos*, 141–70 covers the period's Republican factional divides and their importance to the operation of national politics. Further mention of Conkling within factional politics is made in John M. Dobson, *Politics in the Gilded Age: A New Perspective on Reform* (New York: Praeger Publishers, 1972), 23, 33, 41. Conkling quoted in *Congressional Globe*, 41st Cong., 3rd sess., 630.

Kentucky. He also lost his health. As claims money became more difficult to get, the ability of Hewitt to concentrate exclusively on the claims evaporated. By the end of the summer of 1875, other duties intruded upon the quartermaster. Ten years detached from the Civil War and the more recent threats of federal imposition of martial law, Kentucky had finally reorganized and revitalized its militia. In accordance a state militia act passed in 1873, the legislature created new companies and outfitted them with the most modern breech-loading rifles available. As quartermaster general, Hewitt had to monitor this equipment modernization and evaluate the training of the units. Perhaps most revealing, for the first time in eight years of service, Quartermaster Hewitt had to accompany the state militia in its field-training exercises. The following year, Hewitt resigned, suffering from exhaustion.[77]

The departure of Fayette Hewitt symbolized the changing nature of both Kentucky's struggle for claims and its broader relationship with the United States. For the remainder of the century, there would be fewer and fewer war expenses to claim. Disputes, though frequently contentious, remained confined either to familiar squabbles over Chase's rules or to increasingly arcane controversies over the meaning of the government's 1872 reimbursement legislation. According to the new quartermaster general, Joseph P. Nuckols, the art of getting reimbursement had become more complicated than the "prosecution of an old Chancery suit. . . ." Echoing the frustrations of his predecessor and countless other state agents and quartermasters, the onetime Confederate colonel concluded sadly that "states and governments cannot be hurried."[78]

Perhaps the most noteworthy dispute of the period concerned the state's attempt to gain indemnification for its interest payments on

---

[77] For the militia reorganization and Hewitt's duties, examine the "Quartermaster Report," December 31, 1875, Doc. #14, *Kentucky Documents, 1875*, vol. 2, 5. A brief note on his post-quartermaster activities is contained in Perrin, *Kentucky: A History of the State*, 744.

[78] Governor McCreary's message, January 1, 1878, *Kentucky House Journal, 1877–1878*, 37–38. Nuckols appointment noted in *Tri-Weekly Kentucky Yeoman*, April 8, 1876. Continuing frustration with Chase's rules and the problems with the claims legislation of 1872 are discussed in the quartermaster's report, December 31, 1877, Doc. #11, *Kentucky Documents, 1877*, 6–11. Nuckols quote found in "Adjutant General's Report," February 20, 1880, Doc. #1, *Kentucky Documents, 1880*, 12–13. Biographical information on Nuckols can be found in *The Biographical Encyclopedia of Kentucky* (Cincinnati: J. M. Armstrong and Co., 1878), 588.

the war debt. In 1879, Kentucky joined with three other states—Connecticut, New York, and Illinois—to try to push generic legislation through Congress that would allow the reimbursement of interest. Of the total claim of $2.2 million, Kentucky's share of $973,301 was by far the largest. Like that by Oliver P. Morton in 1871, this attempt at interest indemnification failed, attracting little attention in Kentucky. Indeed, there is only small mention of the effort in any of the official state reports. More telling yet, and for the first time since 1864, war claims merited no mention in the governor's annual message.[79]

Aside from the fact that this episode demonstrated the degree to which interest reimbursement now dominated the state indemnification effort, the particulars of the legislation also help reveal why an interest bill never passed Congress in the nineteenth century. No one, including Kentucky's agents and its military officials, could tell exactly how much the state had expended in interest payments. In 1879, Joseph Nuckols simply calculated a charge of 6 percent on all claims from the time of their initial presentation in Washington. There should be no wonder that Congress recoiled from serious consideration of the legislation.[80]

While controversies with the war claims surfaced occasionally during the next two decades, the claims were clearly on the decline as a politically significant issue. In this fashion, they served as a barometer of Kentucky's more general relations with Washington. In the first few years following the war, claims issues—or more precisely, claims difficulties—reflected the state's contentious dealings with the federal government. As the 1870s and charges of "Grantism" faded from view, so too did Kentucky's openly hostile attitude toward the government. There can be no doubt that war-related tensions often bubbled over in the last two decades of the century, especially during elections when both Republicans and Democrats waved their respective versions of the "bloody shirt." But the partisan nature of the electoral battles no longer stirred administrative tensions. The passage of time—and the election of Democrat Grover Cleveland as

---

[79] Third Auditor to Representative Phil Thompson, December 16, 1879, Letter Press Book, Third Auditor, vol. 6, 291–293, E. 618, RG 217, NA.

[80] "Adjutant General's Report," February 20, 1880, Doc. #1, *Kentucky Documents, 1880*, 11–12.

president in 1884—helped defuse most of Kentucky's lingering anxieties about its place in the Union.

As the state's claims receded even further into the political background, the responsibility for all of Kentucky's outstanding claims would no longer be the sole concern of the quartermaster general. This change reflected, in equal parts, the diminishing importance of the claims and the simple fact that the Kentucky quartermaster had acquired new duties, including those of the adjutant general. Although the quartermaster never fully relinquished his involvement, the most prominent figures in the processing of claims became a shifting mix of lawyers and professional claims agents. In keeping with the patterns of the claims industry as it had developed after the Civil War, these men resided in Washington and represented a variety of states and individuals. In the middle and late 1870s, Kentucky relied upon its general attorneys working in Washington, Albert Pike and Robert Johnson, while throughout the 1880s and until 1892 the state placed its claims with agent Theodore Pettengill.[81]

An efficient claims representative, Pettengill embodied the professional claims agent. Indeed, he embodied the typical civil servant of the period, serving first in government agencies and then pursing what political sociologist Theda Skocpol has described as "careers predominately anchored outside of governments. . . ." For several years, Theodore Pettengill had worked in the third auditor's office as its chief clerk of state war claims. He then parlayed that experience, and the attendant connections, into a thriving private practice as a claims agent. By the time he came to represent Kentucky's interests, he also handled the affairs of Maryland and Michigan. There was also

---

[81] Continuing proof of the activities of the militia hierarchy can be found in various memos accompanying abstracts of Kentucky's claims in 1889 contained in Kentucky State Claims, Box 31, E. 759, RG 217, NA, and in "Adjutant General's Report," December 2, 1889, Document #17, *Kentucky Documents, 1889*, 10. Information on agents and their activities in Pike and Johnson to Governor McCreary, September 10, 1875, Governor's Papers, McCreary, Box 1, F. 2, KSA. Pettengill appears in Pettengill to Sigourney Butler (second comptroller), December 30, 1887, and Pettengill to William J. Stone (congressmen), July 5, 1888, Kentucky State Claims, Box 33, Kentucky State Claims, E. 759, RG 217, NA. Examples of agents representing multiple states include John Trimble and Weston Flint. Trimble served Connecticut and Vermont, while Flint handled the claims of Ohio, Michigan, and New York. See printed circular entitled "Office of Weston Flint" in Lewis V. Bogy Papers, 1866, MHS.

some irony in Pettengill's service as Kentucky's agent. For years, he had been the first person in the third auditor's office to disapprove many of the state's claims.[82]

As Kentucky's struggle for claims reimbursement faded in the late nineteenth century, there are at least two other points to note. First, the transfer of the claims to a professional, and interconnected, claims industry in Washington also signaled a greater degree of interstate cooperation. This manifested itself not only in a general awareness of other states' claims activities but also in the creation of legislation that, if not completely successful, did tie the interests of several states together. A second item to note is that for all its interstate cooperation, the new era in claims did not usher in a new era of actual reimbursement. Although many states had created effective methods for processing claims, and Kentucky had done so both under Fayette Hewitt and later under Theodore Pettengill, successful indemnification depended ultimately upon the government's application of existing precedents. Unfortunately for several states, including Kentucky, the administrative and legislative adherence to claims precedents did not change until 1902. Congress then passed the Dash Act, authorizing the reimbursement of interest claims. The Dash Act thus paved the way for Kentucky to get $661,005 in interest claims.[83]

Nevertheless, the precedent surrounding Chase's rules stood as the dominant feature of the claims process. Throughout the nineteenth century, and indeed even in the adjudication of interest claims

---

[82] Theda Skocpol, "The Origins of Social Policy in the United States: A Polity-Centered Analysis," in *The Dynamics of American Politics: Approaches and Interpretations*, eds. Lawrence C. Dodd and Calvin Jillson (Boulder, Colo.: Westview Press, 1994), 194. Pettengill to Sigourney Butler (second comptroller), December 30, 1887, and Pettengill to William J. Stone (congressmen), July 5, 1888, Kentucky State Claims, Box 33, Kentucky State Claims, E. 759, RG 217, NA.

[83] Evidence of increasing cooperation can be seen in different areas. See Quartermaster Nuckols's calculation in 1877 that the northern states would join Kentucky in trying to revise Chase's rules. This can be found in "Quartermaster Report," December 31, 1877, Doc. #11, *Kentucky Documents, 1877*, vol. 2, 6–11. Further evidence of this cooperation exists in February 1878, when Kentucky's legislature and governor memorialized Congress requesting reimbursement not only for itself but for other states as well. See *Congressional Record*, 45th Cong., 2nd sess., 750. Intergovernmental cooperation can be glimpsed in the multistate interest legislation proposed in 1879. One other example occurred in 1893 when the state agents of Ohio, Kentucky, New York, and Pennsylvania petitioned the secretary of the treasury to modify Chase's rules. Third Auditor to Secretary of the Treasury, December 29 (?), 1893, Letter Press Books, Third Auditor, vol. 14, 159, E. 618, RG 217, NA.

under the Dash Act, the language and decisions of governing officials remained tied to Chase's rules. In 1877, John Sherman, then having risen to secretary of the treasury, declined to modify the rules because of their sixteen years of faithful use. Nine years later in 1886, the solicitor of the treasury concluded that the "rules, which were prescribed almost contemporaneously with the [original July 27, 1861 indemnification] Act . . . and have been followed for so many years, and which are consistent with the terms of the Act, should not now be changed. . . ." Similarly, in 1893, Secretary of the Treasury Charles Foster accepted the advice of an assistant secretary that, although the rules were certainly not "equitable," thirty years of precedent should not be ignored.[84]

During its most controversial moments, Kentucky's often quixotic pursuit of indemnification had both recognized and ignored these circumstances. On the one hand, the state had always noted the rigidity, and the alleged injustice, of Chase's rules. But, on the other hand, until the mid-1870s Kentucky had also always perceived that the government had applied those rules exclusively to the Bluegrass State. Sectional and partisan bias, which so colored Kentucky's larger relationship with Washington, could never be divorced from the claims. It was only the passage of time that allowed Kentuckians to see that Washington had applied its indifference evenly throughout the federal system.

---

[84] Kentucky's reimbursement noted in C. C. Calhoun (state agent) to "accounting officers," June 10, 1902, Kentucky State Claims, Box 34, E. 759, RG 217, NA. Sherman's action noted, and Assistant Secretary Lambertson quoted, in Lambertson to Charles Foster, February 7, 1893, Letter Press Books, vol. 14, 159–167, E. 618, RG 217, NA. Solicitor quoted in S. McCue to Third Auditor, July 21, 1886, Kentucky State Claims, Box 33, E. 759, RG 217, NA.

4

Kansas and Intergovernmental Operations in the Newly Created State

TO THIS POINT, much of what has been described as defining nineteenth-century intergovernmental operations has been the ad hoc efforts of states trying to penetrate a fairly rigid national bureaucracy controlled by both precedent and the popular clamor for retrenchment. An additional characteristic of this system has been the extent to which local issues helped shape an individual state's efforts to crack that national bureaucracy. Within these general parameters, Kansas was no different from any other state. But, at the same time, the experience of Kansas offers a reminder that the states had not developed their administrative capabilities equally. Even in an era of demonstrably limited government, Kansas stood apart because of its almost nonexistent bureaucratic apparatus. It was against this administrative condition that a variety of local issues interacted to shape Kansas' hunt for reimbursement.

Observers of American government have long sensed that structural differences existed in the development of state governments. However, aside from contemporary observers, and as stressed by Ballard Campbell in 1976, few historians have really documented those differences. Within this historiographical context, the limited scope of governing institutions in Kansas at the end of the Civil War cannot be exaggerated. Indeed, when newly elected governor Samuel J. Crawford took office on January 9, 1865, he later noted that "we had nothing with which to set up housekeeping, except the State Seal, a lease on some leaky buildings, and quite an assortment of bills payable." It is also important to note that during those same early weeks of his administration, Crawford saw little need to have any of the above situations repaired, altered, or eliminated. His most prominent fiscal recommendation in 1865 was that the legislature practice "retrenchment where it may be made without prejudice; and a rigid economy in all appropriations."[1]

The comparative weakness of public institutions in the state could be attributed to the war itself. Carved out of the hotly disputed Kansas-Nebraska Territory in January 1861, Kansas had not yet known a moment of peace. Born in the shadow of war, the state had little chance to develop practices and assume responsibilities that other states had spent most of the nineteenth century acquiring. Strapped for cash and credit, the state had to postpone all spending and construction not directly related to the war. Consequently, when Governor Crawford surveyed the scope of his government, he found no capitol building, no state asylum, no penitentiary, and, perhaps most important, no functional method of tax collection. Although the state's total debt of $462,390 in 1865 was small relative to both Missouri and Kentucky, Kansas' inability to collect revenue limited the state's fiscal options. In January 1865, over 35 percent of the state's total assessed tax remained uncollected. Things did not get better the next year when the percentage of uncollected tax skyrocketed to 47 percent. Little would change over the next ten years; in 1875 the state auditor complained that most of the state property tax "is never collected." For most of its early history, perhaps the most effective tax would remain the poll tax, levied at one dollar per head.[2]

That the war produced so little growth in state government is an

---

[1] Early discussion of differences between states, especially in their legislatures, can be found in Bryce, *The American Commonwealth*, 1:458–524, and Albert Shaw, "The American State Legislatures," *The Contemporary Review* 56 (1889): 555–73. Campbell's discussion can be found in his "The State Legislature in American History: A Review Essay," *Historical Methods Newsletter* 9 (1976): 186. Crawford quoted in Mark A. Plummer, *Frontier Governor: Samuel J. Crawford of Kansas* (Lawrence: University Press of Kansas, 1971), 43, and *Journal of the Senate of the State of Kansas, 1865*, 23 (hereafter cited as *Senate Journal*).

[2] Plummer, *Frontier Governor*, 43–44. Information on debt and taxes found in *Senate Journal, 1865*, 17–18. See also *Senate Journal, 1866*, 19. State auditor quoted in Daniel W. Wilder, *The Annals of Kansas, 1541–1885* (Topeka: Kansas Publishing House, 1886), 665. Some material on the nature of the state revenue system and the poll tax can be gleaned from John L. Madden, "The Financing of a New Territory: The Kansas Territory Tax Structure, 1854–1861," *Kansas Historical Quarterly* 35 (Summer 1969): 155–64, and Elbert J. Benton, "Taxation in Kansas," *Studies in State Taxation*, vol. 18, *Johns Hopkins University Studies in Historical and Political Science*, nos. 1, 2, 3, 4 (Baltimore: Johns Hopkins University Press, 1900). A comprehensive account of state finances can be found in James E. Boyle, "The Financial History of Kansas" (Ph.D. diss., University of Wisconsin, 1904), 33–64.

irony of the early political history of Kansas. Noted earlier in the case
of Missouri, the Civil War, like all nineteenth-century American
wars, produced an expansion of executive power. Wartime demands
generally created increased gubernatorial patronage in jobs, services,
and contracts. For the three wartime governors of Kansas there was
no such bonanza of political spoils. Significantly, this void of administrative activity had not been filled by the wartime legislatures. The
state house and senate possessed little patronage and passed few
laws. Indeed, when the legislature met for one month in 1865—an
abbreviated session even by the standards of the time—it passed into
law a small number of acts, the most important of which related to
bond issues, a state census, the incorporation of railroads, and the
settling of war claims.[3]

Whatever expansion of government and administrative authority
that took place during the war fell generally into the hands of the
state congressional delegation. Much of this governing culture originated with the physical isolation of Kansas and the calculated practices of the Lincoln administration. Originally noted by the historian
William B. Hesseltine, Lincoln displaced most state executives
throughout the war, while also expanding his own authority. In Kansas, this routine helped install Senator James H. Lane as the supreme
political ruler of the state. With Kansas far removed from the major
areas of operation, Lincoln readily entrusted the rabidly Republican
state to Senator Lane. Consequently, Lane's power knew few
bounds. Serving at one point as both senator and commissioned general officer, Lane controlled virtually the entire governing machine
of Kansas through political alliances and patronage. Lane's control of
patronage was almost absolute, including even that of the organized
militia, which had been the traditional spoils nest of any given state's
governor. With such a lock on the levers of power, Lane brushed
aside political rivals. By war's end, the senator had succeeded in forcing Kansas' first governor out of office and then engineering the election of the next two chief executives.[4]

The true measure of Lane's role in Kansas politics was that he
essentially limited the administrative function of the governor to that

---

[3] Legislative activities described in Wilder, *The Annals of Kansas,* 417.

[4] There are few studies of Lane. Comprehensive, though dated, is Wendell H.
Stephenson, *The Political Career of James H. Lane* (Topeka: Kansas State Printing
Plant, 1930).

of selling state bonds. Within a three-year period beginning in 1866, Governor Crawford personally negotiated the sale of eleven separate bond issues, most of which required out-of-state travel. Whenever Governor Crawford chose a more visible administrative role, he could be readily blocked by a legislature influenced more by the congressional delegation than gubernatorial power, as was the case when Crawford chose in 1865 to champion immigration into the state. In this case, Governor Crawford sought appropriations to pay for an agent to publicize the state and assist immigrants. The legislature balked, thinking public dollars would be wasted and the governor too eager for the patronage. Still determined to encourage immigration, Crawford spent much of 1865 personally writing a handsome, if unnoticed, brochure touting the wonders of the Sunflower State.[5]

Although the mentally unstable Senator Lane committed suicide in July 1866, the shape of Kansas' political and governing culture had been set for the early years of the Gilded Age. Various governors and their administrative apparatus remained largely inert compared to the power and force exhibited by the state's three-member congressional delegation. This distribution of power stood relatively unchanged until at least 1873. Then, the seemingly ever-present odor of political corruption in Kansas finally toppled Senator Samuel Pomeroy, Lane's successor as king of the state's government. Until that moment in 1873, and for many years following, the state's governing machine remained a minimal affair often paralyzed by political scandals, highly charged senatorial elections, and Indian wars.

Lacking money and thoroughly dependent upon the leadership of the congressional delegation, Kansas turned readily to ad hoc commissions, as it had during the territorial period, to take care of most matters related to claims. So often identified with the later Progressive Era, commissions were inexpensive and temporary—political virtues valued highly in the aftermath of the Civil War. Kansas' claims commissions performed neither the regulatory nor oversight functions that became synonymous with later agencies that monitored everything from railroads to dairy products, but they prefigured those same agencies in that they minimized bureaucratic growth and

---

[5] Wilder lists the various bond issues in *The Annals of Kansas*, 676. Immigration politics described in Plummer, *Frontier Governor*, 53–54.

cost. Manned in equal parts by experts, political cronies, and disinterested citizens, the various claims commissions in Kansas symbolized one aspect of state governance during the Gilded Age. Practical experiments in administration, these particular commissions labored mightily and produced mixed results.[6]

THE PRICE RAID AND EARLY CLAIMS CONFUSION

Given the size of the claims of Missouri and Kentucky, the claims of Kansas appear almost insignificant by comparison. At no time did Kansas possess a cumulative claim exceeding $2 million. Similarly, Kansas did not possess a set of expenses that had been accumulated uniformly throughout the war, as had Kentucky and Missouri. In contrast, Kansas acquired the overwhelming majority of its wartime costs in one raid that occurred in the fall of 1864.

All of this said, the claims of Kansas were no less complex than those of any other state. One example illustrates the point. At the outset of the war, the Sunflower State was among the earliest to petition the federal government for reimbursement when in April 1862 the congressional delegation presented the treasury with a small claim for $12,351. This claim, like so many others in the early stages of the war, met instant rejection because its documentation failed to meet treasury expectations. The state quartermaster general, George W. Collamore, took responsibility for the claim, hoping to acquire the information demanded by the treasury's clerks. Absent any real administrative staff or resources in the state capital at Topeka, Collamore carried the claim and all its attendant documentation with him to his home in Lawrence. While he was there, disaster struck. In August 1863 the Confederate raider William C. Quantrill thundered across the Kansas-Missouri border and attacked Lawrence. Both Collamore and most of the information pertaining to the state's claim were lost in this raid, the most destructive guerrilla action of the war. Collamore suffocated while seeking refuge in his backyard well. The

---

[6] The larger climate favoring retrenchment in the first half of the Gilded Age is covered in Keller, *Affairs of State*, 107–21. The fear of large bureaucratic structures and the substitution of commissions for bureaucracy during the 1880s is discussed in Campbell, *The Growth of American Government*, 20–21.

paperwork disappeared in a fiery inferno that was once the quarter-master's house.[7]

Lawrence provided a severe setback to a state desirous of recouping its war expenses quickly, but the episode was, in some ways, fortuitous. Kansas simply lacked documentation for its claim. The odds of the state ever being reimbursed its whole claim were small based upon the exacting requirements of Secretary Chase's rules. However, the tragedy of Lawrence allowed state leaders to persuade Congress to authorize the treasury, much against Secretary Chase's wishes, to accept copies of some records and the complete reconstruction of others. Based upon this evidence, Congress allowed the treasury to audit and approve sets of the claim in 1870 and 1878. Final payment, or closure, occurred in 1891.[8]

Nonetheless, at the end of the war Kansas devoted very little attention to these claims, no matter their bizarre circumstances. Instead, it sought indemnification for the much larger group of claims that had arisen out of Gen. Sterling Price's invasion of the state in 1864. That summer, Price and his army of 12,000 men struck north from Arkansas into Missouri, aiming to capture St. Louis. Defeated well south of the city at Pilot Knob, Price changed his direction and objective, moving westward along the Missouri River seeking supplies and recruits and trying to reclaim Missouri for the Confederacy. Heading for Kansas and hotly pursued by Union cavalry in his rear, Price ran into a hastily assembled collection of Union soldiers and Kansas militia commanded by Maj. Gen. Samuel Curtis in the vicinity of Kansas City, Missouri. A series of running battles at Lexington, Independence, the Little Blue River, and Westport ensued. After the final engagement at Mine Creek sixty miles south of Kansas City, the combined Union army had shattered Price's command. Price then fled south into Arkansas, thus effectively ending the war in Kansas. No substantial Confederate force ever threatened the state again.[9]

---

[7] Treasury Department, *Report of the Secretary of the Treasury, 1863*, 100; Treasury Department, *Report of the Secretary of the Treasury, 1871*, 150; John C. Nicholson, "Kansas' Account with United States," *Kansas Magazine* 2 (1909): 62; U.S. Congress, Senate Report, 38th Cong., 2nd sess., 1211, S. Doc. 113.

[8] Treasury Department, *Report of the Secretary of the Treasury, 1871*, 150; John C. Nicholson, "Kansas' Account with United States," *Kansas Magazine* 2 (1909): 62; U.S. Congress, Senate Report, 38th Cong., 2nd sess., 1211, S. Doc. 113; *Congressional Globe*, 41st Cong., 2nd sess., 3134, 3289, 4462.

[9] For standard accounts of Price's raid, see Jay Monaghan, *Civil War on the West-*

But even as the loyal citizens of Kansas and Missouri celebrated the defeat of Price, the effects of the raid were only beginning to be felt. For the only time during the war, the governor of Kansas had called forth the entire state militia. Governor Thomas Carney mobilized and placed under Curtis's command 12,612 militiamen. The militia served for eighteen days, whereupon they quickly disbanded once Price had been defeated. Yet this brief mobilization cost Kansas dearly. Besides the human toll of a few hundred casualties among the militia, the state incurred a cost of at least $500,000 in mobilizing, equipping, and paying its citizen-soldiers. The debt was particularly troublesome because cash-poor Kansas staggered under a budget deficit exceeding $126,000. Kansas also possessed small capability of floating a new bond issue without discounting the bonds at a considerable loss. Making matters worse, both the Confederate and Union armies had inflicted considerable property damage all along the Kansas-Missouri border as each side took whatever it needed in food, fuel, and transportation. Eastern Kansas was devastated. Anticipating the high cost of this raid, Governor Carney instructed all citizens to present claims for damages and services rendered to the militia's highest-ranking officer, Maj. Gen. George Dietzler, who would in turn adjust such claims "for payment by the general government." Absent any money to pay his militia, Carney dismissed them with only a promise of future pay once Washington reimbursed the state.[10]

Dietzler did not last long as the chief collection officer for the claims. In November 1864, just one month after the raid, both Dietzler and Carney lost their jobs in bitterly contested elections that were really a plebiscite on Senator Lane's ability to continue his control of state politics. Lane's slate of candidates triumphed easily. In the changeover of gubernatorial administrations that followed, the legislature preempted the newly installed governor, Samuel J. Crawford, in the early management of the claims.

In a one-month session otherwise notable for legislation that aimed

ern Border (Lincoln: University of Nebraska Press, 1955), 307–51; Albert Castel, *A Frontier State at War: Kansas 1861–1865* (Ithaca, N.Y.: Cornell University Press, 1958), 184–202; and Lumir Buresh, *October 25th and the Battle of Mine Creek* (Kansas City, Mo.: Lowell Press, 1977).

[10] Information on the financial condition of Kansas in 1864 can be found in *Senate Journal*, 17–18. Carney quoted in U.S. Congress, Senate Miscellaneous Document, 39th Cong., 1st sess., 1239, S. Doc. 90.

to encourage the planting of trees, the assembly shaped a general plan for gaining reimbursement that would not be superseded in the next twelve years. As a result, the legislature petitioned Congress to indemnify the citizens of Kansas who had suffered by "the acts of our own army" and who could not be provided for "under existing laws." Additionally, it created a commission to receive and audit the claims growing out of the Price raid. This commission would also receive those claims arising from the suppression of hostile Indians along the state's southern and western borders during the summer of 1864. While not substantial, these so-called "Indian" claims became irreversibly fused with the Price claims.[11]

Designed with an eye to frugality, the commission cost little. Composed of the secretary of state, adjutant general, attorney general, and two clerks, the panel consisted of men who were already on the state payroll. Predictably, the legislature determined also to keep the commission on a very short leash. Authorizing legislation was quite explicit as to the scope of activity and deadlines. The commission would have until January 1866 to audit four types of claims associated with the Price raid: services rendered; materials, supplies, and transportation furnished; damages sustained; and miscellaneous claims. Furthermore, the legislature instructed the commissioners to certify only those claims accompanied by some form of corroborative documentation. The owners of valid claims would then receive certificates indicating the type and amount of the approved claim. For those men seeking payment for services rendered, the commission would issue no certificates. The legislature believed that unit payrolls would serve as permanent proof of service. Once the commission had identified all valid claims, it would then forward to the state congressional delegation—through the governor—a detailed statement of the amounts owed to the citizens of the state. Following the plan set forth in the February petition to Congress, the Kansas delegation would then seek an appropriation for the claims.[12]

Hastily created, the indemnification strategy was fraught with problems. In one sense, the plan was sound in that it recognized the proper avenue for having the Price claims adjudicated. This recogni-

---

[11] U.S. Congress, Senate Miscellaneous Document, 38th Cong., 2nd sess., 1210, S. Doc. 32. Hereafter, both the Indian and Price raid sets of claims will be referred to as "Price raid" claims. *Laws of the State of Kansas, 1865,* 124–27.

[12] *Laws of the State of Kansas, 1865,* 124–27.

tion can be seen in the legislature's decision to direct its petition to Congress and not the treasury's third auditor. Evidently, the legislature realized that the Price raid claims did not fall under the limits of the federal act of July 27, 1861. Under Secretary Chase's rules for indemnification, the act covered only those expenses incurred by troops actually mustered into federal service. Because the Kansas militia had not been called out by either the president or his secretary of war, Kansas could not be reimbursed under Chase's interpretation of the July 27, 1861, indemnification act. The only form of redress for the state, as the legislature appears to have realized, was through a special congressional appropriation.[13]

Despite this apparent knowledge of the appropriate forum to present the state's claims, the legislature's plan for indemnification was far from perfect. In fact, it contained a number of weaknesses that caused confusion, fraud, and delay. The first such weakness pertained to the types of claims being pursued. Compared with the requests of other states, Kansas was certainly within the bounds of reason and precedent when it sought indemnification for claims relating to services, materials, supplies, and transportation. However, a problem arose when the legislature instructed the auditing commission to process claims for private-property damages.

By auditing claims for property damages, the legislature committed itself to something it had no realistic hope of achieving. Congress, fearing the ultimate cost of paying such expenses, had consistently displayed an unwillingness to allow any payments for private-property damages. Congress—and the Lincoln administration—believed that the Constitution did not obligate the federal government to cover these claims. Not finding any precedent, Congress then progressively codified the absence of liability for the federal government. In the July 27, 1861, indemnification act, Congress clearly excluded damages to private property from the list of expenses payable by the national government. Two years later in 1863, the treasury rejected Illinois' attempt to receive compensation for private-property damages. The next year, Congress removed this class of claims entirely from the jurisdiction of the United States Court of Claims. Early in 1865, the Kansas legislature and governor had failed

---

[13] U.S. Congress, Senate Executive Document, 51st Cong., 1st sess., 2679, S. Doc. 11.

to recognize that these types of claims would thus go nowhere in Washington.[14]

The gap in knowledge betrayed Kansas' administrative inexperience. It also suggested that the leaders of Kansas had either not learned any lessons from their recent territorial period or that they were a particularly stubborn lot. As early as February 1857, the territorial legislature of Kansas had somehow determined that Washington had unfairly abandoned free-soil settlers during their costly battle with proslavery immigrants. The territorial assembly then created a one-man commission to audit claims for all manner of property damage related to the struggle for "Bleeding Kansas." Asserting that Washington already subsidized proslavery Kansans with policy favoritism and sympathy, the assembly did not allow proslavery citizens to file claims. When this commission and a subsequent three-member body finally completed their audits in 1860, it concluded that the United States owed various Kansans in excess of $600,000. The claims were forwarded to Washington with the righteous endorsement that all the losses had resulted from the negligence of the national government in its failure to protect the people and their property as they were entitled by the Constitution. Two years later in 1862, Quartermaster General Collamore reiterated this charge when he proclaimed that "never did a Territory of the United States pass through its pupilage with so much neglect and abuse from the parent Government. . . ."[15]

Kansas' political leadership therefore possessed definite ideas on the pecuniary responsibilities of the United States. What Kansans regarded as their right during the territorial period remained firm in 1865. The passage of five years and Washington's repeated refusal to allow the territorial claims did nothing to alter the idea that Washington was responsible for individual property damages. Given this mindset, the possibility of confusion in the Price claims was im-

---

[14] *United States Statutes at Large* 12 (1861): 765–68; William A. Richardson, *History, Jurisdiction, and Practice of the Court of Claims,* 2nd ed. (Washington: Government Printing Office, 1885); "Government Claims," *American Law Review* 1 (1866): 657; Third Auditor to Chase, June 19, 1863, Letterbook, Third Auditor, vol. 1, 443–44, E. 617, RG 217, NA; Wiecek, "The Origins of the United States Court of Claims," 401.

[15] Details of the territorial claim can be found in John C. Nicholson, "Kansas' Account with United States," 61. See also Madden, "Financing of a New Territory," 163, and *Report of the Quartermaster General of Kansas,* 1862, 5.

mense, and the auditing commission did not help clarify the picture. Initially unaware of the weakness of claims for property damages, the commission processed those claims. Having then discovered, sometime during the summer of 1865, that Congress would not reimburse these claims, the commission deducted them from their final report to the congressional delegation. Inexplicably, or perhaps not willing to be the bearer of bad news, the commission also failed to inform the legislature of the situation. Making matters worse, subsequent state auditing commissions would repeat this pattern of auditing claims for property damages, while failing to forward them to Washington or report the situation in Topeka. Consequently, throughout the early stages of Kansas' attempt to gain indemnification, which lasted until at least 1872, literally thousands of claimants, and most of the state's political leadership, were under the mistaken impression that they would be reimbursed for property damages. False hopes and high expectations would be the order of the day.

Problems with the legislature's plan did not stop with private-property damages. The appointment of three important state officials was a political and budgetary necessity given the limited funds available and the popular demand for retrenchment. It was also a move that typified nineteenth-century commissions in that they usually were composed of other state officials. According to historian Lawrence Friedman, it was simply a situation of "new labors piled upon old officers." In the case of the new claims commission, the secretary of state, adjutant general, and attorney general were indeed overburdened with work even before the legislature assigned this additional duty. Upon becoming commissioners, these officers naturally delegated most of the massive amount of labor associated with processing the claims—an estimated $2 million worth by October 1865—to their two clerks. Such confidence was misplaced because, according to a legislative report issued in 1868, the clerks became involved in a scheme that eventually "forged and fabricated" a substantial, but unspecified, number of vouchers.[16]

As a consequence of handing the commission to otherwise occupied officials, there would be problems in meeting the legislature's demand for quick completion. The deadline of January 1866 forced

---

[16] *Journal of the Senate of the State of Kansas*, 1886, 328–29; Friedman, *A History of American Law*, 387.

the commission to compile a haphazard report before it had audited all claims and issued the appropriate certification. By the adjutant general's own estimation, $200,000 worth of certificates could still be issued to worthy claimants. But this situation did not prevent the commission from including the nonissue figure in their final conclusion that the United States owed Kansas $505,190. As already mentioned, this figure excluded the legislatively mandated claims for property damages, which amounted to over $91,000.[17]

Kansas' reliance upon commissions for the internal auditing of claims was, by itself, not different from that of other states. On occasion, every state used commissions to audit claims against their public treasuries. However, the difference between the commissions in these states and Kansas was significant. In the other states, the commissions forwarded their information directly to a responsible state-level official, whether it be the state agent or the adjutant general. This individual would then be primarily responsible for the coordination of the indemnification effort. Images of John B. Gray in Missouri and Fayette Hewitt in Kentucky come immediately to mind. In Kansas, the commission became a collection agency for the congressional delegation. The commission audited, allowed, and forwarded claims to the congressional delegation, which then operated as it pleased.

In Washington, the claims fell under the primary control and concern of the junior senator, Samuel Pomeroy. How exactly Pomeroy became the guardian angel of the state's claims is not known, but the situation was indicative of the personalities at work in the delegation. Though always laboring in the shadow of the more flamboyant Senator Lane, Pomeroy was an important politician in his own right. He was a self-proclaimed radical, and one who had served alongside Lane since statehood in 1861. From this position, Pomeroy established a multifaceted reputation. In one respect, he clearly stood as a champion of many of the moral crusades and reforms of the period, whether they concern temperance, orphans, or Sunday "Blue Laws." In Kansas, this posture led some to give him the derisive nickname "Pom the Pious." What drove some of this sneering about Pomeroy's moral rectitude was his association with corruption since the territorial period, an association Senator Lane noted in explaining why

---

[17] U.S. Congress, House Miscellaneous Document, 41st Cong., 1st sess., 1402, H. Doc. 6.

Pomeroy attempted so little to interfere with Lane's dominance of the state. According to Lane, Pomeroy would let Lane "make all the appointments, if he would only let Pomeroy make the money." Yet another part of Pomeroy's reputation pertained to his ability to root out money and subsidies for Kansas. Frequently labeled "Old Subsidy," Pomeroy was particularly adept at providing the necessary inducements to bring the railroads into the state.[18]

Pomeroy therefore emphasized the mundane tasks of office holding, all of which the flamboyant and controversial Senator Lane generally chose to ignore. By the beginning of 1866, the mundane tasks turned out to be most things not related to Reconstruction. Since the end of the war, Lane had taken prominent stands on all the raging national issues. The reauthorization of the Freedmen's Bureau, the Civil Rights Act, the ratification of the Fourteenth Amendment, and the actions of President Andrew Johnson all saw Lane figuring conspicuously, and controversially, in the concurrent debates. The all-consuming nature of Lane's role in these proceedings would become evident during the spring and summer of 1866. Lane determined that the moderate Johnson would triumph over a radically led Congress with his power and prestige enhanced. Lane wanted to ride those coattails. Chameleon-like, he changed his ideological bent from radical to moderate, publicly supporting Johnson down the line. Lane erred, and the switch alienated him quickly from a state that attacked anything related to "Johnsonism." The stress of these events could not have come at a worse time. Almost simultaneously, rumors spread implicating Lane in a bribery scheme connected with Indian contracts. In July, the combination of the two sets of problems launched Lane into a desperate depression. He then placed a pistol in his mouth and pulled the trigger.[19]

---

[18] Pomeroy remains a shadowy figure in Kansas history. Though a prominent figure from "Bleeding Kansas" and the Gilded Age, he lacks a published biography. A biting characterization can be found in Albert R. Kitzhaber, "*Götterdämerung* in Topeka: The Downfall of Senator Pomeroy," *Kansas Historical Quarterly* 18 (1950): 248–55. For a sympathetic portrait, examine Joseph G. Gambone, "Samuel C. Pomeroy and the Senatorial Election of 1861, Reconsidered," *Kansas Historical Quarterly* 37 (1971): 15–32. A judicious, but thin, examination is in Margaret L. Strobel's "A Political Life of Senator Samuel C. Pomeroy of Kansas" (master's thesis, Pennsylvania State University, 1962). Strobel devotes most attention to Pomeroy and subsidies. She makes no mention of his involvement with the claims. Lane quoted in the *Times and Conservative* (Leavenworth), January 25, 1870.

[19] Lane's radical apostasy and financial dealings are covered in Stephenson, *The Political Career of James H. Lane,* 149–59.

Given the preoccupation of Lane in 1865 and 1866, Samuel Pomeroy was thus in position, if by simple default, to work on the most ordinary of tasks facing any politician of the era: shepherding state war claims. In February 1866, Pomeroy got involved in the process when state Adjutant General T. J. Anderson brought the commission's report to Washington and placed it in the hands of the congressional delegation. Once Pomeroy introduced the appropriate legislation into the Senate, the quest for indemnification entered another, no less problematic phase. The claims became bogged down by the flaws in the commission's audits and a general uncertainty of how exactly to secure indemnification. The problem with the audits revealed itself when Senator Pomeroy presented the state's claims for $505,190 in late February. As it turned out, the figure was inflated. Disregarding the fact that claims for damages had been deleted, the state auditing commission's report had not been final. Instead, what had been forwarded to Washington in compliance with the legislature's January 1866 deadline was, in reality, only an interim report. By November 1866, the commission had excised over $13,000 from the final tabulation. Between November and April 1867, at which time the commission released its true final report, another large downward revision had occurred. This time the commission shaved over $150,000 worth of claims, leaving a final audit of $342,145 owed the state. Perhaps the most interesting aspect of the revision was an internal juggle that took place among the claims. The commission reinstituted claims for damages while deleting all those for services rendered. Claims for the militia's pay had been removed in favor of prosecuting those claims for property damage—all without any legislative directive.[20]

Whether for good or evil, Congress never approved Pomeroy's attempted appropriation. At first, the bill traveled successfully through the maelstrom of the Senate's committee system with Pomeroy guiding it every step of the way. The Military Affairs Committee accepted

---

[20] "Adjutant General's Report," 1866, 5; U.S. Congress, Senate Miscellaneous Document, 39th Cong., 1st sess., 1239, S. Doc. 90. Evidence of the interim nature of the report can be found through an analysis of a table found in Wilder, *The Annals of Kansas*, 446. This should be compared with the documentation that accompanied Pomeroy's bill found in U.S. Congress, Senate Miscellaneous Document, 39th Cong., 1st sess., 1239, S. Doc. 90. The internal flip-flopping that occurs here can be seen in a comparison of the various tabulations available in the *Senate Journal, 1886*, 308–13. See also *Congressional Globe*, 39th cong., 1st sess., 979, 1844, 1879.

the validity of the commission's original audit of January 1866 regarding supplies and services rendered by the militia. Rejecting all other claims, the Senate passed legislation on April 11, 1866, authorizing the treasury to audit the claims and pay up to $259,474. This figure represented the commission's original estimation of costs for supplies furnished and services rendered. The Senate's Committee on Military Affairs denied governmental liability for all others. This brief moment of triumph was seen firsthand by Governor Crawford. For most of the spring he had been selling bonds in New York City. On the way back to the state, he stopped in Washington to discuss electoral politics with the congressional delegation. Though optimistic about the ultimate approval of the bill in the House, Crawford was enough of a realist to inform a friend back in Kansas that "nothing is certain in this detestable hole. . . ."[21]

The governor was correct to have reservations. All of Pomeroy's work went to naught. The bill was quickly transferred to the House, where it met the fate of most bills: it was tabled, never to be heard of again. The weight of other items on the legislative calendar certainly had something to do with the tabling. But more importantly, other information slowly dribbled out of the House revealing that the entire indemnification plan worked out by the legislature was missing a vital ingredient. One year later in January 1867, Governor Crawford reported that the legislation died because Kansas had, in fact, not assumed any of the costs of Price's raid. All the state had done was audit the claims of individuals and issue certificates stating that the bearer had a valid claim against the national government. For Crawford and the legislature, it was a revelation that "the Government regards the assumption of the debt by the State as a pre-requisite to any appropriation." It was a critical piece of knowledge that the political leadership of all other states had long possessed.[22]

The failure of this push for indemnification, when connected with the precipitous downward slide of the claims tabulation, prompted the Kansas legislature in February 1867 to reconsider the claims situation. It was not the ideal time to have a legislature reformulate what was essentially an executive branch administrative action. The first

[21] *Congressional Globe*, 39th Cong., 1st sess., 1879–1880. Crawford quoted in Plummer, *Frontier Governor*, 52.

[22] *Congressional Globe*, 39th Cong., 1st sess., 1879, 1893, 1921. "Kansas War Claims," 2. Crawford quoted in *Senate Journal, 1867*, 23.

three weeks of the session were given almost entirely to electoral politics. Both of the state's two senatorial seats were up for election, and a scramble for the seats ensued, during which time money and whiskey flowed liberally. In the end, Samuel Pomeroy retained his place, while Lane's vacated position went to the man whom Governor Crawford had appointed temporarily, Edmund G. Ross.[23]

When finished with this task, the legislature showed itself in no hurry to tackle a busy agenda that included consideration of the Fourteenth Amendment, female and black suffrage, and war claims. Instead, the Senate and House seemed in competition to show which body could display the most irreverent behavior while postponing the most legislative action. The House set the tone. When acting as a Committee of the Whole, members ridiculed an inexperienced chairman with what one newspaperman described as "crude and meaningless motions" designed simply to fluster the embarrassed lawmaker. As part of this exercise, members offered and brought to vote a number of resolutions on how to spell "whole." The Senate showed itself in no less of a playful mood when it offered a resolution to change the name of Representative Przybylowiz to that of Murphy. The House responded with equal zest by resolving to anglicize the name of Senator H. C. Haas to that of House Cat Rabbit. The atmosphere continued in the same vein a few days later when the Senate considered a bill that outlawed the throwing of paper balls within the chamber. Just how seriously the legislature took its business could be seen when allegations began to flow that the just-completed senatorial elections were fraught with vote buying. Soon after the creation of a special committee to investigate the charge, Representative J. R. Goodin put forth a resolution that the committee use the "great phrenologist O. S. Fowler to make an examination of the heads of the members of the House as the most speedy manner of determining" who bribed whom.[24]

Only by the last week of February did the assemblymen, according to one contemporary observer, "suddenly awaken to a realizing sense of the responsibilities resting upon their . . . shoulders." In a last-

---

[23] On the senatorial election of 1867, see Kyle S. Sinisi, "Politics on the Plains: Thomas Carney and the Pursuit of Office During the Gilded Age," *Heritage of the Great Plains* 25 (1992): 27–29, and Plummer, *Frontier Governor*, 101–4.

[24] This paragraph is based upon coverage of the legislature in the *Leavenworth Times*, February 9, 12, and 27, 1867.

minute flurry of activity that saw the House pass forty bills in one day, the legislature revised its war-claims policy. Reflecting a growing realization that the auditing process had been riddled with errors, the legislature acceded to Governor's Crawford's wish that it create a second commission of "disinterested" private citizens—appointed by the governor—to review and revise the work of the first commission. Another, and more significant, addition to policy concerned Congress' desire that the state actually assume war-related debts before receiving indemnification. The legislature's solution was to direct the new commission to issue military scrip, or state IOUs, to each citizen possessing a valid claim.[25]

While, in a technical sense, the issue of military scrip signified that the state had assumed the debt, in actuality nothing of the sort had happened. The state treasurer could redeem the military scrip with currency only when Congress provided Kansas with an indemnity. The legislature had just established its own intention of never actually paying for any of the costs associated with Price's raid. Newspapers took quick note of this, commenting, in one example, that the scrip was "of no benefit" without broader congressional legislation. The best explanation for issuance of the scrip went beyond the legislature's belief that the federal government should, on principle, pay the debt. Foremost, the state treasury was still far too weakened to afford making the initial payment to the claimants. Scrip had by that point in Kansas' history become a well-practiced method of paying bills. Indeed, the legislature paid itself in scrip.[26]

The second commission proceeded quickly and completed its work by the end of July 1867, at which time it invalidated over $100,000 worth of claims. The aggregate for the state—including claims for damages to property—then stood at $240,258. Beginning in late January 1868, the commission issued 61,524 pieces of scrip bearing 7 percent interest annually. Speaking in 1868, Governor Crawford accounted for the large fluctuations in the audits in different ways. Though he proclaimed that there was an "honest difference of opinion" between the two commissions, Crawford also admitted

---

[25] Crawford's recommendation found in *Senate Journal, 1867*, 23. Quote taken from the *Leavenworth Times*, February 19, 1867. See also the edition of February 22.

[26] *Laws of the State of Kansas, 1867*, 63–66; *Kansas Chief* (White Cloud), February 28, 1867.

that many cases of fraud had been uncovered. However it was explained, the second audit remained consistent with the first commission's eventual acceptance of private-property claims and the exclusion-of-service claims, although service claims now reappeared in a line entry separate from the main audit. The amount for services was also a figure conspicuously missing from later legislative and commission reports.[27]

Unfortunately for Crawford and the state, the second commission had not settled the claims problem. Not only did many citizens still doubt the veracity of the new tabulation—especially those who had had claims denied—but the whole claims situation had become a politically charged issue. Spurring this was the poor financial condition of many of the literally thousands of claimants. Aggrieved by either of the two commissions or the federal government's refusal to indemnify the state, claimants turned first to their elected officials. As a result, for the next few years pleas surged into the offices of most Kansas politicians demanding quick federal indemnification. The majority of claimants addressed their state public officials directly, but some enlisted outside aid to press their causes. Citizens turned to lawyers, court clerks, and neighborhood representatives who had proclaimed themselves claims agents. The actual legal function of these claims agents was ill defined if not totally nonexistent. No evidence survives to prove that they took any direct legal action other than to bombard elected officials with inquiries.[28]

The state's executive branch was not immune to the clamor for action. Both the governor and his adjutant general expressed some

[27] *Laws of the State of Kansas, 1867*, 63–66; *The Kansas Chief*, January 30, 1868. For figures produced by the second commission and Crawford's quote, see Wilder, *The Annals of Kansas*, 458. For the different reporting of claims for services rendered, see Wilder, *The Annals of Kansas*, 458; *Senate Journal, 1886*, 310; n.a., *Report of the Price Raid Commissioner* (Topeka: Kansas Publishing House, 1889), iii, hereafter cited as *Price Raid Commissioner*. Amount of scrip listed in *Kansas City Times*, October 4, 1948.

[28] Mrs. Samuel Reynolds to S. J. Crawford, October 31, 1867, Governor's Correspondence, S. J. Crawford, Kansas State Historical Society (KSHS), Topeka; William P. Higginbotham to Congressman Sidney Clarke, November 19, 1867, T. H. McGahey to Clarke, January 8, 1869, H. W. Cook to Clarke, January 14, 1868, Ira D. Bronson to Clarke, February 2, 1868, J. B. Wayant to Clarke, November 10, 1868, Nelson Griswold to Clarke, February 9, 1869, S. R. Anderson to Clarke, February 2, 1870, W. W. Climenson to Clarke, March 2, 1870, Sidney Clarke Collection, Carl Albert Research Center (CARC), University of Oklahoma, Norman.

degree of concern in their reports to the legislature requesting action. Beyond this, their early efforts to gain or organize reimbursement were sporadic at best. Certainly, some of the inertia came from the fact that they were dependent upon the leads of the congressional delegation, the legislature, and the various commissions. However, this by itself does not seem to explain the disengagement. Though there is scant information about the daily schedules of either the governor or adjutant, a reasonable explanation is that they, like Senator Lane before them, were distracted, if not consumed, by other events. Crawford, more than any other governor whom we have examined to this point, was heavily involved in a variety of partisan political crises. In 1866 it was the death of Lane and Crawford's controversial appointment of a successor. In 1867 it was the election of two United States senators and the governor's subsequent involvement in the campaign to grant female suffrage in the state. In 1868 there was the fallout from the failure of Senator Edmund G. Ross to vote for the conviction of President Andrew Johnson. Ross was a friend and ally of Crawford's, and the popular reaction in Kansas was favorable to neither man. Crawford's ties to Ross inevitably ruined the governor's planned attempt to supplant Sidney Clarke as the state's sole congressional representative that same year.

When Crawford did not have partisan fires to put out, he frequently found himself heavily involved in other matters. In early 1865 Crawford appears to have spent most of his energies fighting what he believed was the army's undercounting of state troops against Kansas' draft quota. Later that same year and extending through 1868, the governor engaged in a highly public crusade to modify certain treaties of the United States that disposed of Indian lands along the southern border of the state. Almost simultaneously, Crawford became the center of a corruption investigation over his ties with one railroad—the Union Pacific, Eastern Division. But in terms of simple distraction, none of these issues could have figured as prominently as did Indian depredations. Unlike Missouri or Kentucky, Kansas remained on the edge of one American frontier. It was a frontier that continually offered the threat of Indian uprisings. The rapid expansion of the railroads and the implementation of the Homestead Act aggravated tensions with the Indians, resulting in predictable bloodshed. Between 1865 and 1868, at least 250 settlers and railroad workers lost their lives, with untold hundreds suffering wounds.[29]

Crawford reacted accordingly. A combat-experienced regimental commander during the Civil War, the governor preferred to take literal charge of the situation after each Indian raid. He quickly developed a familiar pattern of operation. Once a raid became known, he called out the local militia, requested United States Army assistance, and offered to mobilize volunteer regiments for mustering into the U.S. army. When possible, this whirlwind of activity took place as Crawford buzzed about the state visiting forts and afflicted regions. This pattern repeated itself throughout the spring and summer seasons of his two administrations. By the fall of 1868, Indian difficulties flared yet again, and Crawford came to a new and, according to his biographer, logical conclusion about what he personally should do. A lame-duck officeholder with no apparent elective future, he resigned as governor to take command of a volunteer cavalry regiment he had finally persuaded the army to accept. It is important to note that Indian difficulties did not cease when Crawford resigned his position. Indian raids remained a constant feature of Kansas life for much of the next six years. Until the 1880s, no governor of Kansas could ever be spared a degree of worry about that part of the frontier.[30]

Where Crawford and succeeding governors had become preoccupied with other activities, so too had their military officials. Though

---

[29] Crawford's messages to the legislature serve as a rough gauge to where the governor applied his energies. These messages can be found in the *Senate Journal* for each year. There is a scattered secondary literature on the Indian depredations. Policy ramifications are covered in Marvin H. Garfield, "The Indian Question in Congress and in Kansas," *Kansas Historical Quarterly* 2 (1933): 29–44. The general military contours of the uprisings are covered in Lonnie J. White's "Indian Raids on the Kansas Frontier, 1865–1875" (master's thesis, Texas Technological College, 1955). His "Winter Campaigning with Sheridan and Custer: The Expedition of the Nineteenth Kansas Volunteer Cavalry," *Journal of the West* 6 (1967): 68–98 is a more detailed approach. See also Marvin H. Garfield's "Defense of the Kansas Frontier, 1866–1867," *Kansas Historical Society* 1 (1932): 326–44 and "Defense of the Kansas Frontier, 1868–1869," *Kansas Historical Quarterly* 1 (1932): 451–69; and Plummer, *Frontier Governor*, 113–34.

[30] Both of Garfield's articles on the defense of Kansas document Crawford's concern and "hands-on" reaction to Indians uprisings. Examples of Crawford's reaction can be found in the *Leavenworth Times*, June through August 1867. The lingering problem of Indian conflicts during Governor James M. Harvey's administration is also noted in Lonnie J. White, "Indian Raids on the Kansas Frontier, 1869," *Kansas Historical Quarterly* 38 (1972): 369–89.

it is difficult to judge how exactly the state military hierarchy and clerical staff were affected by constant mobilizations, it might suffice to note that, aside from California and Minnesota, no other states with war claims encountered this situation. In Missouri and Kentucky, the greatest administrative tasks—outside of war claims—faced by either the adjutant or the quartermaster general were Civil War demobilization and the preservation of records. In reality, these tasks and war indemnification were interrelated, one depending upon the other, which then eased the organization and prosecution of a state's claim. Fortunately, then, for the adjutant general in Kansas, the state sometimes alleviated his command responsibilities. Where in all other states the adjutant general stood as the highest-ranking officer in the militia, in Kansas the legislature, from time to time, authorized the appointment of a commanding general. Nevertheless, this position was never permanent, and the adjutant general, more often than not, stood as the senior officer in the militia. Moreover, like senior militia officers around the country, the workloads of both the quartermaster and adjutant general became magnified by additional duties that invariably got rolled onto their shoulders. For example, in 1865, the legislature expanded the quartermaster's responsibilities to include ordnance and commissary. Within this administrative world, it was easy for the quartermaster to get buried in an area that had no relation to processing claims. Writing in December 1865, Quartermaster D. E. Ballard noted that he had confined most of his efforts during the past year to the ordnance department and that he still had no real idea where the state's ordnance was. The adjutant general was not immune from this type of distraction. In 1868, Adjutant General J. B. McAfee inexplicably became responsible for assisting immigration into the state. In this capacity, the adjutant general soon found himself not only handling the flood of correspondence related to immigration but also the logistical coordination necessary to arrange transportation and the purchase of land in the state. On one occasion, the adjutant general traveled to Chicago, where he purchased advertisements in Swedish-language newspapers. Once that was accomplished, McAfee then worked out the transportation requirements for the prospective immigrants.[31]

---

[31] *Report of the Quartermaster General, State of Kansas, 1865*, 1–2; "Adjutant General's Report," 1868, 9–12.

Thus stretched in their administrative responsibilities, the adjutants and quartermasters general assisted with the claims effort in scattered bursts of activity. Their greatest involvement came soon after the Civil War. In February 1866, Adjutant General T. J. Anderson became the de facto state agent when he relayed the report of the first commission to Washington. A conscientious officer, Anderson nonetheless displayed little early knowledge of either the legislature's instructions or the proper methods for adjudicating the claims. Immediately after his arrival in the capital, Anderson bypassed Congress and presented the state's claim to the War Department for processing under the original indemnification act of July 27, 1861. Not surprisingly—and as anticipated by the legislature—the reviewing official disqualified the claims, stating that because the expenditures were "incurred for troops not mustered into the United States service, they cannot be adjusted at the Treasury without the action of Congress." Following this rebuff, Anderson correctly turned the matter over to the congressional delegation and Senator Pomeroy. He then remained in Washington for about one month, which then proved long enough to testify before the Senate Committee on Military Affairs. After having returned to Kansas in March, Anderson was recalled to Washington in July by Sidney Clarke to testify before James G. Blaine's short-lived Special Committee on the War Debt.[32]

Anderson's work in Washington was the last significant involvement in the claims process that any militia officer would have for the next decade. Again, it appears that other business intruded. Counties failed to provide manpower returns. Camp equipment needed to be collected, weapons distributed, battle flags inscribed, pensioners informed, and official unit histories compiled. But, as with the governors of the state, most working hours would be spent dealing with Indian uprisings. The historical evidence, though scattered and often cryptic, indicates that the senior militia officers spent most of their working hours conducting tours around the state. Throughout the 1860s, Adjutants General Holliday, Anderson, McAfee, Moorhouse, and Whittaker tried frantically to organize local militia companies in

---

[32] *Senate Journal, 1867*, 17; "Adjutant General's Report," 1866, 5–12; n.a., *Kansas War Claims: How they were originated and what Congress has done with them, Representative Clarke's course in the matter, The Soldier's loss and the speculator's gain* (Topeka, Kans.: State Record Steam Printing House, 1870), 2, hereafter cited as *Kansas War Claims*.

reaction to, and anticipation of, Indian trouble. When not working to combat the Indians directly, at least one adjutant general also found himself sorting out the financial mess caused by the uprisings. In 1871, the legislature placed Adjutant General Whittaker on a commission to audit claims for all Indian depredations since Kansas entered the Union in 1861.[33]

Thus prevented from devoting a significant amount of time to the Price claims, the adjutant was, on at least one occasion, able to find a happy convergence of his Indian and Price-related duties. Throughout 1867, the constant mobilizations of the militia had led large numbers of men to keep their state-issued weapons even after being demobilized. Unable to get the return of these vitally needed weapons, Adjutant General McAfee decreed that any militiamen who had not turned in his weapon would also not receive his Price raid scrip, if any were due. Despite its apparent illegality, the mandate appeared to have worked, producing 200 stands of Maynard carbines shortly after the promulgation of the order.[34]

POLITICS, REIMBURSEMENT, AND SCANDAL

By 1868, the issue of the claims had not yet become a controversial political topic. The same events that conspired to distract executive and legislative officials also distracted many citizens struggling to fashion an existence on the frontier. However, by the next year the political nature of the claims began to change even if the results of that change bore little early fruit in terms of reimbursement. Reacting to an apparent increase in public agitation over the claims, especially in the eastern tier of counties, the Kansas legislature in February 1869 authorized yet another commission of what it hoped were "disinterested citizens" to examine all heretofore disallowed claims. By September of that year, this third commission revalidated over $61,000 worth of claims. As of the end of 1869, the officially

---

[33] Evidence of the adjutants' Indian-related activity can be found in Garfield, "Defense of the Kansas Frontier, 1868–1869," 455, 456, 470; White, "Indian Raids on the Kansas Frontier, 1869," 371–89; "Adjutant General's Report," 1867, 1–8; "Adjutant General's Report," 1868, 1–9; and *Senate Journal, 1871*, 28–29. Indian commission mentioned in *Senate Journal, 1872*, 27.

[34] "Adjutant General's Report," 1868, 1–2.

allowed value escalated to $301,480, minus, again, those for services rendered.[35]

The activities of the legislature and the third commission served obviously to muddle the claims picture even more. By this time no one could really say for certain who possessed a valid claim. Seemingly at any moment, the legislature could appoint another commission that could either revalidate or disallow claims that had already been examined three times over. The situation in Washington was no better, revealing only the extent to which the congressional delegation did not communicate with the legislature and its commissions. There, the delegation seemed oblivious to the cyclical fluctuations in the value of the claims. For example, in 1868 Senator Pomeroy introduced a bill for indemnification amounting to $505,190. Attached to this bill was the documentation that had accompanied Pomeroy's first bill submitted in 1866. The essential fact of the attempted appropriation in 1868 was that Pomeroy had inflated the claims owed Kansas by over $260,000, using the tabulations provided by the second commission. Pomeroy guided the claim carefully, defeating the Committee on Military Affairs' attempt to divert all claims-related bills into an even more overworked Committee on Claims, where it would certainly die. Pomeroy's bill eventually passed the Senate, although only at about half of what was originally requested. Just as had happened in 1866, the Senate approved money only for services rendered and supplies furnished. In this case, the language of fiscal restraint governed the decision. According to Senator Henry Wilson of the Committee on Military Affairs, the downward revision of the claim occurred because "we do not want to throw the whole thing open." However, and regardless of the reasoning, the House of Representatives undid the work of Pomeroy when the Speaker of the House, Schuyler Colfax, tabled the measure.[36]

Aside from a general question of why Pomeroy used the wrong figures, this piece of legislative history leads to a question of why Kansas' sole congressman—Sidney Clarke—was unable to push the

[35] *Laws of the State of Kansas 1869*, 159–60; *Senate Journal, 1886*, 311; *Price Raid Commissioner*, iii.

[36] *Kansas War Claims*, 4; *Congressional Globe*, 40th Cong., 2nd sess., 318, 470, 3313. Wilson quoted on 3872 of same. See also U.S. Congress, House Miscellaneous Document, 41st Cong., 1st sess., 1433, H. Doc. 36, and House Miscellaneous Document, 41st Cong., 1st sess., 1402, H. Doc. 6.

1868 bill to passage. The issue gains some importance when it is remembered that Kansas had, if only theoretically, met Congress' demand that the state assume the debt before applying for federal relief. When the House failed, for the second time, to pass Pomeroy's bill, many Kansans pondered Sidney Clarke's role in the whole mess. Their conclusions were not favorable. One popular explanation was that Clarke wanted to delay indemnification for as long as possible. According to this idea, Clarke was part of a ring of speculators that preyed on the holders of military scrip. The longer the delay in indemnification, the more widespread became a belief that the national government would never reimburse Kansas and allow the state treasurer to receive currency in exchange for the scrip. Therefore, claimants desperate for money frequently sold their scrip to speculators at discounts of up to 70 percent. Besieged by speculators, financially destitute claimants turned to Clarke for reassurance. One man queried the congressman: "I desire your advise in regard to this Kanases scrip which was to pay the price raid damiges[.] myself and some of my neighbors have some[.] the speculators says it is wortheless[.] we ask your advise what to do with it. Some says it is clarks falt but we dont believe it. . . ."[37]

Because Clarke had definite senatorial ambitions, the speculation theory became a prominent charge leveled by an opposing faction of the state Republican Party interested in elevating former governor Crawford to Congress. In February 1870, Levi Woodward, a friend of Clarke's and member of the second Price commission, warned the congressman that "your enemies are harping all the time that these claims have rested with you for years. . . ." Some pro-Crawford newspapers, such as the *Lawrence Daily Republican,* charged Clarke with "covertly seeking delay, while his friends were engaging in shaving the scrip." Even Crawford entered the fray as he accused Clarke of never intending to pass any claims legislation and of making profits from the delay in refunding the state.[38]

---

[37] *Kansas War Claims,* 5–7; Willis Barks to Clarke, June 23, 1870, Sidney Clarke Collection, CARC.

[38] Woodward quoted in Levi Woodward to Clarke, February 10, 1870, Sidney Clarke Collection, CARC. Newspaper quoted from the *Lawrence Daily Republican,* August 31, 1870, S. J. Crawford Scrapbook, vol. 2, KSHS. Crawford quoted in clipping, *Kansas State Record,* n.d., S. J. Crawford Scrapbook, vol. 1.

Although no direct evidence substantiates the charge that Clarke made any money by delaying indemnification, several men sought information from Clarke in order to help their own speculative endeavors. In February 1868, one constituent, A. C. Low, wrote Clarke concerning the status of any pending claims legislation. Low asked, "whether in your [Clarke's] opinion it would be safe to buy up the claims of those who served in the Price Raid." Clarke's response is unknown, but later in the same year he received an inquiry from T. J. Sternbergh, a personal friend and prominent local politician in Douglas County, where Clarke also lived. After informing Clarke that he and an associate could "buy the Scrip at about 40 cents on the dollar," Sternbergh wanted to know "if the prospects are favorable" to continuing such speculation.[39]

It is not known to what extent Clarke actually cooperated with these people, but a no less plausible explanation exists for the House's failure to pass the Senate's appropriation. It is also an explanation that helps assess the early inability of Kansas to receive indemnification. In a state where the power of the congressional delegation was paramount, a small three-man delegation was bound to have a great deal of inner turmoil. Jealousy and ambition, especially between Clarke and Pomeroy, mixed to create a political atmosphere where legislative sabotage then became commonplace. To one observer, "a member of one body has but to set a foot a measure to have the member of the other body tilt at it with a force to destroy it." This same Washington-based critic went on to note that nothing of benefit to Kansas could ever pass both houses.[40]

No matter the motive, Sidney Clarke allowed Pomeroy's bill to die. He received the bill from the Senate in late July, just as the session wound to a close. Instead of accepting the bill as the Senate had revised and reduced it, Clarke chose to press for the amount originally requested by Pomeroy, a number already two-years and three-commissions old. As reported by Governor Harvey, Clarke believed Pomeroy's bill "totally inadequate, . . . [and its] passage was not pressed before the House." To reconcile this difference required too

---

[39] Low quoted in A. C. Low to Clarke, February 12, 1868, Sidney Clarke Collection, CARC. Sternbergh quoted in T. J. Sternbergh to Clarke, December 23, 1868, Sidney Clarke Collection, CARC.

[40] *Times and Conservative*, February 5, 1870.

much time, and the Senate bill simply faded away as the session ended.[41]

The failure of the indemnification effort in 1868 marked a slight change in the involvement of the state executive branch. With popular pressure mounting and the inauguration of a new governor less militarily inclined than Samuel Crawford, executive branch officials became a more visible presence in claims activities. The result was tighter coordination between officials in Kansas and the congressional delegation. Governor Harvey, Auditor A. T. Thoman, Adjutant General Thomas Anderson, Senator Pomeroy, and Congressman Clarke made a partial political peace, joining together in a new effort to get a federal auditing commission appointed along the lines of the commission created in 1866 to take care of Missouri. Clarke's involvement with this new movement was both legislatively practical and politically necessary—especially considering his ambitions to run for United States senator when the legislature convened in January 1871. Following his abandonment of Pomeroy's indemnification bill in 1868, Clarke felt constituent pressure acutely. One of Clarke's friends, H. F. Tower, reminded the congressman of the importance of the claims when he wrote: "You are probably aware that the interest felt in that direction [the Price claims] is much greater in your district than in any other in the state, . . . and the active influence of our member in that direction cannot fail to have its influence, for those claims will put thousands of dollars into the pockets of the poorer classes, while a delay only works a forfeiture of their support. . . ." State Auditor Thoman reiterated these sentiments when he informed Clarke in April 1870 that a federal commission was "the next best thing" to Pomeroy's appropriation and that "if you succeed in this . . . it will politically be very nearly as good a point for you, as if the direct Payment was ordered."[42]

After several attempts to pass legislation, Kansas finally received in February 1871 what it had asked for. Congress authorized a com-

---

[41] *Congressional Globe*, 40th Cong., 2nd sess., 3928, 4491. James Harvey quoted in *Senate Journal, 1870,* 17–18. See also U.S. Congress, House Miscellaneous Document, 41st Cong., 2nd sess., 1433, H. Doc. 36, and clipping, n.a., n.d., box 05A, folder 1-g, Sidney Clarke Collection, CARC.

[42] Clarke to James Harvey, December 29, 1869, Governor's Correspondence, James Harvey, KSHS; Harvey to Clarke, June 17, 1870, Letter Press Book, Governor Harvey, KSHS. H. F. Tower to Clarke, January 17, 1870, and A. T. Thoman to Clarke, April 15, 1870, Sidney Clarke Collection, CARC.

mission appointed by the War Department, although such action was not in time to save Sidney Clarke's political career in Kansas. As H. F. Tower predicted, the constant delay had undermined Clarke's popularity. To be sure, problems with the claims were not his only liability. Clarke had been accused by some of being a tool of the railroads and of not getting better terms for the citizens of Kansas in the national government's sale of Indian lands. Just as bad, Clarke had alienated the Republican Party establishment in Leavenworth, the largest city in Kansas and the political center of gravity of the party. In some ways this alienation developed simply because Clarke hailed from Lawrence in Douglas County and thus apparently never showered Leavenworth with political goodies. This mattered greatly to party members in Leavenworth, who by 1870 had already worked up a Christmas wish list for the next session of Congress and proclaimed loudly that "Leavenworth has favors to ask of the next Congress." "We want a Custom House, Post Office, and United States Court room." No less important for creating ill will in Leavenworth, Clarke had much earlier come out for repudiating the state debt, a stance far ahead of mainline Republican thinking in Kansas at the time. The most widely read newspaper in the state, *The Times and Conservative* of Leavenworth, denounced Clarke, proclaiming that he would "have to swallow or take back [the position] if he ever appears before the people of this state."[43]

Notwithstanding Clarke's reception in Leavenworth, his wider popularity had slid steadily downhill since the death of Lane. During the final years of the war, Clarke had been a rising star in the state Republican Party, but the passage of time had gathered him a great many enemies. This list included Pomeroy, former governors Crawford and Thomas Carney, and Republican State Central Committee

---

[43] The twisting trail to passing this legislation in both houses in 1871 can be followed in the *Congressional Globe*, 41st Cong., 1st sess., 29, 74; 41st Cong., 2nd sess., 3083, 3182, 4511, 4960, 5596; 41st Cong., 3rd sess., 569, 716, 739, 755, 906. See also U.S. Congress, House Miscellaneous Document, 41st Cong., 1st sess., 1433, H. Doc. 36; U.S. Congress, Senate Miscellaneous Document, 41st Cong., 2nd sess., 1408, S. Doc. 61; *Kansas War Claims*, 4–5. Clarke's record in the disposition of Indian lands is excoriated in the *Lawrence Daily Republican*, August 31, 1870, S. J. Crawford Scrapbook, vol. 2, KSHS. For more information on Indian and railroad allegations, consult Plummer, *Frontier Governor*, 113–34. Wish list found in the *Leavenworth Daily Times*, November 8, 1870. Repudiation quote found in the *Times and Conservative*, October 28, 1869.

chairman Daniel R. Anthony. They were all enemies that his onetime patron, Senator Lane, could no longer shield from him. The political opposition smelled blood, and in 1870 it descended with full force. The *Times and Conservative* thundered that Clarke was "a big booby and dishonest demagogue" who speculated in war claims. The opposition also produced an inflammatory pamphlet notable for more than its long-winded title: "Political Affairs in Kansas, A Review of the Official Acts of our Delegation in Congress, Shall Inefficiency and Corruption be Sustained? A New Deal and Less Steal." The pamphlet helped drown out anything positive that Clarke might either have accomplished or claimed to have accomplished. Accused of "land gobbles," "Indian steals," and stonewalling the war claims, Clarke stood defenseless. Consequently, in September 1870 the Republican Party rejected Clarke's bid for renomination on the party's fall ticket. Perhaps worse, Kansans also selected a legislature that would be entirely hostile to Clarke's bid for the Senate three months later in February 1871. Sidney Clarke had been pushed from statewide office. Although Clarke would manage to be elected to the state house in 1879, charges of corruption and vote selling in the senatorial election of 1871 finished his political career in Kansas.[44]

The destruction of Sidney Clarke was not the only political casualty of the elections of 1870 and 1871. In the most direct sense, the charges of vote buying that snared Clarke also caught every other candidate in the race. Indirectly, the election canvass also highlighted the state Republican Party's increasing dissatisfaction with Senator Pomeroy. The preelection charges of corruption that so dogged Clarke easily became attached to Pomeroy. So too did the allegations that petty infighting had prevented the entire congressional delegation from functioning. Though the reality of the situation was that the delegation did manage to produce legislation—involving

---

[44] *Times and Conservative*, January 27, 1870. Clarke's failed reelection bid is mentioned briefly in Plummer, *Frontier Governor*, 136. For information on the electoral scandal of 1871, see Sinisi, "Politics on the Plains," 31–35. Clarke would find political success elsewhere. He soon left for Oklahoma, where he became active in territorial politics. There is no satisfactory biography of Sidney Clarke. For essential information, see George L. McCoy, "The Congressional Career of Sidney Clarke" (master's thesis, Oklahoma State University, 1962). McCoy addresses Clarke's electoral difficulties and the impact of the pamphlet "Political Affairs. . . ." on pages 74–77. Other biographical data can be examined in the *Biographical Directory of the American Congress, 1774–1961*, 702.

railroads and Indians—of some arguable benefit to the state, the highly visible lack of indemnification stuck with important Republicans. Over and over, the *Times and Conservative* castigated the delegation for its internal bickering and the attendant inability to deliver indemnification. In one edition, the paper asserted that "if we had a good delegation in Congress the whole amount [of the Price claims] would be paid by the general government and Kansas would be out of debt." Later, but in the same spirit, the paper reported that other states had received their war claims because their congressmen did not work for "private swindlers." This steady chorus echoed through other papers, eventually resulting in a Republican-sponsored resolution in the state House demanding that the entire Republican congressional delegation resign. Such emotion still bubbled over when in September 1870 a mob burned Pomeroy in effigy outside the Republican State Convention.[45]

What is revealing about this contemporary reaction to the congressional delegation and its handling of the claims is the degree to which the other parts of the state government emerged unscathed. At no time was there any tangible complaint directed to either the legislature or the executive branch. This is striking in that the press, both Democratic and Republican, rarely hesitated to attack their state officials. The Republican press, in particular, frequently denounced the Republican-dominated legislature on issues ranging from corruption to general laziness. Republican Sol Miller and his paper, the *Kansas Chief*, were unsparing. Whether it be skewering the legislature for adjourning just "to get on a drunk" in 1867, or accusing them of employing too many janitors, clerks, and secretaries in 1868, Miller typified the criticism of even "friendly" papers. Nevertheless, the perception was that the legislature generally did what needed to be done, even if in a corrupt and indolent fashion. Popular opinion clamored for fiscal retrenchment, and the legislature usually delivered. Within this context, the *Times and Conservative* could laud "the masterly inactivity" of the legislature, while condemning the congressional delegation for the general failure to reimburse.[46]

---

[45] Various quotes found in the *Times and Conservative*, October 13, 1869 and January 22, 1870. Burning of the effigy described in the *Kansas Chief*, September 15, 1870.

[46] *Kansas Chief*, January 24, 1867, February 20, 1868; *Times and Conservative*, October 13, 1869, February 11 and 12, 1870.

Two points can be made about this. First, satisfaction with state policies diffused any potential call for the employment of a state agent. No apparent tension existed on this issue between any prominent political factions or lobbying groups in the state. Second, the legislature had acted in a reasonable and pragmatic manner. The universal demands for retrenchment could not be ignored, and the legislature generally answered the call on everything from debt restrictions at the state and county levels to the use of biennial sessions. But at the same time, the legislature rarely hesitated to increase its spending, even as Sol Miller called for reducing spending by half and taxation by a quarter. Similarly, the legislature showed some willingness to hire various agents to handle the vagaries of state finances and claims. While in one case it refused Samuel Crawford's call for an immigration agent, the legislature hired agents throughout the 1860s and early 1870s to buy and issue grain to destitute farmers and settle claims for railroad lands with the United States.[47]

Perhaps most telling regarding the legislature's efforts to untangle the claims was its decision in 1869 and 1870 to authorize the governor to appoint a war-claims agent. Only after traveling to Washington and investigating the condition of the claims did Governor Harvey refuse to appoint an agent. His decision reflected the belief that an agent would not help the creation of a commission by the federal government to audit the claims, and also the popular conviction that temptation to defraud might overcome the agent. Harvey's mistrust of agents was not merely playing to the emotions of the crowd. Examples abounded where private agents slipped into the world of scandal. So too did examples of state agents gone astray. Such indeed was the case in 1867 when J. C. Walker, agent for New York, collected indemnification moneys and then fled the country. Given this background, Harvey's reasoning easily muted any potential criticism of state officials. The message, then, was the same: resolving an intergovernmental issue, like the claims, depended upon the congressional delegation. In the only known case of not pinning the blame on the delegation, conventional wisdom held that some other congressman was to blame. Writing in March 1871, Sol Miller faulted

---

[47] Retrenchment emphasized in the *Times and Conservative,* February 13, 1870. The *Kansas Chief* discussed it in the issue of January 9, 1870. Various agents mentioned in Wilder, *The Annals of Kansas,* 446, 468, 501, 636; *Senate Journal, 1870,* 17–18; *Times and Conservative,* March 1, 1870.

Representative James A. Garfield of Ohio with holding up a claims appropriation for the state. To Miller, the only thing that could explain such an action was that Garfield was a man "who keeps his hide well filled with whisky all the time."[48]

Such emotion and controversy over the claims did not stop even when the delegation produced legislation creating a commission to audit the claims. Chaos continued to reign over the Price claims, although fortunately for the congressional delegation it was nothing that could be placed on their shoulders. At first, positive action occurred: a military auditing commission arrived in Kansas on March 14, 1871, and by April 5 it reported to Congress. The next year, on August 13, Governor Harvey received the indemnification payment for the Price raid. But on closer examination, problems developed with both the federal audit and the eventual disbursement of the federal moneys to the individual claimants.[49]

In the case of the audit, Kansas did not receive quite what it wanted. General James A. Hardie's auditing commission, which consisted of himself and two other officers, went through all available records in Kansas and concluded, not surprisingly, that much in the previous state audits had been in error. Documentation had been forged, claims had been improperly classified, and militiamen had been credited with more time in service than was possible under the aegis of Governor Thomas Carney's executive orders. Perhaps most important, the Hardie Commission finally made it clear that claims for damages would not be accepted. According to Hardie, "there is no responsibility for payment on the part of the United States" for all claims pertaining to property damages. Hardie's bottom line, then, was a surprise to most every Kansan either directly or indirectly connected with claims. The total figure allowed was over $337,000, yet this amount consisted, in large part, of moneys for paying the militia, which Hardie deduced to be $260,241. Hardie disallowed the vast majority of those claims that had been accepted by the various state commissions. Because Kansas had issued over $560,000 worth of

---

[48] Wilder, *The Annals of Kansas,* 446, 468, 501, 636; *Senate Journal, 1870,* 17–18; *Times and Conservative,* March 1, 1870. Walker mentioned in the Report of the State Treasurer of Indiana, October 31, 1867, Governor's Papers, Thomas Bramlette, Sec. 2, Box 174, Roll 206, KHS. Miller quoted in the *Kansas Chief,* March 18, 1871.

[49] *Price Raid Commissioner,* xxiv; Wilder, *The Annals of Kansas,* 575.

scrip for state-allowed claims, hundreds of Kansans were left holding scrip that the state could not—and would not—redeem.[50]

As if this situation was not sufficient to cause discontent among interested claims holders, state treasury officials mismanaged most affairs having anything to do with the Price claims. In successive administrations during the 1860s and 1870s, corruption and misman-agement swirled around this department. Bond scandals and the fre-quent misappropriation of public money only marked the beginning of evils laid at its feet. In the case of the claims, things turned sour after the state treasury received the Price indemnification late in 1872. Intended only for those claims allowed by the Hardie Commis-sion, the money never did reach all the right pockets. Where earlier claims difficulties could be blamed on a variety of people, problems of disbursement fell squarely upon the state treasurer, Josiah Hayes. The treasurer misused the federal funds in various ways. He only casually supervised the whole disbursement process and redeemed countless pieces of duplicated or forged scrip. Likewise, he accepted numerous claims that had been disallowed by the Hardie Commis-sion. According to Hayes's chief clerk, J. C. Collins, this reauditing was done in the belief that several claims had been improperly la-beled as damages when they should have been placed in another category. Finally, Hayes allowed the Price indemnification to be used in paying other unrelated claims pending against the state. The exact amount of money that Hayes thus misallocated is not known, with estimates ranging between $20,000 and $49,000. But as indicated by impeachment charges filed against Hayes during the spring of 1874, his troubles transcended the Price claims. The impeachment covered a multitude of abuses, including the loaning of public money to friends. However, before Hayes could be convicted, he resigned his office. The legislature never tried him.[51]

---

[50] Hardie quoted in *Price Raid Commissioner*, xxv. See also pages xxv–xxvi in same.

[51] The actual appropriation of money is traced in the *Congressional Globe*, 42nd Cong., 2nd sess., 1704, 1711, 2834, 3869, 4303, 4315, 4459. Some treasury scandals covered in *Senate Journal, 1869*, 526–60. The tribulations of Hayes are documented in *Journal of the Proceedings of the Court of Impeachment Sitting for the Trial of Josiah E. Hayes, Treasurer, Together with the Testimony Taken in New York, and a Detailed Statement of the Price Raid Scrip Paid* (Topeka, Kans.: State Printing Works, 1874), 4, 29, 62, 80–81. The exact amount of the misallocation is unknown. Three reports issued after the impeachment vary greatly as to the proper figure. One speci-

After Hayes's impeachment, controversy over the Price claims continued. As it became expressed in letters and newspaper editorials, the controversy generally concerned three groups of people: those who had been robbed of their money by Hayes; those who had their claims disallowed by the Hardie Commission; and those who presented entirely new Price related claims after 1872. But for all purposes, a climax had already been reached when the federal government reimbursed the state in 1872. From that point until well into the early twentieth century, the claims issue surfaced only in spurts of popular and political clamor. Dependent as the issue was upon agitation, a basic political fact was that the claims were easily buried when other items swamped the legislature. Such was the situation in 1873 when outrage over Hayes's handling of the reimbursement might have translated into some type of legislative action. This was never the case, as that session became consumed by a bribery scandal that eventually brought down Senator Pomeroy. In succeeding years, the legislature, in particular, became anxious to put the whole affair behind it. In 1876, Ward Burlingame, the personal secretary of Governor Thomas Osborn, indicated the slackening importance of the issue when he informed one disgruntled claimant that the Price claims were "agitated to a greater or lesser extent each session of the Legislature" with little anticipated result.[52]

Any further attempt by the state to gain indemnification for the Price raid became intertwined with, and subservient to, other claims that Kansas held against the United States. In 1877 the state had begun to recover from a decade-long plague of financial panic, drought, and grasshoppers, but the public treasury was still in a weakened condition. The legislature thus readily sought windfall income. The potential for this windfall lay in a variety of claims that Kansas had accumulated since statehood. The lure of this money

fies $49,088.40, another specifies $21,308.13, while yet another lists "approximately $20,000.11." See respectively: *Report of the Committee on Claims on Senate Concurrent Resolution, #9, 1877; Senate Journal, 1886,* 30; and *Senate Journal, 1889,* 44–45.

[52] Information on the senatorial scandal of 1873 can be found in Gambone, "Samuel C. Pomeroy and the Senatorial Election of 1861, Reconsidered," 15–32; Kitzhaber, "*Götterdämerung* in Topeka: The Downfall of Senator Pomeroy," 243–78; and James C. Malin, "Some Reconsiderations of the Defeat of Senator Pomeroy of Kansas, 1873," *Mid-America* 48 (1966): 47–57. Burlingame quoted in Ward Burlingame to H. J. Skinner, February 15, 1876, Letter Press Book #6, Governor's Correspondence, Thomas Osborn, KSHS.

proved enough for the legislature to embark in a new administrative and bureaucratic direction: it authorized the governor to appoint a state agent to prosecute claims against the United States. The areas in which this agent could act were broad. He could pursue "five-percent claims," which, according to the terms of statehood, were 5 percent of the proceeds of the sale of all lands by the federal government in the state. The agent could also pursue claims for school lands, which descended from another statehood provision setting aside certain sections of land grants for schools. The federal government had long-since sold these lands, prompting the state to seek reimbursement. Finally, the legislature empowered the new agent to prosecute all types of war claims.[53]

Soon after this authorization, Governor George T. Anthony appointed Samuel J. Crawford as agent. In some ways, the appointment was odd. Former governor Crawford had become a quixotic figure in Kansas politics, migrating from wartime radicalism to liberal republicanism to greenbackism. He had even denounced Governor Anthony during the election of 1876. Anthony's political motives for the appointment are not known, though he may have been trying to shuttle the persistent and ambitious Crawford away from the state. But at the same time, valid reasons existed to hire Crawford. He was a practicing attorney with contacts in Washington who had also come to dabble in the state's claims soon after his loss of public office. Crawford believed, correctly, that his compensation of 10 percent of all reimbursement secured was inferior to other state agents of the time, but he accepted the appointment.[54]

Crawford was a meticulous man, and his selection proved one of the more profitable administrative decisions taken by the government of Kansas during the nineteenth century. Headquartered in Washington, Crawford moved primarily on the land claims. By the time he had been forced out of the agency in 1891 by the rise of the Farmer's Alliance in the legislature, Crawford had secured $345,470 in school lands claims and almost $756,000 in five-percent land claims. With the military claims, Crawford had mixed success. In one

---

[53] The economic condition of the state is detailed in John L. Madden, "The Kansas Economy in Historical Perspective, 1860–1900" (Ph.D. diss., Kansas State University, 1968), 9–95. Creation of a state agent covered in Plummer, *Frontier Governor*, 157–58.

[54] Compensation of Crawford discussed in Plummer, *Frontier Governor*, 159.

sense, he accomplished much in prosecuting military claims unrelated to the Price raid. By 1891 he had pushed through the treasury
and gained special congressional appropriations for over $372,000 in
military claims. This indemnification covered less than half of Kansas'
claimed federal expenses in raising volunteer regiments, repelling
Confederate invasions, and countering Indian uprisings.[55]

In another sense, Crawford met failure in all attempts to clarify
and gain reimbursement for the Price raid claims. A small part of this
failure occurred when Crawford fell into many of the same traps that
other states and agents had already stumbled into. Early in his tenure
he wasted his time pushing claims for property damages. This was an
issue long settled, and indeed one settled during his own administration. Similarly, Crawford early on became mired in the forms and
abstracts required by the treasury. Quite simply, it took him repeated
attempts to organize his claims according to the practices of the treasury. If these distractions and delays were not frustrating enough for
both Crawford and any prospective claimants, he at times failed also
to coordinate with state executive branch officials, who often possessed the documentation necessary for indemnification.[56]

A bigger part of the failure to straighten out the Price claims was
the limited scope of Crawford's responsibilities when it came to management of war claims. Unlike either the agents or even the adjutants
general who shepherded the claims of other states, Crawford's control was limited to presentation in Washington. Beyond that, he was
totally dependent upon the state government and other officials to
collect and process the information in its early stages. It was in this
area that the state remained tied to its previous administrative
course. The legislature would appoint a succession of four new commissions between 1873 and 1903 to audit and revise the audits of

---

[55] The figures for indemnification are found in Frank W. Blackmar, *Kansas Cyclopedia of State History*, 3 vols. (Chicago: Standard Publishing Co., 1912), 1:353. Crawford's combined war-claims settlement includes a single payment of $332,308 in
1885. The process of securing this amount can be followed in Third Auditor to
Crawford, February 27, 1885, Letter Press Book, Third Auditor, vol. 8, E. 618, RG
217, NA.

[56] The following correspondence reveals a problem in the coordination and dupli-
cation of effort with state officials and a general weakness in the organization of the
state's claims: Third Auditor (U.S.) to Third Auditor (Kans.) P. D. Bonebrake, June
8, August 26, October 13, 1879, and March 23, 1880, Letter Press Book, Third Auditor, vol. 6, E. 618, RG 217, NA.

claims so that they could then be sent to Washington. Each new commission served, in the end, only to allow newly presented claims and provide reports on the activities and errors of previous commissions.[57]

While the commissions conducted their business, Agent Crawford labored mightily on the Price claims. In the beginning, he did not lack for help from the state's governor, George T. Anthony. In October 1877, Anthony forwarded an extended request—twenty-five pages worth—to Congress asking for a complete indemnification in the interests of a "long-delayed justice." This impassioned and detailed petition, coupled with Crawford's lobbying in Washington, produced some favorable results, although at least one Illinois newspaper termed the whole episode just one more "Kansas grab" designed to "abstract money from the pockets of taxpayers." Congress agreed to audit all claims in question with the provision that all outstanding scrip be forwarded to the War Department accompanied by all documentation. Unfortunately, the task of gathering together all scrip and documentation proved impossible for the state. The appropriate documentation was in disarray. Two years earlier in 1875, Governor Osborn had noted that many of the records "form a huge, unwieldy mass on the top of one of the [state] Treasury safes." By 1878, those records that had not vanished were, according to one state adjutant general, "greatly worn and mutilated," with some being so worn as to be "past copying."[58]

Throughout the 1880s, Agent Crawford appears to have devoted less and less attention to the Price claims, preferring instead to concentrate on the far more lucrative, and less convoluted, land and general military claims. He did, however, continue to forward relevant information to the governors and to suggest possible methods for solving the Price riddle. Among his suggestions was a proposal in

---

[57] *Senate Journal, 1879,* 30–31; W. C. Smith to Governor George Glick, February 5, 1884, Governor's Correspondence, George Glick, Box 6, F-9, KSHS.

[58] Anthony quoted in George A. Anthony, "A statement relating to the claims of the State of Kansas. . . ." (Topeka: Kansas Publishing House, 1877), 23. Quote of Illinois newspaper found in unidentified clipping, n.d., S. J. Crawford Scrapbook, vol. 1, 21. *Report of the Adjutant General of the State of Kansas, 1876, 1877, 1878,* 14–15; Prentis Noble to John Brown, June 15, 1878, Letter Press Book #12, Governor's Correspondence, George Anthony, KSHS. Osborn quoted in *Senate Journal, 1875,* 41–42. Last quote taken from the Fifth Biennial Report of the Adjutant General of the State of Kansas, 1885–1886, 70–71, in *Kansas Public Documents, 1886.*

1886 to abandon the commission system and create, instead, a court of claims "with full power to adjudicate" all claims before finally sending them on to Washington. An imaginative proposal, Crawford's state court of claims had just as much chance of being approved as it had of working, if ever actually implemented. The disorganization of old documentation, the taint of corruption, and the innumerable pieces of scrip floating around spelled doom for any administrative entity or agent attempting to process claims related to the Price raid. Thus while the state would continue to collect indemnification for its other wartime expenses beyond the turn of the century, the Price raid became synonymous less with a valiant defeat of a desperate Confederate invasion than an administrative tangle no one could unlock. Though the state managed considerable success in getting indemnification for other war-related expenses after the turn of the century, such that the money could even finance the building of the Grand Army of the Republic Memorial Hall, the Price raid claims remained forever a riddle.[59]

In its general outline, the process of recovering indemnification for Kansas had been limited by much of what had affected other states. There was the unbending wall of Chase's rules at the entrance to the treasury. There was the basic unwillingness of Congress to establish new precedents, especially concerning private property and a state's obligation to first assume debt. There was also, and just as importantly, the shaping influence of local concerns and conditions. For Kansas, this meant that the distractions of the frontier, the early dominance of the congressional delegation, and inexperience with intergovernmental administration would all mold the state's reimbursement proceedings more than any other consideration. The result was often administrative confusion as the state groped its way through the intergovernmental tangle. Congressmen, governors, ad-

---

[59] For the actions and attitudes of the governors towards the problems associated with the claims, see, in particular, the various governor's messages to the legislature from 1877 through 1893, S. J. Crawford to Jas. Minnear, March 5, 1883, W. C. Smith to Glick, February 5, 1884, Governor's Correspondence, George Glick, KSHS; George A. Martin to Crawford, September 2, 1885, Crawford to Martin, September 5, 1885, Crawford to Martin, September 14, 1885, Crawford to Martin, December 10, 1885, Governor's Correspondence, George A. Martin, KSHS. For Crawford's quote see, *Report of the Honorable Samuel J. Crawford the Governor of Kansas, in the matter of the State Claims, 1886,* 6. Evidence of the inactivity of the claims can be found in *Senate Journal, 1891,* 50.

jutants and quartermasters general, and claims commissioners all became part of a rudderless effort remarkable for its lack of a centrally
responsible administrative figure. Not until the appointment of Samuel J. Crawford as state agent in 1877 would the state create that
administrative figure. Though this boded well for all manner of
claims, it did little for the Price raid claims. As late as the 1950s,
holders of the Price raid scrip still presented their pieces of paper
to state officials and newspaper correspondents—some still seeking
reimbursement, others wondering what exactly the funny-looking
pieces of paper were.[60]

---

[60] The legacy of the Price claims found in the *Daily Capitol* (Topeka, Kans.), March
2, 1954.

5

Conclusion

THE SLOW PACE OF reimbursement for most states lasted until the turn of the twentieth century. At that time, Congress began to display considerably less interest both in watching over the issue of reimbursement and in carefully guarding the doors of the treasury. An increasingly bureaucratized institution with broader interests and duties found it much easier to hand off responsibility for war claims than had Congresses in the early years of the Gilded Age. Just as Congress had loosened its grip on veterans' pensions and benefits throughout the 1880s and 1890s, so too had it eventually seen its way to liberalizing the flow of indemnification to the states.

First there was the Dash Act of 1902, which finally authorized payment of interest on bond issues. Ten years later, Congress followed with the Dent Act, transferring jurisdiction over state claims to the United States Court of Claims and expediting most cases, if not those of the Price raid, where documentation was in order. The net effect was a flood tide of money to the states that would total almost $15 million by 1930. It was this round of reimbursement that helped build a Grand Army of the Republic Memorial and Library in Topeka, Kansas, and a state capitol in Frankfort, Kentucky. Even Nevada benefited from the new largess when it received over $500,000 in 1930. Within the paradigm established by Daniel Elazar, a more "cooperative" period in intergovernmental operations had arrived.[1]

Despite real success, problems and disputes remained during this new period, the tenor and issues of which were the same as those seen between 1861 and 1880. Kansans still pursued the Price raid claims, while Missourians still struggled in vain to have the Crafton claims, and others, recognized. Throughout the Great Depression of

---

[1] U.S. Statutes at Large, 40 (1919), 772; Brainerd Dyer, "California's Civil War Claims," Southern California Quarterly 45 (1963): 1–24; Kansas City Times, October 4, 1948; Bayless E. Hardin, "The Capitols of Kentucky," The Register of the Kentucky Historical Society 43 (1945): 173–200.

the 1930s and even well into the 1990s, Missourians queried officials in Washington and Columbia about their scrip. Perhaps most aggrieved were Californians. Stuck on the fringes of the war and contending more with hostile Indians than rebellious Confederates, California accumulated a debt, with interest, totaling nearly $9 million. The state pursued this claim all the way to the U.S. Supreme Court in 1953. Despite the Court ruling adversely, California persevered until at least the late 1990s in trying to recover its war debt. Although quite relevant to contemporary citizens with claims to press, the issue and controversies of state indemnification have become little known and little remarked upon. They have, in a sense, assumed a position in the history of the Civil War much like that of the still-living widows of Confederate veterans, who continue to surface in quirky human-interest segments in the contemporary news media. The war claims and the widows have thus become mere footnotes and trivia to the war itself.[2]

To recover the history of the claims, I posed a series of questions at the outset of this study. The questions concerned both simple procedure and the larger context within which indemnification took place. The subsequent discussion suggests that careful distinctions need to be made when describing governance in the Gilded Age. For most of the twentieth century, a conventional wisdom has ruled the historical treatment of the period. It has been a none too favorable treatment and one defined by what Ballard Campbell has called the "indictment thesis"; that is, the Gilded Age was a time synonymous with corruption and government held hostage by Robber Barons. Even where recent scholarship on the period has downplayed the role of corruption and Robber Barons, its analysis of governmental operations has still tended to the negative. Since the late 1970s, scholars have poked and prodded the early Gilded Age for evidence

---

[2] *Kansas City Times,* October 4, 1948, describes the continuing efforts of Kansans to get scrip redeemed. For Missouri's attempts to secure reimbursement through the Great Depression, see C. C. Calhoun, Attorney for the State of Missouri, to the Comptroller General of the United States, July 20, 1933, Comptroller to Calhoun, November 29, 1933, Calhoun to Comptroller, January 30, 1934, E. Y. Mitchell Collection, R. 95, F. 3674, WHMC. A most recent example of an individual's attempt to redeem the Crafton scrip can be found in Thomas E. Morris, Securities Examiner, Department of the Treasury, to Frank Taggart, December 3, 1992, copy in author's possession. California's difficulties traced in Dyer, "California's Civil War Claims," 1–24.

of modernization, or what Theodore Lowi and others have labeled "development." With some notable exceptions, but most prominently Richard Bensel, these researchers have found neither modernization nor development in the years before at least 1877. Their related criticism of the period's administrative capacity has been strong, especially as that capacity compares to what scholars believe reformed governance could have achieved in all matters from social provision to the running of the United States Department of Agriculture. To Daniel Carpenter, nineteenth-century administrative capacity was "minimally sufficient . . . to distribute federal largesse to electorally favored constituencies." Richard Bensel has concluded that the post–Civil War patronage-based bureaucracy "was incompatible with administrative competence." And ultimately, Mark Summers has argued that the limited government of the Gilded Age "could no longer do all the tasks that were expected of it either efficiently or competently."[3]

The history of the claims allows for a more nuanced view of postwar administration. Beyond a doubt, state government exhibited no small measure of the old "indictment thesis." Fraud and inefficiency in the state executive agencies occur just enough to taint the image of governance in all states. The Crafton Commission in Missouri and the first Price raid commission in Kansas illustrated virtually all that could go wrong in a state's handling of its administrative tasks. Nevertheless, the natural tendency to focus on the controversial obscures whatever virtues there were in state-level administration. In terms of personnel, for every example of a corrupted official such as John

---

[3] The literature on Gilded Age politics and government is voluminous. For a critical summary, consult Charles W. Calhoun, "The Political Culture: Public Life and the Conduct of Politics," in *The Gilded Age: Essays on the Origins of Modern America*, ed. Charles W. Calhoun (Wilmington, Del.: Scholarly Resources, 1996), 185–213. See also Ballard Campbell, "Public Policy and State Government," in same. However, these articles leave out the mushrooming scholarship of the "state-centered" theorists. The best recent analysis of this can be found in Dodd and Jillson, *The Dynamics of American Politics: Approaches and Interpretations*. See particularly Theodore Lowi's foreword to this volume, "Political History and Political Science." Quotes found in Carpenter, *The Forging of Bureaucratic Autonomy*, 46; Bensel, *Yankee Leviathan*, 237; Summers, *The Era of Good Stealings*, x. It should also be noted that not all historians have denounced the competency of nineteenth-century patronage bureaucracy. Consult, for example, Yearley, *The Money Machines*, 101, and Michael Nelson, "A Short, Ironic History of American National Bureaucracy," *The Journal of Politics* 44 (1982): 747–78.

Crafton or Josiah Hayes, there was a John B. Gray, George C. Bingham, or Fayette Hewitt, each of whom pursued indemnification doggedly and with great success. More importantly, the resulting mixed bag of administrative efficiency was exactly what the public was willing to tolerate in exchange for other items in its governing culture. On the one hand, this meant procedures, or administrative structures, that reflected local concerns, whether they be of a heightened fear of lobbyists or the existence of external threats to the security of the state. On the other hand, the absence of any significant demand for state-level reform justifies the states' tendency to flirt with an innovation—the use of private agents—that did not threaten the existing administrative system. The electorate's often skeptical treatment of this administrative patch, to borrow Stephen Skowronek's terminology, suggests strongly that the people valued simple economy in governmental affairs more than elaborate governing structures and the potential reimbursement it might deliver. In shaping their administrative methods, elected politicians met the public's demand for retrenchment, which then revealed perhaps the greatest virtue of small spoils-based governing structures: a responsiveness to the popular will.[4]

Less ambiguous is an evaluation of the executive agencies of the national government. Simply put, they performed well and at a capacity that satisfied the polity. Though both the Treasury and War Departments would not be without their well-documented troubles during this time, their record with the claims was remarkable. Time after time, the accounting clerks subjected each entry in each claim to a level of scrutiny that produced not malfeasance but howls of protest for the unbending nature of the examination. This type of performance came in an organization lacking any of the characteristics of a modern bureaucracy. Low-level bosses created office routines. Standardized hours of work were hard to find. Rationalized subdivisions of labor did not exist, and worker specialization was unheard of; most clerks did most jobs within the office. Working above the clerks was a parade of politically appointed chief clerks and auditors who not only managed a system that had dispensed over $40 million by 1873, but who also spent immeasurable amounts of time answering the inquiries of impatient agents and congressional com-

---

[4] Skowronek, *Building a New American State*, 37–162.

mittee chairmen. If not lightning fast (form letters and typewriters would not appear until the late 1880s), these premodern bureaucrats were tireless. By 1883, the third auditor's office had been reduced to a total of eight clerks. The office had also by that time been given the responsibility for auditing all individual war claims related to the loss of horses during the Civil and Indian Wars. These clerks then received, in that year alone, over 8,000 horse claims and $5 million worth of state war claims. Compounding this mountain of paper, the office received 6,206 letters of inquiry, while initiating 17,400 of its own. Such a tide of numbers, claims, and explanations could have either choked the office or led it easily down a road of corruption. However, absolute adherence to basic precedents simplified case dispositions and allowed consistency in judgment. By any measure, this administrative system had functioned exceptionally within a political culture that emphasized fiscal retrenchment. It was, in other words, a government that did not require Mark Summer's healing prescription of "a more activist judiciary [and] a professional bureaucracy."[5]

Although the executive departments were hardly without their difficulties, congressional scandals dwarfed all others both in contemporary news accounts and historical inquiry, with the Credit Mobilier debacle coming to symbolize the depravity of the institution. Nevertheless, the processing of the claims in Congress provides some surprises as well. Congressional dealings with the claims, similar to those of the treasury, were never tainted by anything approaching even a minor scandal. Just as important, congressional management of the claims reveals something about the relative insularity of the states and their congressional delegations.

War indemnification had the potential to be among the biggest pork-barrel bonanzas of the postwar period. It was an issue that in 1865 held forth the promise of over $468 million in payments to the different states. Deal making and coalition building among the states should have been inevitable conditions to insuring that all got the appropriate pieces of pork. And yet, legislative logrolling, so often

---

[5] Insight into clerical life and office functions can be found in Aron, *Ladies and Gentlemen of the Civil Service*, passim, but especially 78–79, 81. Aron's focus is, however, more on gender relations in the modern office than administrative efficiency. Workload statistics found in T. E. G. Pettengill to Third Auditor, March 24, 1885, Letter Press Book, Third Auditor, vol. 8, E. 618, RG 217, NA. Summers, *The Era of Good Stealings*, x.

seen by historians of the nineteenth century, was nowhere to be found. Good opportunities abounded for state delegations both to trade votes and to craft broad enabling legislation. However, the only significant attempt to create legislation that would cover all states came in December 1865 with the establishment of James G. Blaine's ill-fated select committee in the House. After Blaine's proposal for a generic remedy died with little fanfare, few proposals, let alone multistate alliances, emerged to smooth the path to reimbursement.[6]

Within the sample of states explored in this study, there was sufficient commonality among sets of claims such that the three states could have tried to fashion mutually beneficial legislation. Nothing of the sort came to pass. Instead, what became more obvious, through at least the 1870s, was just how destructive other interested states could be when one state sought its own reimbursement. State mercantilism—which had been so evident before the war, on issues ranging from canal building to mining—trumped all thoughts of logrolling legislation. For example, from March 1862 to July 1865, Missouri's first attempts to generate legislation were sabotaged by Kentucky and Pennsylvania. The delegations of these two states tacked on amendments that would have applied the provisions of the different bills to their own states. More than ten years later, the fratricidal nature of claims legislation became evident again when yet another Missouri reimbursement bill got smothered in Kentucky's abortive attempt to craft legislation favoring the indemnification of interest. Both states failed to support each other's bills.[7]

The one early episode that seemed to offer the greatest opening for broad-based interstate cooperation, including Missouri and Kentucky, came in January 1871. At that time, Oliver Morton of Indiana pushed forward his proposal to indemnify interest on war-related bond issues. Unfortunately, Morton's effort did not represent any great shift in actual cooperation among the states. He crafted his bill narrowly to favor Indiana, while failing to persuade any other state

---

[6] Morton Keller has observed the "traditional demands of pork barrel" in *Affairs of State*, 323. See also Calhoun, "The Political Culture: Public Life and the Conduct of Politics," 185–213.

[7] *Congressional Globe*, 37th Cong., 2nd sess., 3272–73; 38th Cong., 2nd sess., 1865, 1264–67. Antebellum state mercantilism described in Scheiber, "Federalism and the American Economic Order," 97–98. Missouri's and Kentucky's problems in 1876 revealed in Bingham to Hardin, April 20 and 25, 1876, Governor's Papers, Hardin, CFD-165, F. 15294, MSA.

delegations of the bill's inherent value to them. Not until 1879 would scattered legislation appear in both houses that sought to group together the claims of different states and territories.[8]

The lack of interstate cooperation, or, better yet, a sense of corporateness, can be explained in at least four ways. First, it was simply the traditional way of doing business. The creation of legislation was a very particularistic, if not localistic, action. The concerns of the majority of congressmen rarely crossed state lines, leading few to see the possibilities of logrolling legislation. Second, there was the even more traditional impulse of fiscal responsibility that worked against the type of corporate action necessary to pass potentially expensive bills. Third, both major political parties remained ambivalent about the claims, weakening any movement to craft broad legislation. The task of building alliances within a party was hard enough without having to build similar support outside the party. Fourth, and perhaps most important, as all states chased a limited quantity of dollars, an intense competition developed that produced few allies and many rivals. The larger notion that all states shared interests and a corporate identity would have to wait until the 1920s, symbolized by the birth of lobbying groups such as the Public Administration Clearinghouse, the National Governors' Association, and the National Conference of State Legislatures.[9]

It is in this last regard that the nature of administrative federalism also comes into sharper focus. In her work on lobbying, Margaret Thompson made distinctions between what she characterized as the "old lobby" and modern interest-group politics. To Thompson, the lobbying of private interest groups in the nineteenth century bore little resemblance to that developing after the turn of the century. What separated the "old lobby" from modern interest groups was

---

[8] *Congressional Globe*, 41st Cong., 1st sess., 29; 41st Cong., 2nd sess., 1076; 41st Cong., 3rd sess., 115, 509, 549–53, 599. An example of claims legislation that grouped together several states was a bill "for the benefit of the states of Texas, Colorado, Oregon, Nebraska, California, Kansas, and Nevada, and the Territories of Washington, and Idaho, and Nevada when a Territory." *Congressional Record*, 49th Cong., 1st sess., 123. Prominent legislation linking a number of states did not appear again until 1893. Third Auditor to Secretary of the Treasury, December 29 (?), 1893, Letter Press Books, Third Auditor, vol. 14, 159, E. 618, RG 217, NA.

[9] On the difficulties of creating legislation, see Thompson, *In the "Spider's Web,"* 112–13. State lobbying groups are mentioned in Jonathan Walters, "Lobbying for the Good Old Days," *Governing* 4 (1991): 33–37.

their organizational structure and the degree of corporate identity. During the early Gilded Age, groups with common interests lacked both qualities, which ultimately led Thompson to describe them as simple clienteles rather than interest groups. Even the most powerful groups—Union veterans and the railroads—suffered from the inability to create a single front and a coherent agenda for legislative action. Internecine warfare then broke out as, in the case of the veterans, different fraternal organizations pursued scattershot legislation that ultimately left the individual veteran isolated in his pursuit of private pension bills.[10]

The states in pursuit of their claims were no different. Their executive officials and congressional delegations communicated little among each other, perceiving not allies, but rivals in the war for reimbursement. The one opportunity for the states to coexist peacefully over the claims came in July 1865. At that time, nearly all states heeded the call of Massachusetts to assemble their adjutants general in Boston. While there would be socializing, excursions to the White Mountains, and debates about what to do with captured battle flags, there was also frequent discussion of how to maintain records uniformly. The meeting even produced a resolution to turn each adjutant into his own state's official agent for pension claims. The convention closed with a resolution to gather the following year to discuss matters of continuing interest. Needless to say, the adjutants never did meet again. However, it is not difficult to divine the reason for the dissolution of the group: the supreme crisis of the Union had passed, as did the need for civil servants to engage in what could readily be perceived as a tax-supported vacation.[11]

The short-lived existence of the adjutants' convention highlights the idea that administering the federal system was an ad hoc affair. This situation descended in no small part from the rhetoric of constitutional dual federalism. It was a concept that had survived the Civil War, despite the war's obvious obliteration of a federal system weighted toward its peripheral states. The vitality and resiliency of

---

[10] Thompson, In the "Spider's Web," 136–37, 164, 256.

[11] Report of the Adjutant General of the State of Kansas, 1865, 14; Frankfort Commonwealth, July 14, 1865. The different state militias would meet again in 1878, but at that time it was to form a group dedicated to preserving the militia system from attacks of military professionals bent on reforming, or abolishing, the militia. Stephen Skowronek discusses this in his Building a New American State, 92–95.

dual federalism had the inevitable result in the postwar era, as it always did, of minimizing actual intergovernmental contact and, perhaps more importantly, the idea that there could be extensive intergovernmental contact. At bottom, state leaders, regardless of party, viewed each instance of contact as only temporary and therefore not warranting the creation of a bureaucratic apparatus capable of dealing with the government in a systematic fashion. All solutions, then, to intergovernmental matters not involving the congressional delegation were to be temporary and, of course, inexpensive. Agents and preexisting state officials fit these needs well. Their use has been well documented pertaining to reimbursement, but they could be seen again and again in the few administrative matters involving the national government. Because intergovernmental administration in the early Gilded Age translated simply to the extraction of benefits and not the subsequent maintenance of reports or regulations, states could utilize agents or specially detailed public officials when specific issues arose. These officials, therefore, became notable figures in episodes ranging from the disposition of Indian treaty lands to the acquisition of a variety of land and money grants owed as part of the admission of new states.[12]

Whether the states chose agents or specially detailed civil servants was a matter dependent upon a uniform set of questions that had local answers. For example, could a particular state afford an agent? How deep were popular and political sentiments about the possible corruption an agent could bring to the system? What were the relationships between congressional delegations, governors, and legislatures when it came to the dispensation of power or patronage? And ultimately, what was the simple competence of the agents or military officials involved? These issues influenced Missouri, Kentucky, and Kansas in different ways, but they were still yet important in forging a state's administrative response.

No less important in shaping intergovernmental relations were

---

[12] The wide variety of activities an agent could find himself engaged in is best represented by Samuel J. Crawford of Kansas. See Plummer, *Frontier Governor,* 157–69. Other examples of the responsibilities can be found in the numerous letters of application for the job of state agent. See particularly Congressmen George Adams and L. Trimble to John W. Stevenson, April 12, 1870, Stevenson Family Papers, vol. 29, LC; William Brown to Stevenson, March 31, 1870, and George Evans and John Trimble to Stevenson, April 22, 1870 Governor's Papers, Stevenson, Box 1, F. 3, KSA.

local political, economic, and military concerns. For Missouri, reimbursement was an economic urgency. Governor Thomas Fletcher's willingness to bypass the legislature when hiring an agent indicated a virtual state of panic over a public debt that exceeded $24 million. Kentucky's indemnification proceedings would always be controlled by the legacy of the war and the state's strained relations with a federal government led by the supposedly malicious Republicans. Radical Kansas carried none of this baggage into any of its federal dealings, but it did bear an equally important set of local influences. Its governing machine lacked experience and institutional knowledge of intergovernmental affairs. The congressional delegation often dwarfed the power of the governor and legislature. Most significantly, state officials were overextended with a variety of troubles related to taming a frontier. The claims would always compete with Indian raids for the attention of adjutants, quartermasters, and governors.

No matter how these types of localistic concerns affected an individual state's response to intergovernmental operations, all states were ultimately compelled to face a federal government that was not terribly sympathetic to their plights. Such a reality is different from that suggested by Daniel Elazar, who has postulated that the federal government used war claims as a vehicle to aid the states. To the contrary, the universal demand for retrenchment and a genuine impulse to guard the national treasury from any legislation that might unlock its carefully guarded doors meant that Washington would not go out of its way to provide money to the states. There was also no corresponding sense among public officials that indemnification provided a golden opportunity to circumvent the restrictions of dual federalism, a point also suggested by Elazar. The national government's officials did not manipulate indemnification so as to solve, or ameliorate, a variety of state problems unrelated to war claims. By the same token, state officials did not attempt to gain leverage in their arguments by proposing to use indemnification moneys for public services or internal improvements.[13]

Absent, then, an administrative system reliant upon hidden deals and agendas, intergovernmental operations depended upon simple organization at the state level and the attendant ability to bring organized pressure, and knowledge, to bear in Washington. It is here that

---

[13] Daniel Elazar, *The American Partnership*, 302.

the experience of any given state becomes no different than that of most modern special-interest groups. Administrative operators, or lobbyists, carried the burden of making the case for legislation and executive decisions. Whether they be agents or specially detailed state officials, these administrative operators worked all branches of the national government and both sides of the partisan aisle.

Indeed, in an era known for its partisan party activity and the importance of party in distributing public largesse, the agent demonstrated the limits of party influence. Moving within the bureaucracy of the executive offices and the halls of Congress, the agent, or other state military official, carried with him no plainly identifiable party tag. A nonpartisan representative of a state, the agent occupied a safe position from which to lobby civil servants and elected officials. When partisanship did become an issue in a state's reimbursement—as it did with Kentucky's claims—party influence, and its organizing strengths, mattered little to the final outcome. Though many within Kentucky believed that partisan political machinations had controlled the destiny of their claims, the real fate of Kentucky's reimbursement was determined elsewhere.

Successful indemnification ultimately occurred within the committee rooms of Congress and, especially, the clerical offices of the Treasury and War Departments. In the committee rooms, overt partisanship would get a lobbyist nowhere. Even that most rabid of political partisans, Fayette Hewitt of Kentucky, realized this and receded far into the background when his state's claims reached Congress for a decision. But it was in the clerical offices of the executive branch, where most claims decisions were made, that Secretary Chase's impersonal rules trumped all other concerns, including that of party. The lack of party influence would become even more apparent throughout the Gilded Age as the states relied increasingly upon professional agents, who often represented multiple states exhibiting different political preferences. In an administrative era stamped so clearly by the antebellum characteristics of limited government, patronage, and ad hoc procedure, the shadowy and technocratic role of the state agent hinted at the future shape of lobbying. The modern bureaucratic world was just around the corner.

APPENDIX

CHRONOLOGICAL LISTING OF CONGRESSIONAL APPROPRIATIONS
FOR THE PAYMENT OF STATE CLAIMS ARISING OUT OF INDIAN
INVASIONS AND HOSTILITIES, 1797–1860

Date	State	Payment
March 3, 1797	Georgia	$ 70,496.35
	Kentucky	3,386.76
	South Carolina	8,400.25
February 21, 1812	Louisiana, Kentucky, and Indiana Territory	32,800.00
March 2, 1827	Georgia	129,375.66
March 2, 1829	Illinois	856.55
February 11, 1830	Pennsylvania	13,795.54
March 2, 1831	Missouri	9,085.54
April 5, 1832	All states participating in the Seminole War	120,000.00
June 15, 1832	Illinois (and "neighboring states")	300,000.00
July 14, 1832	Illinois (and "neighboring states")	100,000.00
September 8, 1841	Florida	19,388.02
	Florida	297,213.92
	Georgia	78,495.92
August 11, 1842	Georgia	175,000.00
	Louisiana	175,000.00
August 29, 1842	Louisiana	61,378.15
August 10, 1846	Alabama	13,455.32
July 21, 1852	Texas	80,741.00
May 31, 1854	Kentucky	1,000.00
	Louisiana and Texas	18,060.49
	Florida	7,241.93
August 5, 1854	California	924,259.65
March 3, 1856	Texas	25,000.00
June 30, 1856	Texas	137,755.38
March 3, 1857	Arkansas	1,212.00
March 3, 1859	Massachusetts	227,176.48
	Texas	123,544.51
June 21, 1860	New Mexico	74,009.00
	Iowa	18,988.84
Total		$3,247,117.26

Summary of Reimbursement Payments Registered in the Office of the Third Auditor for the War of 1812

State	Total Payment as of 1859
Connecticut	$ 119,069.29
Delaware	41,075.72
Maryland	672,500.44
Massachusetts	657,924.74
Mississippi	4,585.64
New Hampshire	58,000.00
New York	191,318.93
North Carolina	77,000.00
Pennsylvania	343,369.40
Rhode Island	42,422.57
South Carolina	312,259.16
Vermont	4,421.18
Virginia	1,958,918.17
Total	$4,482,865.24

Summary of Reimbursement Payments Registered in the Office of the Third Auditor for the Mexican War

State	Total Payment as of 1859
Alabama	$ 9,951.44
Illinois	299.00
Indiana	8,287.46
Louisiana	32,688.79
Maine	10,308.28
Michigan	19,638.99
Mississippi	1,699.26
North Carolina	3,084.84
Ohio	14,623.54
Pennsylvania	1,569.39
South Carolina	5,936.64
Tennessee	23,247.21
Texas	9,171.76
Virginia	11,601.87
Total	$152,108.47

Summary of Reimbursement Payments for the Civil War

State	Paid Through the Office of the Third Auditor	Paid Through the Office of the Second Auditor	Total Amount Paid Through 1884
Colorado Territory	$ 55,238.84		$ 55,238.84
Connecticut	2,096,950.46		2,096,950.46
Delaware	31,988.96		31,988.96
Illinois	3,080,442.51		3,080,442.51
Indiana	2,668,529.78	$1,073,208.51	3,741,738.29
Iowa	1,039,759.45		1,039,759.45
Kansas	384,138.15		384,138.15
Kentucky	3,504,466.57		3,504,466.57
Maine	1,027,185.00		1,027,185.00
Maryland	133,140.99		133,140.99
Massachusetts	3,660,483.07	7,608.88	3,668,091.95
Michigan	844,262.53		844,262.53
Minnesota	70,798.45	276.75	71,075.2
Missouri	7,580,421.43		7,580,421.43
Nebraska	485.00		485.00
New Hampshire	976,081.92	450.00	976,531.92
New Jersey	1,420,167.35	96,859.44	1,517,026.79
New York	3,957,996.98	198,938.52	4,156,986.98
Ohio	3,245,319.58		3,245,319.58
Pennsylvania	3,204,636.24	667,074.35	3,871,710.59
Rhode Island	723,530.15		723,530.15
Vermont	832,557.40		832,557.40
Virginia	48,469.97		48,469.97
West Virginia	471,063.94		471,063.94
Wisconsin	1,035,059.17		1,035,059.17
Total	$42,093,173.89	$2,044,416.45	$44,137,590.34

Schedule of Payments Registered in the Office of the Third Auditor for Missouri, 1861–1884

| | Authorizing Legislation | | | | |
Date	Act of July 17, 1861 (Advances)	Act of July 27, 1861	Act of Apr. 17, 1866	Act of Jan. 27, 1879	Amount
Oct. 6, 1862	$125,000.00				$ 125,000.00
Apr. 24, 1867			$ 3,023.00		3,023.00
Apr. 24, 1867			645,331.08		645,331.08
July 17, 1867			1,696,391.46		1,696,391.46
Aug. 22, 1867			1,000,000.00		1,000,000.00
Sept. 4, 1867			1,817,864.66		1,817,864.66
Sept. 27, 1867			1,128,807.25		1,128,807.25
Sept. 9, 1867		$646,958.23			646,958.23
Oct. 24, 1867			78,044.60		78,044.60
Oct. 24, 1867			171,960.86		171,960.86
Aug. 12, 1868			32,445.40		32,445.40
Aug. 9, 1882				$234,407.10	234,407.10
Aug. 9, 1882				187.00	187.00
Total		$771,958.23	$6,573,896.10	$234,594.10	$7,580,421.43

Schedule of Payments Registered in the Office of the Third Auditor for Kentucky, 1861–1884

Date	Act of July 1861 (Advances)	Act of July 27, 1861	Act of June 8, 1872	Act of March 3, 1877	Amount
		Authorizing Legislation			
May 20, 1862	$ 315,000.00				$ 315,000.00
June 27, 1862	436,000.00				436,000.00
June 3, 1863	100,000.00				100,000.00
Mar. 8, 1864	200,000.00				200,000.00
Feb. 8, 1867		$ 155,115.09			115,115.09
Feb. 8, 1867		606,641.03			606,641.03
Apr. 24, 1867		40,398.30			40,398.30
June 5, 1867		79,674.75			79,674.75
Aug. 26, 1867		40,623.39			40,623.39
Oct. 15, 1867		83,412.64			83,412.64
Mar. 9, 1868		34,341.78			34,341.78
June 11, 1868		40,823.56			40,823.56
Aug. 25, 1868		31,812.53			31,812.53
Aug. 5, 1869		14,308.48			14,308.48
Apr. 27, 1870		28,174.51			28,174.51
Oct. 22, 1870		145,710.00			145,710.00
May 29, 1871		50,119.75			50,119.75
June 17, 1871		130,543.60			130,543.60
Aug. 20, 1872			$525,258.72		525,258.72
Mar. 16, 1874		30,588.53	58,199.32		88,787.85
Apr. 18, 1874			6,728.25		6,728.25
Nov. 2, 1874		3,568.23	35,490.65		39,058.88
July 13, 1875		24,817.23	33,739.93		58,557.16
Dec. 17, 1875		4,538.85	8,411.33		12,950.18
June 13, 1876		25,531.94	7,046.38		32,578.32
Nov. 25, 1876		4,967.08	390.27		5,357.35
May 9, 1877				$101,121.05	101,121.05
June 1, 1877		10,452.27	4,114.53		14,566.80
Mar. 19, 1879		6,091.85			6,091.85
July 1, 1880			15,000.00		15,000.00
Aug. 9, 1882		36,211.81			36,211.81
Mar. 13, 1883		29,498.94			29,498.94
Total	$1,051,000.00	$1,657,966.14	$694,379.38	$101,121.05	$3,504,466.57

SCHEDULE OF PAYMENTS REGISTERED IN THE OFFICE OF THE THIRD AUDITOR FOR KANSAS, 1861–1884

Date	Authorizing Legislation		Amount
	Act of July 27, 1861	*Acts of Feb. 2, 1871 and June 8, 1872*	
Mar. 19, 1970	$ 9,360.82		$ 9,360.82
Apr. 18, 1871		$ 110.00	110.00
Apr. 18, 1871		110.00	110.00
Apr. 18, 1871		110.00	110.00
Aug. 14, 1872		336,817.37	336,817.37
Feb. 4, 1878	2,073.34		2,073.34
June 14, 1881	26,604.05		26,604.05
Aug. 9, 1882	8,952.57		8,952.57
Total	$46,990.78	$337,147.37	$384,138.15

Bibliography

Manuscripts

Benecke, Louis. Papers. Scrapbooks. Western Historical Manuscripts Collection. Columbia, Mo.

Bogy, Lewis V. Papers. Missouri Historical Society. St. Louis.

Bristow, Benjamin. Papers. Library of Congress. Washington, D.C.

Brown, B. Gratz. Papers. Western Historical Manuscripts Collection. Columbia, Mo.

Clarke, Sidney. Papers. Newspaper clippings. Carl Albert Research Center. University of Oklahoma. Norman.

Cockrell, Francis. Papers. Western Historical Manuscripts Collection. Columbia, Mo.

Gibson, Charles A. Papers. Missouri Historical Society. St. Louis.

Hyde, Ira. Papers. Western Historical Manuscripts Collection. Columbia, Mo.

Minor, Francis. Papers. Missouri Historical Society. St. Louis.

Miscellaneous Manuscripts. Western Historical Manuscripts Collection. Columbia, Mo.

Mitchell, E. Y. Papers. Western Historical Manuscripts Collection. Columbia, Mo.

Rollins, James S. Papers. Western Historical Manuscripts Collection. Columbia, Mo.

Sherman, John. Papers. Library of Congress. Washington, D.C.

Stevenson Family. Papers. Library of Congress. Washington, D.C.

Archives

General Orders Kentucky Volunteers, 1865. Military Records and Research. Frankfort.

Governor's Papers. Charles Hardin. CFD-165. Missouri State Archives. Jefferson City.

Governor's Papers. George A. Martin. Kansas State Historical Society. Topeka.

Governor's Papers. George Anthony. Kansas State Historical Society. Topeka.

Governor's Papers. George Glick. Kansas State Historical Society. Topeka.

Governor's Papers. James Harvey. Kansas State Historical Society. Topeka.

Governor's Papers. John W. Stevenson. Kentucky State Archives. Frankfort.

Governor's Papers. Samuel J. Crawford. Kansas State Historical Society. Topeka.

Governor's Papers. Thomas Bramlette. Kentucky State Archives. Frankfort.

Governor's Papers. Thomas C. Fletcher. CFD-159. Missouri State Archives. Jefferson City.

Governor's Papers. Thomas McCreary. Kentucky State Archives. Frankfort.

Governor's Papers. Thomas Osborn. Kansas State Historical Society. Topeka.

Missouri Adjutant General's Office. Correspondence. Boxes 210 and 211. RG 133, Missouri State Archives. Jefferson City.

U.S. House Committee on Claims. Minutes. 39th Cong. through 42nd Cong. RG 233. National Archives. Washington, D.C.

U.S. House Committee on Military Affairs. Minutes. 39th Cong. RG 233. National Archives. Washington, D.C.

U.S. Senate Committee on Military Affairs. Papers. Box 44. S. 43A-E10. RG 46. National Archives. Washington, D.C.

U.S. Treasury. Records of the Accounting Officers of the Department of the Treasury, State Claims, 1861–1890. Kentucky. E. 759. RG 217. National Archives. Washington, D.C.

U.S. Treasury. Records of the Accounting Officers of the Department of the Treasury, State Claims, 1861–1890. Missouri. E. 759. RG 217. National Archives. Washington, D.C.

U.S. Treasury. Records of the Third Auditor. E. 604. RG 217. National Archives. Washington, D.C.

U.S. Treasury. Records of the Third Auditor. E. 618. RG 217. National Archives. Washington, D.C.

U.S. Treasury. Records of the Third Auditor. E. 758. RG 217. National Archives. Washington, D.C.

FEDERAL PUBLIC DOCUMENTS

Congressional Globe, 1861–1872.
Congressional Record, 1873–1904.
Commonwealth v. Boutwell, 13 Wallace 526 (1871).
Houston v. Moore, 5 Wheaton 1 (1820).
United States v. New York, 160 U.S. Reports 598 (1895).
U.S. Department of the Treasury. *Report of the Secretary of the Treasury on the State of the Finances for the Year Ending,* 1861 through 1890.
U.S. Department of War. *War of the Rebellion: The Official Records of the Union and Confederate Armies.* 3 series. 70 vols. Washington: Government Printing Office, 1880–1901.
U.S. House. 25th Cong., 2nd sess., 1838. H. Rept. 465.
U.S. House. 28th Cong., 2nd sess., 1845. H. Rept. 108.
U.S. House. 39th Cong., 1st sess., 1866. H. Misc. Doc. 43.
U.S. House. 39th Cong., 1st sess., 1866. H. Rept. 16.
U.S. House. 41st Cong., 1st sess., 1869. H. Misc. Doc. 6.
U.S. House. 41st Cong., 1st sess., 1869. H. Misc. Doc. 36.
U.S. Senate. 32nd Cong., 1st sess., 1852. S. Rept. 329.
U.S. Senate. 38th Cong., 2nd sess., 1852. S. Misc. Doc. 32.
U.S. Senate. 38th Cong., 2nd sess., 1852. S. Rept. 113.
U.S. Senate. 38th Cong., 2nd sess., 1865. S. Rept. 107.
U.S. Senate. 39th Cong., 1st sess., 1866. S. Misc. Doc. 90.
U.S. Senate. 39th Cong., 1st sess., 1866. S. Rept. 12.
U.S. Senate. 41st Cong., 2nd sess., 1870. S. Misc. Doc. 61.
U.S. Senate. 43rd Cong., 1st sess., 1874. S. Rept. 70.
U.S. Senate. 50th Cong., 1st sess., 1888. S. Rept. 1286.
U.S. Senate. 51st Cong., 1st sess., 1890. S. Ex. Doc. 11.
U.S. Statutes at Large 5 (1816): 252–53.
U.S. Statutes at Large 5 (1817): 251–52, 378.
U.S. Statutes at Large 10 (1846): 111, 115.
U.S. Statutes at Large 12 (1861): 276.
U.S. Statutes at Large 12 (1861): 765–68.
U.S. Statutes at Large 14 (1866): 38–39.

U.S. *Statutes at Large* 14 (1867): 565.
U.S. *Statutes at Large* 17 (1872): 346.
U.S. *Statutes at Large* 40 (1919): 772.

STATE PUBLIC DOCUMENTS

Missouri

Annual Reports of the Adjutant General of the State of Missouri, 1863–1874. Jefferson City, 1864–1875.

Avery, Grace and Floyd Shoemaker, eds. *The Messages and Proclamations of the Governors of the State of Missouri.* Vols. 3, 4, 5. Columbia: State Historical Society of Missouri, 1922–1924.

Heard, John T. *Report of the Honorable John T. Heard, Agent for the State Claims to the Fund Commissioners.* Jefferson City: State Journal Co., 1883.

Journals of the House of Representatives of the State of Missouri
Journals of the Senate of the State of Missouri
Laws of the State of Missouri
Missouri Adjutant General, Acting Quartermaster and Paymaster General's Report, 1877 and 1878. Jefferson City, 1879.

Missouri Constitution (1875)

Report of the Adjutant General of Missouri Upon Certificates Issued by the Missouri War Claims Commission of 1874. Jefferson City: Stephens Printing Co., n.d.

Kentucky

Acts of the General Assembly of the Commonwealth of Kentucky, 1863–1872.
Journal of the House of Representatives of Kentucky, 1861–1880.
Journal of the Senate of Kentucky, 1861–1880.
Kentucky Documents, 1863–1889.
Report of the State Agent for Kentucky, at Washington, made to the Governor, January 1, 1867. Legislative Document #8. Frankfort: Kentucky Yeoman Office, 1867.

Kansas

"Fifth Biennial Report of the Adjutant General of the State of Kansas, 1885–1886." *Kansas Public Documents, 1886.*

Journal of the Proceedings of the Court of Impeachment Sitting for the Trial of Josiah E. Hayes, Treasurer, Together with the Testimony Taken in New York, and a Detailed Statement of the Price Raid Scrip Paid. Topeka: State Printing Works, 1874.

Laws of the State of Kansas, 1865.

Report of the Adjutant General of the State of Kansas, 1865, 1866, 1868, 1876, 1877, 1878.

Report of the Honorable Samuel J. Crawford the Governor of Kansas, in the Matter of the State Claims, 1886.

Report of the Price Raid Commissioner. Topeka: Kansas Publishing House, 1889.

Report of the Quartermaster General of the State of Kansas, 1862, 1865.

Senate and House Journals of the Legislative Assembly of the State of Kansas, 1861–1886.

Georgia

Acts of the General Assembly of the State of Georgia, 1842.

NEWSPAPERS

Columbia (Mo.) Statesman
Daily Capitol (Topeka, Kans.)
Daily Kentucky Yeoman (Frankfort)
Daily Republican (Lawrence, Kans.)
Daily Tribune (Jefferson City, Mo.)
Frankfort (Ky.) Commonwealth
Kansas Chief (White Cloud)
Kansas City (Mo.) Times
Leavenworth (Kans.) Times
Liberty (Mo.) Tribune
Missouri Republican (St. Louis)
Missouri State Times (Jefferson City)
Missouri Statesman (Columbia)
Observer and Reporter (Lexington, Ky.)
People's Tribune (Jefferson City, Mo.)

Times and Conservative (Leavenworth, Kans.)
Tri-Weekly Kentucky Yeoman (Frankfort)
Weekly Eagle (Booneville, Mo.)
Weekly Peoples Tribune (Jefferson City, Mo.)

BOOKS, PAMPHLETS, AND UNPUBLISHED
THESES AND DISSERTATIONS

Anderson, William C. *The Price of Liberty: The Public Debt of the American Revolution.* Charlottesville: University of Virginia Press, 1983.

Anthony, George A. "A statement relating to the claims of the State of Kansas. . . ." Topeka: Kansas Publishing House, 1877.

Aron, Cindy S. *Ladies and Gentlemen of the Civil Service: Middle-Class Workers in Victorian America.* New York: Oxford University Press, 1987.

Bates, Edward. *The Diary of Edward Bates, 1859–1866.* Edited by Howard K. Beale. Washington: Government Printing Office, 1933.

Bensel, Richard F. *Yankee Leviathan: The Origins of Central State Authority in America, 1859–1877.* Cambridge: Cambridge University Press, 1990.

Biographical Directory of the American Congress, 1774–1961. Washington: Government Printing Office, 1961.

The Biographical Encyclopedia of Kentucky. Cincinnati: J. M. Armstrong and Co., 1878.

Blackmar, Frank W. *Kansas Cyclopedia of State History.* 3 vols. Chicago: Standard Publishing Co., 1912.

Bogue, Allan. *The Congressman's Civil War.* Cambridge: Cambridge University Press, 1989.

Bolles, Albert S. *The Financial History of the United States From 1861–1885.* New York: D. Appleton and Co., 1886.

Boorstin, Daniel J. *The Americans: The Democratic Experience.* New York: Random House, 1973.

Bowling, Kenneth R. *Politics in the First Congress, 1789–1791.* New York: Garland Publishing, 1990.

Britton, Wiley. *The Aftermath of the Civil War.* Kansas City, Mo.: Smith, Grieves and Co., 1924.

Brock, William R. *Investigation and Responsibility: Public Responsi-*

bility in the United States, 1865–1900. Cambridge: Cambridge University Press, 1984.

Brown, Thomas H. "George Sewall Boutwell: Public Servant (1818–1905)." Ph.D. diss., New York University, 1979.

Bryce, James. *The American Commonwealth.* 2 vols. Chicago: Charles H. Sergel and Co., 1891.

Bullock, Charles J. *Historical Sketch of the Finances and Financial Policy of Massachusetts from 1780–1905.* Publications of the American Economic Association, series 3, vol. 8, no. 2. New York: MacMillan Co., 1907.

Buresh, Lumir. *October 25th and the Battle of Mine Creek.* Kansas City, Mo.: Lowell Press, 1977.

Burton, Theodore. *John Sherman.* New York: Houghton, Mifflin and Co., 1906.

Calhoun, Charles W., ed. *The Gilded Age: Essays on the Origins of Modern America.* Wilmington, Del.: Scholarly Resources, 1996.

Campbell, Ballard. *Representative Democracy: Public Policy and Midwestern Legislatures in the Late Nineteenth Century.* Cambridge: Harvard University Press, 1980.

Campbell, Ballard. *The Growth of American Government: Governance from the Cleveland Era to the Present.* Bloomington: Indiana University Press, 1995.

Carpenter, Daniel P. *The Forging of Bureaucratic Autonomy: Reputations, Networks, and Policy Innovation in Executive Agencies, 1862–1928.* Princeton, N.J.: Princeton University Press, 2001.

Castel, Albert. *A Frontier State at War: Kansas 1861–1865.* Ithaca, N.Y.: Cornell University Press, 1958.

Chandler, Ralph C., ed. *A Centennial History of the American Administrative State.* New York: The Free Press, 1989.

Clark, Dan Elbert. *Samuel Jordan Kirkwood.* Iowa City: State Historical Society of Iowa, 1917.

Clary, David A. and Joseph W. A. Whitehorne. *The Inspectors General of the United States Army 1777–1903.* Washington: Government Printing Office, 1987.

Cooling, Benjamin F., ed. *The New American State Papers: Military Affairs.* 19 vols. Wilmington, Del.: Scholarly Resources, 1979.

Coulter, E. Merton. *The Civil War and Readjustment in Kentucky.* Chapel Hill: University of North Carolina Press, 1926.

Cunningham, Noble E., Jr. *The Jeffersonian Republicans: The Forma-*

tion of Party Organization, 1789–1801. Chapel Hill: University of North Carolina Press, 1957.

Current, Richard N. *The Civil War Era, 1848–1873.* Madison: State Historical Society of Wisconsin, 1976.

Davis, William C. *The Orphan Brigade: The Kentucky Confederates Who Couldn't Go Home.* Garden City, N.Y.: Doubleday and Co., 1980.

Dearing, Mary R. *Veterans in Politics.* Baton Rouge: Louisiana State University Press, 1952.

Dobson, John M. *Politics in the Gilded Age: A New Perspective on Reform.* New York: Praeger Publishers, 1972.

Dodd, Lawrence C. and Calvin Jillson, eds. *The Dynamics of American Politics: Approaches and Interpretations.* Boulder, Colo.: Westview Press, 1994.

Elazar, Daniel. *The American Partnership: Intergovernmental Co-operation in the Nineteenth Century United States.* Chicago: University of Chicago Press, 1962.

Eldersveld, Samuel J. and Hanes Walton Jr. *Political Parties in American Society.* 2nd ed. Boston: Bedford/St. Martin's, 2000.

Ferguson, E. James. *The Power of the Purse: A History of American Public Finance, 1776–1790.* Chapel Hill: University of North Carolina Press, 1961.

Friedman, Lawrence M. *A History of American Law.* New York: Simon and Schuster, 1973.

Friedman, Milton and Anna J. Schwartz. *A Monetary History of the United States, 1867–1960.* Princeton, N.J.: Princeton University Press, 1963.

Grodzins, Morton. *The American System: A New View of Government in the United States.* Chicago: Rand-McNally, 1966.

Hall, Kermit. *The Magic Mirror: Law in American History.* New York: Oxford University Press, 1989.

Hamm, Richard F. *Shaping the Eighteenth Amendment: Temperance Reform, Legal Culture, and the Polity, 1880–1920.* Chapel Hill: University of North Carolina Press, 1995.

Hemphill, W. Edwin, et al., eds. *The Papers of John C. Calhoun.* 16 vols. Columbia: University of South Carolina Press, 1975.

Hesseltine, William B. *Lincoln and the War Governors.* New York: Alfred A. Knopf, 1948; reprint, Gloucester, Mass.: Peter Smith, 1972.

Hoffer, Peter C. *The Law's Conscience: Equitable Constitutionalism in America.* Chapel Hill: University of North Carolina Press, 1990.

Holloway, J. B., ed. *Laws of the United States and Decisions of the Courts Relating to War Claims.* Washington: Government Printing Office, 1908.

Hoogenboom, Ari. *Outlawing the Spoils: A History of the Civil Service Reform Movement, 1865–1883.* Urbana: University of Illinois Press, 1961.

Huntington, Samuel P. *Political Order in Changing Societies.* New Haven, Conn.: Yale University Press, 1968.

Janda, Kenneth, et al. *The Challenge of Democracy: Government in American.* 2nd ed. Boston: Houghton Mifflin Co., 1989.

Jones, Robert B. *Tennessee at the Crossroads: The State Debt Controversy, 1870–1883.* Knoxville: University of Tennessee Press, 1975.

Josephson, Matthew. *The Politicos, 1865–1896.* New York: Harcourt, Brace and World, 1938.

Julian, George W. *Political Recollections, 1840 to 1872.* Chicago: Jansen, McClurg, and Co., 1884.

Kammen, Michael G. *A Rope of Sand: The Colonial Agents, British Politics, and the American Revolution.* Ithaca, N.Y.: Cornell University Press, 1968.

Kansas War Claims: How they were originated and what Congress has done with them, Representative Clarke's course in the matter, The Soldier's loss and the speculator's gain. Topeka, Kans.: State Record Steam Printing House, 1870.

Keller, Morton. *Affairs of State: Public Life in Late Nineteenth-Century America.* Cambridge, Mass.: Harvard University Press, 1977.

Klement, Frank L. *Wisconsin and the Civil War.* Madison: State Historical Society of Wisconsin, 1963.

Klingberg, Frank W. *The Southern Claims Commission.* Berkeley: University of California Press, 1955.

Lincoln, Abraham. *The Collected Works.* Edited by Roy P. Basler. 9 vols. New Brunswick, N.J.: Rutgers University Press, 1953–1955.

Lutz, Donald S. *The Origins of American Constitutionalism.* Baton Rouge: Louisiana State University Press, 1988.

McCormick, Richard L. *The Party Period and Public Policy: American Politics From the Age of Jackson to the Progressive Era.* New York: Oxford University Press, 1986.

Mahon, John K. *History of the Militia and the National Guard.* New York: Macmillan Publishing Company, 1983.

Martin, Lewis D. *Lumberman from Flint: The Michigan Career of Henry D. Crapo 1855–1869.* Detroit: Wayne State University Press, 1958.

Monaghan, Jay. *Civil War on the Western Border.* Lincoln: University of Nebraska Press, 1955.

Morgan, H. Wayne. *From Hayes to McKinley: National Party Politics, 1877–1896.* Syracuse, N.Y.: Syracuse University Press, 1969.

Noyes, Alexander D. *Thirty Years of American Finance: A Short Financial History of the Government and People of the United States Since the Civil War 1865–1896.* New York: G. P. Putnam's Sons, 1900; reprint, New York: Greenwood Press, Publishers, 1969.

Ostrom, Vincent. *The Meaning of American Federalism: Constituting a Self-Governing Society.* San Francisco: Institute for Contemporary Studies, 1991.

Parrish, William E. *A History of Missouri, Volume 3, 1860–1875.* Columbia: University of Missouri Press, 1973.

Parrish, William E. *Turbulent Partnership: Missouri and the Union, 1861–1865.* Columbia: University of Missouri Press, 1963.

Perrin, W. H., et al., eds. *Kentucky: A History of the State.* 5th ed. Louisville, Ky.: F. A. Battle and Co., 1887.

Peterson, Norma L. *Freedom and Franchise: The Political Career of B. Gratz Brown.* Columbia: University of Missouri Press, 1965.

Plummer, Mark A. *Frontier Governor: Samuel J. Crawford of Kansas.* Lawrence: University Press of Kansas, 1971.

Raff, George W. *The War Claimant's Guide: A Manual of Laws, Regulations, Instructions, Forms and Official Decisions . . . Growing Out of the War of 1861–1865.* Cincinnati: Robert Clarke and Co., 1866.

Rash, Nancy. *The Paintings and Politics of George Caleb Bingham.* New Haven, Conn.: Yale University Press, 1991.

Ratchford, Benjamin U. *American State Debts.* Durham, N.C.: Duke University Press, 1941.

Richardson, William A. *History, Jurisdiction, and Practice of the Court of Claims.* 2nd ed. Washington: Government Printing Office, 1885.

Riker, William H. *Soldiers of the State.* Washington: Public Affairs Press, 1958; reprint, New York: Arno Press, 1979.

Rothman, David J. *Politics and Power: The United States Senate, 1869–1901*. Cambridge, Mass.: Harvard University Press, 1966.

Scheiber, Harry. *The Condition of American Federalism: An Historian's View*. Washington: Government Printing Office, 1966.

Schouler, William. *A History of Massachusetts in the Civil War*. 2 vols. Boston: E. P. Dutton, 1868–1871.

Schultz, Stanley K. *Constructing Urban Culture: American Cities and City Planning, 1800–1920*. Philadelphia: Temple University Press, 1989.

Scott, William A. *The Repudiation of State Debts: A Study of the Financial History of Mississippi, Florida, Alabama, North Carolina, South Carolina, Georgia, . . .* New York: Thomas Crowell, 1893.

Shade, William G. *Banks or No Banks: The Money Issue in Midwestern Politics, 1832–1865*. Detroit: Wayne State University Press, 1982.

Sifakis, Stewart. *Who Was Who in the Civil War*. New York: Facts on File Publications, 1988.

Skocpol, Theda. *Protecting Soldiers and Mothers: The Political Origins of Social Policy in the United States*. Cambridge, Mass.: Belknap Press of Harvard University Press, 1992.

Skowronek, Stephen. *Building a New American State: The Expansion of Central State Authority, 1877–1920*. Cambridge: Cambridge University Press, 1982.

Sproat, John G. *"The Best Men": Liberal Reformers in the Gilded Age*. Chicago: University of Chicago Press, 1982.

The Statistical History of the United States from the Colonial Times to the Present. Stamford, Conn.: Fairfield Publishers, 1965.

Staudenraus, P. J. *Mr. Lincoln's Washington: Selections from the Writings of Noah Brooks, Civil War Correspondent*. South Brunswick, N.J.: Thomas Yoseloff, 1967.

Stephenson, Wendell H. *The Political Career of James H. Lane*. Topeka: Kansas State Printing Plant, 1930.

Stone, Richard G. *A Brittle Sword: The Kentucky Militia, 1776–1912*. Lexington: University Press of Kentucky, 1977.

Studenski, Paul and Herman E. Kross. *Financial History of the United States: Fiscal, Monetary, Banking, and Tariff*. New York: McGraw-Hill, 1963.

Summers, Mark. *The Era of Good Stealings*. New York: Oxford University Press, 1993.

Tap, Bruce. *Over Lincoln's Shoulder: The Committee on the Conduct of the War.* Lawrence: University Press of Kansas, 1998.

Tapp, Hambleton and James C. Klotter. *Kentucky: Decades of Discord, 1865–1900.* Frankfort: Kentucky State Historical Society, 1977.

Teaford, Jon C. *The Unheralded Triumph: City Government in America, 1870–1900.* Baltimore: Johns Hopkins University Press, 1984.

Thelen, David. *Paths of Resistance: Tradition and Democracy in Industrializing Missouri.* Columbia: University of Missouri Press, 1986; paperback edition, 1991.

Thompson, Margaret S. *The "Spider's Web": Congress and Lobbying in the Age of Grant.* Ithaca, N.Y.: Cornell University Press, 1985.

Trachtenberg, Alan. *The Incorporation of America: Culture and Society in the Gilded Age.* New York: Hill and Wang, 1982.

Webb, Ross A. *Benjamin Helm Bristow: Border State Politician.* Lexington: University Press of Kentucky, 1969.

Weeden, William B. *War Government, Federal and State, in Massachusetts, New York, Pennsylvania, and Indiana, 1861–1865.* New York: Houghton, Mifflin and Company, 1906.

White, Leonard. *The Jeffersonians: A Study in Administrative History, 1801–1829.* New York: The Free Press, 1951.

White, Leonard D. *The Republican Era: A Study in Administrative History, 1869–1901.* New York: The Free Press, 1958.

White, Leonard D. *The States and the Nation.* Baton Rouge: Louisiana State University Press, 1953.

Wiecek, William M. *The Guarantee Clause of the U.S. Constitution.* Ithaca, N.Y.: Cornell University Press, 1972.

Wilder, Daniel W. *The Annals of Kansas, 1541–1885.* Topeka: Kansas Publishing House, 1886.

Wilmerding, Lucius. *The Spending Power: A History of the Efforts of Congress to Control Expenditures.* New Haven, Conn.: Yale University Press, 1943.

Wubben, Hubert H. *Civil War Iowa and the Copperhead Movement.* Ames: Iowa State University Press, 1980.

Yearley, C. K. *The Money Machines: The Breakdown and Reform of Governmental and Party Finance, 1860–1920.* Albany: State University of New York Press, 1970.

JOURNAL AND PERIODICAL ARTICLES

Bates, Whitney K. "Northern Speculators and Southern State Debts, 1790." *William and Mary Quarterly*, 3rd series, 19 (1962): 30–48.

Benton, Elbert J. "Taxation in Kansas." *Studies in State Taxation*, vol. 18, *Johns Hopkins University Studies in Historical and Political Science*, nos. 1, 2, 3, 4 (Baltimore: Johns Hopkins University Press, 1900).

Bond, Beverly. "The Colonial Agent as a Popular Representative." *Political Science Quarterly* 35 (1920): 372–92.

Broden, Thomas F. "Congressional Committee Reports: Their Role and History." *Notre Dame Lawyer* 33 (1958): 209–38.

Brown, Harry James. "Garfield's Congress." *Hayes Historical Journal* 3 (1981): 57–77.

Campbell, Ballard. "The State Legislature in American History: A Review Essay." *Historical Methods Newsletter* 9 (1976): 185–94.

Chamberlain, Robert S. "The Northern State Militia." *Civil War History* 4 (1958): 105–18.

Connelly, Thomas L. "New-Confederatism or Power Vacuum: Post-War Kentucky Politics Reappraised." *Register of the Kentucky Historical Society* 64 (1966): 257–69.

Dyer, Brainerd. "California's Civil War Claims." *Southern California Quarterly* 45 (1963): 1–24.

Gambone, Joseph G. "Samuel C. Pomeroy and the Senatorial Election of 1861, Reconsidered." *Kansas Historical Quarterly* 37 (1971): 15–32.

Garfield, Marvin H. "Defense of the Kansas Frontier, 1866–1867." *Kansas Historical Society* 1 (1932): 326–44.

Garfield, Marvin H. "Defense of the Kansas Frontier, 1868–1869." *Kansas Historical Quarterly* 1 (1932): 451–69.

Garfield, Marvin H. "The Indian Question in Congress and in Kansas." *Kansas Historical Quarterly* 2 (1933): 29–44.

Gibson, Betty. "'Reconstruction' and 'Readjustment': Some Comparisons and Contrasts." *Filson Club History Quarterly* 35 (1961): 167–73.

Glazer, Walter S. "Wisconsin Goes to War: April 1861." *Wisconsin Magazine of History* 50 (1967): 147–64.

"Government Claims." *American Law Review* 1 (1866): 653–67.

Hardin, Bayless E. "The Capitols of Kentucky." *Register of the Kentucky Historical Society* 43 (1945): 173–200.

Harrison, Robert. "The Hornet's Nest at Harrisburg: A Study of the Pennsylvania Legislature in the Late 1870s." *Pennsylvania Magazine of History and Biography* 103 (1979): 334–55.

Hume, John F. "Responsibility for State Roguery." *North American Review* 139 (1884): 563–79.

Kincaid, John. "From Cooperation to Coercion in American Federalism: Housing, Fragmentation and Preemption, 1780–1992." *Journal of Law and Politics* 9 (1993): 333–433.

Kitzhaber, Albert R. "*Götterdämerung* in Topeka: The Downfall of Senator Pomeroy." *Kansas Historical Quarterly* 18 (1950): 248–55.

Kravitz, Walter. "Evolution of the Senate's Committee System." *Annals of the American Academy of Political and Social Science* 411 (1974): 27–38.

Loeb, Isidor. "The Development of Missouri's State Administrative Organization." *Missouri Historical Review* 23 (1928): 49–60.

Luraghi, Raimondo. "The Civil War and the Modernization of American Society: Social Structure and Industrial Revolution in the Old South Before and During the War." *Civil War History* 18 (1968): 230–50.

Madden, John L. "The Financing of a New Territory: The Kansas Territory Tax Structure, 1854–1861." *Kansas Historical Quarterly* 35 (1969): 155–64.

Malin, James C. "Some Reconsiderations of the Defeat of Senator Pomeroy of Kansas, 1873." *Mid-America* 48 (1966): 47–57.

Nelson, Michael. "A Short, Ironic History of American National Bureaucracy." *Journal of Politics* 44 (1982): 747–78.

Nicholson, John C. "Kansas' Account with United States." *Kansas Magazine* 2 (1909): 60–64.

Northrup, Jack. "Governor Richard Yates and President Lincoln." *Lincoln Herald* 70 (1968): 193–206.

Peele, Stanton J. "History and Jurisdiction of the United States Court of Claims." *Records of the Columbia Historical Society* 9 (1915): 2–21.

Potter, Marguerite. "Hamilton R. Gamble, Missouri's War Governor." *Missouri Historical Review* 35 (1940): 25–71.

Renick, Edward I. "Assignment of Government Claims." *American Law Review* 24 (1890): 442–56.

Scheiber, Harry. "American Federalism and the Diffusion of Power: Historical and Contemporary Perspectives." *University of Toledo Law Review* 9 (1978): 619–80.

Shaw, Albert. "The American State Legislatures." *Contemporary Review* 56 (1889): 555–73.

Sinisi, Kyle S. "Politics on the Plains: Thomas Carney and the Pursuit of Office During the Gilded Age." *Heritage of the Great Plains* 25 (1992): 25–38.

Tanner, E. P. "Colonial Agencies in England." *Pacific Studies Quarterly* 16 (1901): 24–49.

Walters, Jonathan. "Lobbying for the Good Old Days." *Governing* 4 (1991): 33–37.

Welch, Richard E., Jr. "George Edmunds of Vermont: Republican Half-Breed." *Vermont History* 36 (1968): 64–73.

Whalon, Michael W. "Israel Washburn and the War Department." *Social Science* 46 (1971): 79–85.

White, Lonnie J. "Indian Raids on the Kansas Frontier, 1869." *Kansas Historical Quarterly* 38 (1972): 369–89.

White, Lonnie J. "Winter Campaigning with Sheridan and Custer: The Expedition of the Nineteenth Kansas Volunteer Cavalry." *Journal of the West* 6 (1967): 68–98.

Wiecek, William M. "The Origin of the United States Court of Claims." *Administrative Law Review* 20 (1968): 387–406.

Wilson, James Q. "The Rise of the Bureaucratic State." *The Public Interest* 41 (1975): 77–103.

INDEX